The Verbal Games of
Pre-school Children

The Verbal Games of Pre-school Children

Susan Grohs Iwamura

51552

ST. MARTIN'S PRESS   NEW YORK

ISBN 0-312-83877-8

Library of Congress Cataloging in Publication Data

Iwamura, Susan Grohs.
   The verbal games of pre-school children.
   Bibliography: p.
   Includes index.
   1. Language acquisition. I. Title.
P118.19 1980   401'.9   79-22384
ISBN 0-312-83877-8

CONTENTS

TABLES

EXAMPLES

Example Number	Date Recorded
1	4 Sept.
2	7 June
3	30 Oct.
4	12 Sept.
5	13 May
6	13 May
7	8 Oct.
8	7 June
9	21 May
10	22 May
11	22 May
12	17 June
13	14 June
14	4 Oct.
15	30 Oct.
16	18 June
17	21 May
18	12 June
19	21 June
20	30 Aug.
21	30 Aug.
22	2 Nov.
23	13 May
24	20 May
25	20 May
26	10 June
27	17 June
28	21 June
29	11 Sept.
30	8 Oct.
31	19 Oct.
32	12 Oct.
33	12 Sept.
34	13 June
35	18 Sept.

Example Number	Date Recorded
36	14 May
37	17 Sept.
38	12 June
39	30 May
40	18 June

EXAMPLES IN CHRONOLOGICAL ORDER

Date Recorded	Example Number
30 Aug. a.m.	20
30 Aug. a.m.	21
4 Sept. p.m.	1
11 Sept. a.m.	29
12 Sept. a.m.	4
12 Sept. a.m.	33
17 Sept. a.m.	37
18 Sept. p.m.	35
4 Oct. p.m.	14
8 Oct. a.m.	7
8 Oct. a.m.	30
12 Oct. a.m.	32
19 Oct. p.m.	31
30 Oct. p.m.	15
30 Oct. p.m.	3
2 Nov. a.m.	22
13 May p.m.	5
13 May p.m.	6
13 May p.m.	23
14 May a.m.	36
20 May p.m.	24
20 May p.m.	25
21 May p.m.	9
21 May p.m.	17
22 May p.m.	10
22 May p.m.	11
30 May a.m.	39
7 June p.m.	2
7 June p.m.	8
10 June p.m.	26
12 June a.m.	18
12 June a.m.	38
13 June a.m.	34
14 June a.m.	13
17 June p.m.	12

Date Recorded	Example Number
17 June p.m.	27
18 June p.m.	16
18 June p.m.	40
21 June a.m.	28
21 June a.m.	19

PROLOGUE

Once upon a time, and a very good time it was, there were two little girls named Suzy and Nani. They were very good friends and they loved to talk to each other. They went to pre-school every day. Back and forth, back and forth, in the car. They talked and talked and talked. To pass the time they made up games. Nani's mommy sometimes listened to them playing the games and she thought what an interesting thing it would be to study their conversation. So, sometimes, when she was driving, Nani's mommy recorded what the girls were saying on a tape-recorder. Later, Nani's mommy listened to these recordings and wrote about the games that Suzy and Nani had invented to pass the time.

PREFACE

Sources of ideas are difficult to identify. A book such as this has been influenced by the direct and indirect contributions of many people. The most direct contributors were the two children whose conversations are examined here. I am grateful to Suzy's parents for permitting me to record her speech and to Suzy and my daughter, Nani, for being such lively interlocutors. I also appreciate their friend Eero's contributions and his parents' permission to include him in this study. I have not tried to hide the identity of the children behind pseudonyms, although I intentionally omitted surnames. The phonetic shape of the names sometimes influenced the shape of the discourse and an arbitrary change in the names might have affected the analysis. As for my own child, she seems to enjoy being in her mother's book.

I am indebted to a number of people who have influenced my work. My interest in the field of first language acquisition began in a seminar taught by Dr Michael Forman, who has encouraged me to continue my work in this area. Dr Ann Peters guided the research that led to the PhD dissertation on which this book is based. Insightful criticism and personal encouragement also came from Dr Susan Fischer, Dr Stephen Boggs and Dr Ronald Scollon. I also appreciate the supportive commentary I received from Dr Lily Wong Fillmore and from Dr Jenny Cook-Gumperz. Additional advice on transcription came from Dr Anatole Lyovin. I am grateful to Marie Strazar and Dr George Grace for reviewing and commenting on the manuscript.

An informal seminar has been meeting at the linguistics department at the University of Hawaii since 1973. It has been an arena for critical discussion and I have derived much benefit from participating in it. The membership has varied somewhat over the years and I find it impossible to name all the participants whose ideas have influenced my present views.

Special appreciation is due my husband, Jim, for encouragement throughout the writing of this book and for help in the preparation of the manuscript.

While I am happy to share the credit, the responsibility for the final product is mine. No doubt the ideas presented here will be challenged by other views of how children acquire language. If the development of such views is encouraged by this book, I shall be satisfied that it has served its purpose.

1 INTRODUCTION

1.1 Linguistic Theory and Theories of Acquisition

During the last two decades, developments in the study of language acquisition have paralleled developments in linguistic theory in several important respects. In both areas the focus of interest was at first almost totally limited to syntactic and phonological structure. More recently, the study of semantics and linguistic context has been included. The initial concentration on syntactic and phonological structure was to some extent a response to the publication of Chomsky's *Syntactic Structures* in 1957. Before this book appeared, the goal of many linguistic studies had been the description of a finite corpus of data. Chomsky proposed a different objective: the prediction of the structures of an infinite set of sentences. He also suggested that children are born with an innate ability of constructing the rules capable of generating the correct structures of whatever language they hear. The studies of child language which were done in the sixties, such as the early work of Brown and his colleagues (1960, 1963, 1964), centred on the child as a developing grammarian who is in the process of learning how to construct sentences of increasing complexity.

Discussion of the meaning of these increasingly complex structures was not given a prominent place in studies such as Brown's. Nor was semantics a major focus of Chomsky's work in 1957 and 1965, because he believed that whenever a choice must be made between analyses, syntactic criteria should outweight consideration of semantics. Semantics, however, became more prominent as researchers pursued another of Chomsky's goals — 'explanatory adequacy'. Some theorists gave semantics central importance in order to explain relations between sentences. Among the first to feature semantics prominently were Lakoff (1965) and McCawley (1968). Another was Fillmore, whose theory was based on semantically relevant case categories (1968). Shortly after semantics became more important in linguistic metatheory, the study of children's language began to expand in similar directions. This expansion was evident in the work of Macnamara (1972) and Bloom (1970). These researchers pointed out that syntactic rules were discovered by the child with the aid of meaning. According to Bloom, 'children develop certain conceptual representations of regularly occurring experiences and then learn whatever words (and, subsequently, syntactic structures) conveniently code such conceptual experiences' (p. 113).

The ideas of Bloom, Fillmore and others affected the thinking of other researchers. Brown, for example, was influenced by their work when he began to write *A First Language* in 1969. He said that Bloom's thesis and Fillmore's article in addition to the work of I. M. Schlesinger (1971), Beatrice and Allan Gardner (1969), and Melissa Bowerman (1973)[1] persuaded him to consider semantics as well as grammar in his approach to the data. Brown called this approach 'the method of rich interpretation' (1973, p. ix) and contrasted it with the method he had used earlier in the sixties (1963, 1964). In discussing the development of the method of rich interpretation, Brown said he had moved from 'early, non-semantic, "lean" characterizations, [such as] telegraphic speech and pivot grammar, to various semantic, "rich" characterizations in terms of relations, cases, operations, and the like' (p. 63).

Brown (1973) based the use of 'semantically aware kinds of grammar' (p. 65) on evidence that a child learning a language can express semantic relations which are appropriate to a given context. (This is what Halliday (1977) called 'learning to mean'.) Interest in the expression of meaning in context has been a concern of sociolinguists such as Labov, Hymes and Ervin-Tripp. Knowledge of structures must not be a sufficient condition for language mastery because, as Hymes (1974) said, 'A child from whom any and all of the grammatical sentences of a language might come with equal likelihood would of course be a social monster' (p. 75).

Since normal children develop into socially normal adults, it is obvious that more than the learning of grammatical structure is involved in the acquisition of a first language. This view of language learning has led researchers to begin to see the child as more than a grammarian devising grammatical constructs. The tendency now is to see the child as a partner in ongoing communicative activity during which she discovers rules of usage as well as rules of grammatical construction. This view now seems to represent the orientation of much recent language acquisition research because, as Bruner pointed out, 'Neither the syntactic nor the semantic approach takes sufficiently into account what the child is trying to do by communicating' (1974/5, p. 283).

In this book, I will examine what two young children were 'trying to do by communicating' with each other in a natural but restricted context over a period of several months. My approach to the data is similar to Brown's 'rich interpretation' because I agree that the learning of grammatical structures does not take place outside social context and also because I am interested in the process which produces normal adults instead of 'social monsters'. I will focus on those sections of the data I collected which illustrate most clearly the learning of rules of grammar and rules of conversation in the context of social usage.

1.2 Theory and Method

The choice of how and where to collect data for this study was determined by my desire to investigate children's acquisition of these two types of rules: grammatical construction and social usage. Most of the recent research which has resulted from an interest in language acquisition as an interactive response to others has focused on adult-child speech. Once researchers began to see the child as a partner in communicative activity, they discovered that adults respond differently to other adults and that they also respond differently to different children. Differences in adult response can be motivated by adult concern for children's special linguistic needs (Berko-Gleason, 1975) either without direction from children or in response to children's reactions. Children are able to control conversation to an increasing extent as they master both rules of grammar and rules of social interaction (R. Scollon, 1974; Keenan, 1974a,b; Halliday, 1973; Chou-Allender, 1976). The rules of usage can be either some form of adult rules, such as those involved in turn-taking or greeting sequences, or they can be new rules invented by children to be used in conversation. In adult-child interactions, a child is always younger, smaller, and of inferior social status and linguistic ability. There is no reason to believe that only adult-child interactions contribute to the language acquisition process. Indeed, the ability to interact effectively with one's peers may be more important to a child at some stages of development due to social pressures such as adjusting to school or simply the desire to enjoy the company of peers. Interactions between children can be sustained and coherent (Keenan, 1974a). In the study of child-child interactions, we can observe the growth of adult-like patterns and also patterns of the children's own design. In both of these sets of patterns, we can also examine the relationship between rules of grammatical construction and rules of social usage.

Patterns which are unique to children — those which adults do not share — suggest ways in which children organise their perceptual world as well as their verbal expressions of these perceptions. I disagree with those researchers who dismiss as immature children's speech which is inconsistent with adult speech. Researchers such as Bloom (1970), Brown (1973) and McNeill (1970) tended to see the child as a passive learner. By taking this view, they failed to appreciate the child's success in influencing her environment and in communicating her own perceptions. Other researchers (Bever, 1968, 1970, 1975; Slobin, 1973, 1975) have seen the child as a more active learner (Fischer, 1976, p. 75). My experience in studying my own data and in interacting with children makes me much more sympathetic to an approach which views the child as an active learner (not to mention: *teacher*). I also feel that we must learn a great deal more about the forms and patterns children invent — apparently without direct adult models — which enhance their ability to confront and manipulate their world. This we must accomplish before we can make the kind of claims which some theorists try to make about whether children's speech is reconstructed out of adult deep structure (McNeill) or adult surface structure (Bloom).

There are, however, special conditions which prevail when the linguist focuses on the very forms which are least like adult forms. The distance between the system of the linguist and the system[2] of the child is probably greatest in these areas. The linguist should not, I believe, discount the feeling that she is dealing with an 'exotic language' as Dale (1976) refers to children's speech. Unlike linguists who write grammars of 'exotic' adult languages, the linguist who studies children's language does not have available to her either bilingual informants or the potential to become a speaker of the language she is studying. Even when the assumption is granted that the linguist and the child belong to the same language community, the linguist must find a way to establish the degree to which her system and the child's system coincide. Internal evidence is one way of doing this. By internal evidence, I mean internal to the child's system and not based on external prompting by the linguist or eager parents. An adult may recognise a child's word as a cognate of an adult word, but the child may or may not *use* the word in the same context or with the same meaning as the adult. *Use* is therefore one kind of evidence of how closely the child's system coincides with the adult's system.

A study of children's language can be improved if the possibilities for internal justification or explanation can be optimised. An optimal situation for collecting this kind of data would therefore be one in which the child — without external prompting — explains her own language in her own terms. This type of situation provided the data that are examined here. The recording situation included two children and excluded 'external prompting' by an additional speaker. The observable data included not only the speech of each child free from direct adult influence, but also the structure that the two children used to organise their conversation. Suzy and Nani, the children whose speech was recorded, were very interested in communicating accurately with one another. The ways and means they found to explain themselves to each other provided internal evidence about how closely or how distantly their systems coincided with the adult system. They developed a process for self-explanation and knew when such explanation was and was not necessary. We will see in these processes aspects of the interconnection between social demands placed on language and the linguistic forms that are used to fulfil these needs. Observation of this area is possible because child-child data do include evidence for interpreting children's speech.

In a naturalistic study such as this, one seeks to reduce the sources of variability. Arbitrary elimination of variables is not desirable because (1) we do not know in advance which factors are relevant, i.e., determine or influence the patterns we are looking for; and (2) any change we impose on the natural setting could alter it and render it unnatural. The choice of which variables to include and which to eliminate must therefore come out of the nature of the setting itself. This reduces the possible settings in which data can be collected, but it ensures that no relevant factors will be eliminated and no unnatural factors will be imposed.

In the setting in which data were collected for the present study, variables were limited because of the nature of the setting itself, not because I chose to eliminate anything. The data collection procedure, which will be explained below (section 2.1), captured a complete system without reducing the natural number of dimensions. At the same time, the natural conditions could remain unchanged by the data-collecting procedure (except for the presence of the tape recorder), thereby eliminating no factors until some of them could be proven irrelevant to the question under study. Even the investigator had a natural role. My participation was crucial — the activity (riding in the car) could not take place without me. Furthermore, the fact that I was Nani's mother was a consideration often overriding my role as investigator.

In looking for ways to characterise what Suzy and Nani were doing with language, I first considered the role of dialogue in the language-learning process. Participation in dialogue is clearly based on social awareness, since dialogue involves adoption and assignment of communication roles which can be accomplished only in and through language (Halliday, 1973). The language-learning process is stimulated by the ability to interact socially and linguistically, because new forms are available and new forms are also required. New forms may appear in a child's speech because she needs them to construct discourse. *Dialogue*, since it is participatory by definition, requires that the utterances of the involved parties be related. This relationship is realised as coherent discourse. In the construction of discourse, a child shows an awareness not only of the relationship between utterances and the non-linguistic setting, but also of the relationship among utterances.

The amount of information speakers share determines the possible levels of informality of their dialogue. They may choose to be formal even though they know each other well and share a great deal of information, but they would find it difficult to understand each other's informal style if they were strangers. Style can be recognised as (among other features) points along a continuum of explicitness which is inversely related to the amount of information that interlocutors share (Joos, 1961). That is, the more they know about each other's frame of reference, the less they must explain explicitly. Explicitness, as it is used here, is a kind of redundancy in the sense that parts of a set of utterances are potentially redundant with regard to other parts, depending on the presuppositions that the parties bring to the dialogue. If explicitness is redundant with respect to these presuppositions, then a violation in speech style will occur. People can be offended if someone is over-explicit. If a person expects to be addressed in consultative style and to have her opinion requested, she will not be happy to be given instructions in formal style. A person might also resent being talked down to when she is told what she already knows. A friend might resent being treated like a stranger.[3] Overlap or redundancy would then exist because the presuppositions have already provided the information which is repeated in a too formal (over-explicit) choice of style.

In children, language-learning and socialisation can be observed in the crucial activity of dialogue. In dialogue, a child learns to take on communication roles (e.g. questioner and answerer) as well as social roles (daughter, granddaughter, peer, sibling). Furthermore, engaging in conversation is a way of integrating one's own personality and ideas with those of another person. Informal styles use 'casual devices which are designed out of the mere fact that one person is not another person' (Joos, 1961, p. 40). A child must learn how to differentiate between what she knows and shares with another person and what she does not share with someone else. She learns to refer to shared information by means of casual devices such as words or phrases that have special applications for her and those she is conversing with. She must also learn how to ask for information she lacks and how to interpret and respond to another's request for missing information. She must also master the casual devices[4] for expressing these requests and responses. All of this must be learned through the process of observing and participating in dialogue. My data show that the process of using such devices involves at least three steps: (1) monitoring one's own and another's speech, (2) providing someone else with appropriate information about what she is saying,[5] and (3) responding to what others say about one's own speech. This process will be discussed in detail below.

In learning to communicate through dialogue, a child is also learning how to choose an appropriate style; that is, how to balance explicitness against shared information. A successful participant in a dialogue knows when to use full explanations and specific references (consultative style) and when and to what extent such references will be redundant with respect to known facts, attitudes, and experiences. Joos points out that casual and intimate styles are not merely short cuts or detours but derive their forms from the full explanations which exist in consultative style. 'Huh?', for example, might be a quick way of saying, 'I don't understand. Please repeat what you just said.' The use of ellipsis, pronominal forms, codes or jargon and other abbreviations is typical of what has been called 'restricted' code in the literature (Bernstein, 1964, 1970). A lack of pronouns and the repetition of nouns would make an utterance typical of an 'elaborated' code. The latter type of utterance would be acceptable if it were found in, say, the speech of a museum guide talking to a tour group whose membership is varied with regard to knowledge of the subject-matter and whose numbers may change constantly because some people move through a museum faster than others. Such an utterance would be completely inappropriate if the guide were going through the museum with an expert or a close friend. Then that explicitness, however necessary during the guided tour, would be a signal to the expert that his expertise was in question and to the friend that the closeness of the friendship was in doubt. (I am ignoring here other differences between speech to the friend and to the expert.)

Neither Bernstein nor Joos applied his terms to the early development of language. The question of how the hypothetical museum guide learned when and to what extent explicitness was either required or redundant has been explored very little in the literature. In fact, the literature tends to support the position that there is a negative correlation between child-child interaction and increases in language complexity and maturity (Bates, 1975; Nelson, 1973). Lack of explicitness, which might be considered an indication of ellipsis in adult speech, has usually been seen as immaturity in a child. The child has been seen as an egocentric being who is unable or unwilling to take another person's point of view. The possibility that the child's lack of explicitness is *intentional* usually has not been considered. By looking carefully at child-child interaction as we will do here, we will be able to see the development of mastery of the non-explicit/explicit continuum which is part of what Slobin (1975) called 'rhetorical expressiveness'. Slobin defined this term as the ability to monitor and adjust one's own speech on the basis of what others think, feel and know.

I question the practice of researchers (e.g. Bernstein, 1970) who have assumed that when a child answers with minimal information she cannot express the full thought. I suggest that it might be the case that the child is aware of a choice and chooses the less full answer because the fuller one would be redundant in the context. The examination of the context of child-child interaction provides valuable clues which indicate whether an utterance is short simply because the child chooses to make it short or whether she simply has not mastered the linguistic structures required to express the idea fully.

Measuring linguistic complexity on the basis of mean length of utterance (MLU), for example, has been used a great deal and is, by definition, a measure only of whatever superficial forms the child chooses to use. Elliptical sentences may involve deletion transformations and are therefore more complex than sentences which have no ellipsis.

Since MLU measures only what remains after such transformations apply, it 'penalizes the more mature child who may have learnt discourse rules for deleting redundant material in his utterances' (Cross, 1975, p. 119). (Other problems in comparing Suzy and Nani's speech with the speech of children described in the literature will be discussed. See section 2.2.) MLU is therefore in some ways inversely related to the mastery of intimate speech styles in which redundant material is deleted and to the mastery of discourse. That is, the more *intimate* a style is, the less *explicit* it is, because in intimate style a speaker not only replaces nouns with pronouns (and uses other anaphoric devices) but she replaces whole references with 'jargon' (in Joos's terms, an abbreviation appropriate to the intimate dyad or group). In the development of routines,[6] in my data, a routine came to be ritualised[7] when Suzy and Nani developed their own terminology. If a ritualised routine were analysed for linguistic complexity as measured by fully developed, explicit sentences, it would score very low. For example, in the Hiding Game (Chapter 7), 'Let's hide' was a code-phrase for an invitation to start playing the game. To express this explicitly, one of the children would have had to say, 'I want to play the Hiding Game now. Let's get down on the floor and pretend that a monster is chasing us.' Such explicit expression would score well on any scale of linguistic complexity but would have ruined the game because it would have violated the intimate nature of the girls' relationship and the shared experience of having developed the game. Explicitness in this case would have been the same as the museum guide giving her standard lecture to the visiting expert or her close friend.

The use of a measure such as MLU also obscures the richness of 'vertical' constructions, that is successive utterances by one child (R. Scollon, 1974). Svenka, Savic and Jocic (1972; referred to in Bates, 1975) analysed dialogues between twins and suggested that the impoverished nature of individual twin utterances is deceptive. Their claim, based on examination of successive utterances, is that twins share 'deep structures'[8] with the effect that they demonstrate an underlying capacity for linguistic forms that would be expressed in a series of phrases by single children who do not share such underlying structures. Bates concluded that the notion of 'shared deep structures' may not be typical of twins alone (p. 5). As this study illustrates, children who know each other well can use verbal forms to refer to underlying ideas which they share. (In the case of the Hiding Game, Suzy and Nani continued to refer to an underlying narrative that was never explicitly stated.) Such children can understand each other with a minimum of elaborate explanation. This lack of explicitness in their speech to each other corresponds to the most intimate style identified by Joos (1961). The fact that inexplicit, intimate styles as well as more explicit styles can be found in child-child interaction indicates that the children are developing control over at least one aspect of the range of styles that are available to adult speakers.

While my data indicate that some children begin to interact effectively in dialogue before the third birthday, Slobin (1975) shares with other researchers the view that children below four years cannot participate in effective discourse due to a limited ability to 'decenter' in the Piagetian sense. However, Slobin is aware that

> Most studies of child language comprehension put the child into a situation where there are no contextual cues to the meanings of utterances, but in real life there is no reason for a pre-school child to rely heavily on syntactic factors to determine the basic propositional and referential meaning of what he hears. (p. 29)

Slobin suggests that the emphasis on syntax in most child language research may obscure the possibility that mastery of grammatical complexities is 'attributable, to a large extent, to a growing need to comprehend aspects of messages and to communicate expressively — that is, to direct [a] listener's attention skillfully in discourse, trying to maintain interest, attention, and understanding' (p. 31).

Slobin proposes a framework for exploring the relationship between grammatical elements and social interaction from a developmental point of view. This framework is made up of four demands which he claims all languages must fulfil (see below). He compares language change in the areas of child language, historical linguistics, languages in contact, and the evolution of pidgins and creoles. His focus is to 'clarify the psycholinguistic processes which make language possible by studying the way language changes as the speech of a child approaches the speech of his community, as the speech of one community approaches that of another', as languages change due to internal pressure and external pressure and as pidgins develop and become creoles (1975, p. 1).

Slobin points out that a theory of change cannot be separated from a theory of structure because both are bound by the same psycholinguistic and sociolinguistic constraints. An investigation must therefore begin with a characterisation of the cognitive and communicative determinants of the nature of human language. Slobin suggests that as a result of these determinants a fully developed language must fulfil four conditions:

(1) be clear: strive for 'semantic transparency' (the shortest path between surface and meaning);
(2) be humanly processible in ongoing time: provide necessary cues to underlying structures to ensure ongoing parsing of sentences;
(3) be quick and easy: conflate whenever possible;
(4) be expressive: (a) semantically expressive: express propositional and referential content and (b) rhetorically expressive: provide alternate ways of expressing notions.

Of the four, 1 and 2 initially influence child language and pidgins the most due to the fact that both these transitional types of language are characterised by relatively simple forms (are transparent semantically) and by restrictions of function in comparison with more developed linguistic systems such as creoles and the language of older children. Conditions 3 and 4 provide impetus for change and movement towards full development, while conditions 1 and 2 constrain the directions of change of a given language system with a small range of possibilities. For example, a gain in compactness (Condition 3) or expressiveness (Condition 4) is often purchased at the expense of ease of processing (Condition 2) or semantic transparency (Condition 1) of the message.

The two children in my study were at the stage (2;9 and 3;0 to 3;5 and 3;8 respectively) where their language fulfilled the first two of the four conditions well enough for them to develop ways of handling the second two. The beginning of this stage of language development overlaps the earliest manifestations of dyadic interaction. The routines which we will examine here exhibit tension between Slobin's four requirements for a fully developed language. Routines allowed Suzy and Nani at the same time both to take verbal shortcuts (Condition 3) and to be more expressive (Condition 4). As a routine was used more frequently, the speech used to implement it became less transparent (Slobin's Condition 1 was less influential). When the speech became more compact as well as more familiar, the routine became a better vehicle for directing the listener's attention, thus becoming more rhetorically expressive.

In some routines (to be discussed below) the children's interest centred on the trade-off between transparency (Condition 1) and expressiveness (Condition 4). The process of the diminishing need to fulfil Conditions 1 and 2 (semantic transparency and processibility) and the increasing need to meet Conditions 3 and 4 (compactness and expressiveness) affected many of the routines to some extent. Suzy and Nani's growing control over a variety of styles allowed them to find alternate ways of expressing ideas, thus fulfilling Slobin's Condition 4. One way of using language expressively is choosing the right style at the right time.

Joos's concern with ellipsis and other shortened forms in intimate and casual speech coincides with Slobin's Condition 3, compactness. In order to choose an appropriate style which is neither too compact nor over-explicit, a speaker must take into account another's state of mind. A speaker cannot make decisions about whether her listener will understand a shortened form or will need an expanded expression of an idea unless the speaker has access to information about the listener's knowledge of and attitude towards the topic under discussion.

Learning to perceive someone else's inner state of mind is part of learning how to communicate expressively. Once a child has begun to interact as a speaker/hearer, she becomes aware that others react not only to what she says but to how she says it. This awareness of another's reaction is part of what Pittenger *et al*. (1960) call 'immanent reference'. That is, 'no matter what else human beings may be communicating about, *they are always communicating about themselves, about one another, and about the immediate context of the communication*' (p. 229, emphasis theirs). In my data, I found that Suzy and Nani made maximum use of their awareness of each other's knowledge and attitudes when they developed and used routines such as the Hiding Game (see above, p. 24 and below, Chapter 7). The successful use of these routines depended on the intimate understanding by each girl of what the other had in mind. Within the parameters of their relationship, Suzy and Nani were able to monitor their own and each other's speech, provide each other with metalinguistic feedback, and adjust their speech in response to this feedback. Examination of these data from child-child interactions also reveals that a process of ritualisation[9] occurred in which certain routines came to be used only when Suzy and Nani accurately accounted for each other's state of mind. When this occurred, they were able to use abbreviated, jargon-like forms to initiate and maintain a familiar routine.

The data to be discussed in the next few chapters were especially rich in ritualised routines because of the closeness of Suzy and Nani's relationship and the situation in which these data were collected. These factors contributed to the quality of the girls' verbal interactions. In the process of ritualisation of a routine, short forms developed which represented for Suzy and Nani longer explanations. In order to use short forms meaningfully, each girl had to be aware of how the other understood the routine and the unexpressed explanations. Each girl also had to know what the other expected her to say and do. The development of such expectations was no doubt enhanced by the closeness of their relationship and the frequency with which they were in a situation that encouraged verbal integration (daily rides in the car). Suzy and Nani had optimal conditions for developing complex verbal structures. The object of this study is to describe these structures and the processes by which Suzy and Nani developed them.

Notes

1. Brown had access to pre-publication drafts of work which appeared subsequently.
2. I am using *system* in a broad sense to include all that a person knows about the structure and use of her language. I will delineate below (p. 51) the specific areas within this definition of *system* that will be examined here.
3. All three of these examples involve more than explicitness. Explicitness is,

however, an important measure of formality of style and I will continue to use it as such in this discussion.

4. Sacks *et al*. (1974) called one set of these devices 'repair mechanisms'. Keenan and Schieffelin (1976) discussed the use of some of these devices by children to improve communication. I have found in my data that 'Huh?' is used frequently to request repetition and/or clarification. In addition to repair mechanisms such as 'Huh?', Suzy and Nani had their own casual devices which took the form of special words and phrases which they used to refer to shared information. This will be discussed in Chapter 7.

5. Grace calls this phenomenon 'metalinguistic feedback' (1976, Ch. VII, p. 7). Devices such as 'Huh?' allowed each girl to give the other an outside view of her own speech. The ability of the girls to provide each other with metalinguistic feedback and to adjust their speech according to the feedback each received from the other was an important part of their interaction.

6. I will use Boggs' (1975) definition of 'routine': 'standardized forms of speech that have a particular function but can be differently combined in a more encompassing discourse' (p. 8). 'Standardization' in this book means accepted by Suzy and Nani as a familiar unit in their conversation. The manifestations of such acceptance will be discussed with reference to specific routines. Usually acceptance was shown by both girls manipulating some aspect of their verbal exchange in similar ways.

7. 'Ritual' and 'ritualized' will be further explained below (p. 28).

8. I assume these 'deep structures' are not the same as grammatical deep structures which underlie sentences in generative grammar as in Chomsky (1957, 1965).

9. I share with Goffman the feeling that the term ' "ritual" is not particularly satisfactory because of connotations of other worldliness and automaticity' (1976, pp. 266-7). Goffman points out that 'ritual' is nevertheless useful because it refers to concerns which are 'patently dependent on cultural definition and can be expected to vary quite markedly from society to society'. In the case of ritualisation to be discussed here, I am interested in the private society which Suzy and Nani shared (to the exclusion of others). I will show that automaticity is a very important part of ritualised routines in their private social interactions, that it is dependent on the negotiated cultural values that existed between the children, and that it is realised by adjustments in the verbal manifestations of these special routines. Furthermore, development of private ritual was based on increased understanding of what each girl knew the other expected of her. (See also Chapter 2, footnote 19.)

2 COLLECTION AND ANALYSIS OF DATA

2.1 Data Collection

The recording environment was composed of the subjects, the adult data collectors, the setting, and the equipment.

The subjects were two girls: Nani, my daughter, was 2;9 at the beginning of the study, and her friend, Suzy, was 3;0. The parents of both children shared the chore of driving them to and from the pre-school which the girls attended from eight to five, five days a week. Each family drove once each day, mornings one week and afternoons the next. A third child, Eero, a boy, was present at five sessions in September and October.

The girls knew each other very well since they had spent a great deal of their first two years together. Suzy's mother had been hired to care for Nani in her home every weekday from the time Nani was six weeks old and Suzy was four months old. Thus, the children shared much of the same environment until Suzy was two (September 1972) and started pre-school. Although the girls subsequently saw very little of each other until Nani began to attend the same pre-school almost a year later, this did not seem to affect their feelings of closeness and, if it did, the shared experiences in pre-school (they were always in the same group) and in riding to and from school together, combined with their desire to communicate, made their interaction intense and, at times, urgent. They were often impatient when communication failed or proved difficult, although they usually found a way to repair misunderstandings.

Since neither child had siblings and they both lived in apartments where there were few if any children their age to play with, Nani and Suzy probably saw each other more than either of them saw any other child. Their family backgrounds and environments were similar. They both came from homes where they were exposed to both General American English (GAE) and Hawaiian English (HE), varieties of American English which are spoken in Hawaii.[1] In both homes the parents had some years of college education and were middle-class in terms of socio-economic background and life-style.

Of the 66 recorded sessions, 5 included a third child, Eero, who was four months older than Suzy. He was better acquainted with Nani than with Suzy, who had known him only during the few months when he attended the pre-school. The sessions recorded when he was present provide comparison data.

The idea of collecting data while I was driving the girls to pre-school occurred to me two or three weeks after we had started the car pool. Listening to the girls as I drove made me realise that the situation could be one which encouraged active child-child interaction while limiting the variables in a natural way.

I stopped collecting data after the first nine weeks (August- November) because I wanted to consider more carefully the kind of data I was getting and to see whether I could detect any change in the girls' behaviour after the recording equipment was removed.

During the five-month period before I began to record again, I noticed that some of the routines[2] I had noticed earlier were still being used and that there was no difference in the girls' behaviour that I could observe once the tape-recorder and microphone were gone. My decision to record another series of daily sessions was based on these informal observations and on the discovery that in the recorded data, topics and routines tended to carry over from one day to the next rather than being dropped after one day and picked up again a week or so later. This indicated that daily recording sessions would be more likely to pick up data on the development of routines than weekly ones. The second series of recordings was almost seven weeks long, nearly the same length as the initial series. At the end of that time, Suzy left the pre-school because her family decided to move to New Jersey.

All sessions (except one) were recorded in the same car during the ride between home and pre-school in Honolulu. Supplementary information was obtained from time to time from observations (mostly of Nani) in other settings. I recorded these observations in a notebook and used them occasionally to clarify data collected on tape. I refer to the information in this notebook as field notes. Sessions occurred almost daily on weekdays and were ten to fifteen minutes long. Table 1 gives the dates and number of sessions.

The car in which all but one recording was made had bucket seats in the front with a low divider or console which was at the level of the seats and extended from the gear shift stick to four inches behind the front seats. This divider was quite low — too low to be an arm rest — and below the level of the girls' faces as they sat on the bench seat in the back.

The same recording equipment was used throughout this study. Recordings were made on a Sony TC-110 tape-recorder which was powered by a Sony BF-9 battery pack. The tape-recorder was placed

on the passenger seat within easy reach of the driver while a Sony
ECM-19B microphone was inserted in a stand that was attached to the
centre divider. The microphone stand held the microphone at an angle
pointing towards the back seat where the children always sat. I tried to
prevent them from sitting on the edge of the seat because they were
both small and light and could be easily thrown by a sharp turn if they
did not sit against the back of the seat.

Table 1: Data Collection Schedule

Dates	28 Aug. - 2 Nov. 1973	8 May-28 June 1974
Number of weeks	9	7
Number of sessions	35	31[b]
Ages at start	3;0 (S)	3;8 (S)
	2;9 (N)	3;5 (N)
	3;4 (E)[a]	

a. Ages are computed by month of birth, not day of birth. Abbreviations are
   S = Suzy, N = Nani, E = Eero.
b. This includes one session recorded by Suzy's mother (15 May) and five
   recorded by my husband (20-24 May).

I wanted the children's behaviour to be as little influenced as possible by the fact that I was recording what they were saying. The situation itself — the drive between home and the pre-school — would have
existed whether or not the tape-recorder was present. My informal
observations of periods during which the tape-recorder was not present
indicated that the recorder made very little, if any, difference in the
way the girls behaved (except when the microphone caught their attention and they sang directly into it). I also wanted to know if they
would behave differently when another adult was driving. I checked
this by asking Suzy's mother and my husband to record when they
were driving. This was done on six occasions. Of these, Suzy's mother
recorded one session in her car and my husband recorded five in the
car I usually drove. Although the drivers were in fact available for interaction, very little adult speech is present in the data. When the drivers
spoke, they usually used GAE with the occasional use of HE intonation
and lexical items. In instructing the other adults to behave as naturally
as possible, I explained that it was not essential to encourage the children to talk or to refrain from contributing themselves. The minimal

participation by the adults was acknowledged by the children. On one occasion, for example, Nani, referring to me, told Suzy, 'She's driving. Cannot talk to her now.' (See Appendix B, Analysis of 12 June, Utterance 52.) I found no difference in the data collected by different adults. In fact, the tendency of some topics to recur during consecutive or nearly consecutive sessions continued in spite of changes in cars and drivers. (See Examples 23 and 24, 13 May p.m. and 20 May p.m., section 6.2.1.)

During the single attempt to record in Suzy's mother's car, the quality of the recording was very poor due to the noise level of her car, a VW beetle, and to the absence of an adequate surface on which to attach the microphone stand. (There was no centre divider between the front bucket seats.)

The children were aware of the tape-recorder and knew that I carried it to and from the car, inserted the microphone into the stand or removed it, and that I turned the recorder off and on. What interested them most about the equipment was the microphone, which prompted them to sing. (They were familiar with singers on television singing into a microphone.) They could not reach the tape-recorder, but they did try to remove the microphone. Although I did not stop them from speaking or singing directly into the microphone, I scolded them if they tried to remove it.

Except for occasional attempts to remove the microphone and to sing directly into it, the children ignored the equipment. I never transcribed when Nani was at home and made no other use of the equipment in her presence. Informal observation of their behaviour during the five months when no recordings were made revealed that the only effect of the presence of the equipment was the availability or non-availability of the microphone to be sung into. When the equipment reappeared in May, the girls noticed it by testing to see if the rule about not touching the microphone still operated. After they found out that it did, they continued to behave exactly as they had before the reappearance of the recording equipment.

2.1.1 Transcription

One of the questions that comes up immediately in the study of any natural system is how to handle the data so as to preserve as much of its naturalness as possible. The first step, the recording of data on tape, is itself a transformation of the speech behaviour being studied. Each step in the transcription and analysis of the recorded data adds a layer of artificiality to the final product of a study such as this. The closeness of fit between the real world and the conclusions reached here depends, to a large extent, on keeping these layers of artificiality in focus. I feel that the reader can better evaluate my conclusions if he or she is aware of how I handled the transcription of the data.

The data were transcribed in conventional orthography on the backs of used computer paper. The reason for using this paper — apart from the fact that it was readily available and cost nothing — was that it was wider than most other paper that I might have used. The width of paper permitted the use of vertical columns. By transcribing one speaker's speech in each column, I was able to show overlapping of the speech of different speakers, simultaneous speech, and discrete turns which did not overlap. I was also able to reserve one column (the right-most) for a running commentary on contextual, non-verbal information or points of interest in my transcription that I thought I might return to for comparison with other data. I used this column to record such information as exceptionally long periods of silence, verbal tone that was not indicated directly in the transcription (e.g. 'petulant'), and information that might provide insight into what the girls were talking about (e.g. a birthday party, the weather, etc.). A facsimile of this columnar format is shown in Table 2. I also kept a notebook for more extensive comments and explanations. Comments on the general tone of the session — happy, argumentative — were useful in interpreting the data. Some information that was specific to a particular word or sentence was indicated in parentheses within the column assigned to the speaker.

I tried to transcribe the tapes immediately after recording. Regardless of whether this was possible, I took notes in the notebook of unusual events that the girls had discussed. These notes were useful in determining what the children were talking about when I transcribed the data. For example, a discussion of candy or a toy might have been difficult to understand if I had not noted that there had been a birthday party at the school that day and the girls were discussing the contents of the 'packages' (bags filled with prizes and candy) they had received. (See section 4.2.2, Example 8.) I also made special notes and phonetic transcriptions when I noticed that the phonetic shape of certain words or phrases had direct effects on the discourse.

At times intelligibility of the recorded data was a problem. In order to represent as much of the communication between the children as possible, I used the notation (?) to indicate words or phrases that I could not transcribe but which were treated as an utterance by the children. Although I was unable to assign a phonetic shape or a semantic

Table 2: Facsimile of Transcription Format

12 Oct. a.m.

Nani (spitting)	Eero (spitting)	Suzy	Driver	Comment
		(slowly) somebody, wake up.	Hey, hey, hey, no spitting. Come on.	
		(faster) somebody, wake up.		
	Boo, boo.			
(?) Here (?)				
	wee-ee go.			
Oh! Oh! Oh!				
		Wha? Somebody's asleep.		
Hm?				
		Somebody's asleep (whisper) Sh-h-h.		
Ah.				
		(whisper) Sh-h-h. Be quiet. (?) O.K. Here.		
(giggle) Yeah somebody awake yeah.		Now, Ima.		
		I'm monster.		Old game[a]

a. This was an early observation on my part of what I later realised was a well developed routine, the Hiding Game. (See Chapter 7.)

value to these short sounds, they often helped to indicate that the flow of conversation was uninterrupted. In some cases, they seem to be requests for repetition or clarification which kept the conversation going. (The specific functions of (?) and 'Huh?' were similar and will be discussed with reference to repair sequences. See sections 4.4.2 and 7.3.2.)

In giving transcriptions here, I have converted the columnar format into a horizontal one for the purposes of discussion. Data presented in horizontal format are easier to read and take up less space, especially when only two speakers are involved and it is clear what each speaker is responding to.

I used conventional orthography except where the flavour of speech could be better expressed by slight alterations. I used IPA for those cases where more explicit information was necessary. Many of the elements of the recorded data which I felt were the most remarkable could not be expressed either in IPA or conventional orthography. To capture such elements as voice quality, rising pitch, and chanting and other forms of rhythm, I explained in parentheses what the speaker was doing. I had originally put these explanations in the running commentary of the transcription (the right-most column) or in the notebook. Words that were spoken in a very unusual manner or were sung I placed within quotation marks (here as well as in the original transcription) and the manner in which they were spoken or sung I explained in parentheses. When stress is exceptionally strong or used in an unusual way, the stressed segment is in italics. If three degrees of stress were used (normal, heavier, heaviest), the segment receiving the heaviest stress is in bold. In my original transcription I tried various conventions for showing excessive stress (accent marks, capital letters), but I decided to use italics here because it seems to be the easiest to read.

Punctuation marks are used to show pauses and meaningful intonational contours. A period (.) indicates a long pause or an intonation pattern that showed that the speaker was ending an utterance. A comma (,) indicates that the speaker separated one word from others either by a pause or an intonational contour. If no punctuation is shown at the end of an utterance, this indicates that the speaker stopped or was interrupted before completing a thought or intonation pattern. Decisions in the placement of punctuation are generally subjective because they involve simultaneous interpretation of several aspects of speech. It is often difficult to know which of these aspects coloured the interpretation in which way.

2.1.2 Evaluation of Data Collection Method

The recording situation had certain advantages as well as disadvantages. The greatest advantage was that factors such as physical setting, the identity of the participants and their relationship to each other, and the intentions or needs of the participants which motivated their presence were constant because of the natural situation and not in spite of it. Therefore, control of variables was not artificial, but came from the recording environment itself. The actual complexity of natural systems involves many dimensions, only some of which can be considered in any one study. In this study, the natural situation itself was made up of reduced dimensions; it focused naturally on what I was interested in:

how young children talk to each other when they have nothing else to do.

The situation as well as the intimacy of the girls' relationship contributed to the complexity of their verbal encounters. There was very little to do in the car besides talk. They could move from one side of the back seat to the other or move to and from the floor and the seat. Although they made as much use as possible of the physical space available (see Chapter 7), the possibilities for movement were severely limited. Physical restrictions were therefore an important factor for at least two reasons: (1) the girls could not wander away from the recording equipment; and (2) they had to depend on their own verbal skills to keep themselves entertained.

It is possible that the lack of physical freedom and the unpleasantness of quarrelling when the trip became tedious stimulated the girls to create highly complex discourse. The object of this study was to exploit the situation and to analyse as accurately as possible the conversation[3] which they created.

The disadvantages of the data collection method concerned the degree and type of detail I could record. These were primarily technical and did not significantly reduce the value of the data for the type of study I was doing. Traffic and engine noises reduced the technical quality of the tapes to the extent that phonetic transcription was often not possible and occasional words and phrases were unintelligible. Narrow phonetic transcription was, however, not needed because the focus of the analysis was on the girls' use of words, sentences and routines in discourse, rather than on phonology. Since I was driving, I could not see most of what was happening in the back seat and I could not take running notes during the session. I was able to compensate for my limited access to non-verbal cues and references by noting after each session the events (such as a birthday party or rainy weather) which might have influenced the girls' conversation. There were also audible indications of what was happening, as when the girls moved around the back seat or unwrapped candy and ate it. The girls were aware that my ability to watch them and to interact with them was limited by my reason for being there. Not only was my role necessary at the time of the recording, but it kept me occupied with driving and limited my direct influence on their speech. They were left dependent on their own resources for entertainment. This controlled yet another variable: the direct influence of adult speech on the speech of the children.

Daily recording sessions of ten to fifteen minutes over a period of several weeks yielded a kind of data that would be difficult if not impossible to obtain in longer weekly sessions or in occasional sessions which took place over a period of months or years. Data from a normal, daily situation allowed for the study of how long certain topics, structures and routines continued to occur and whether those that occurred frequently over a period of days, weeks and months changed or stayed the same. An additional advantage to frequent recording came from the situation itself. Because the girls saw each other every day, their conversations contained themes and references that were familiar only to themselves in the context of their daily interactions. The variety of speech styles they used included the least formal of the styles described by Joos (1961). The data therefore included casual and intimate speech styles and new as well as old themes, topics and procedures.

2.2 Suzy and Nani's Language

I feel that a discussion of how Nani and Suzy compare with other children is needed before I describe how I approached the data which I had collected. This comparison will be based on descriptions of other children's language that have appeared in the literature. The most extensive of these were accomplished by Brown and his colleagues and I will refer to their work.

It is not sufficient to compare only chronological age because chronological age has been shown to be only a rough indicator of level of language development (Brown, 1973). Brown and his colleagues have used a variety of measures of complexity to determine rates of growth and to compare the three children in their study — Adam, Eve and Sarah — with each other. These measures showed that Eve spoke as maturely at age 26 months as Adam did at 34 months and as Sarah did at 40 months. In order to estimate the maturity of Suzy and Nani's speech at the time I was collecting data, I attempted to apply some of Brown's techniques to the data I collected. In doing so, I hoped to provide a measure by which Suzy and Nani could be compared with each other and with other children.

My initial attempts at using Brown's techniques failed. I did not believe that measures involving the use of MLUs would be useful for the reasons I discussed in Chapter 1. I believe that the reason for my inability to compare my data to Brown's findings in areas that did not involve MLUs was that my data and Brown's differ in at least two ways: (1) the children we studied were in different communities and exposed to different dialects; and (2) the recording situations were different. I described above (section 2.1) the setting in which the data were collected for this study and I will return to this point below. I will expand here the points I mentioned with regard to the community in which Suzy and Nani were learning to speak (p. 30). Both girls were exposed to a mixture of dialects which ranged from General American English (GAE) through varieties of AE spoken with an accent typical of Hawaii (Standard and Non-Standard Hawaiian Dialect; Tsuzaki, 1971, p. 330) to Hawaiian Creole English (HCE). HCE is a descendant of the English-based pidgin formerly (and presently) spoken among immigrants. HCE has characteristics significantly different from GAE (Tsuzaki, 1971; Perlman, 1973; Carr, 1972; Bickerton and Odo, 1976). The language being learned by Adam, Eve and Sarah in Brown's study appears to have been GAE. At least Brown does not describe any difference between the speech of the children's parents and what generally seems to accepted as GAE.

Defining HCE involves making divisions along the continuum of Hawaiian English (HE) which has the English-based pidgin of immigrants and other non-native speakers at one end and moves through various stages of creolisation and de-creolisation towards a standard form that varies only slightly from GAE. HCE has been further defined (Odo, 1972, p. 235) as a useful abbreviation for a set of creole features, but not as the language variety of any speaker or speech community in Hawaii. The distribution of these features along the HE continuum shows a heavier clustering of creole features at one end and a total or nearly total absence of these features at the other end. The proportion of creole features to GAE features indicates the point on the continuum of a given speech sample. I found in the speech of Suzy and Nani many features which occur in HE but not in GAE. This indicates that the girls were exposed to and were learning these features. My knowledge of the backgrounds of the two children supports this indication and I believe it a major reason for difficulties that arose when I attempted to measure the language development of Suzy and Nani against the language development of Adam, Eve and Sarah as reported by Brown.

I have no reason to believe that Suzy and Nani were exposed, to any extensive degree, to the pidgin or heavily creole end of the spectrum. However, it is important to note that every speaker of HE commands a range of the continuum and moves up and down the range to conform with the demands of communicative situations (Perlman, 1973, p. 241). Informal speech to close friends or relatives requires movement along the range that an individual commands to a variety of speech that contains as many creole features as the speaker is able to use, while formal speech requires the use of as few creole features and as many standard features possible.[4] Perlman calls this movement 'style shift'. R. Scollon (1975) says that style shifting is not only a function of the formality or informality of speech situations among peers, but also of the relative age of the participants. Adults have style(s) which they use predictably for communicating with children.[5] HCE features are available to speakers of HE to mark the style(s) they use in talking to children. The information I need in studying the language of children in Hawaii includes the features that speakers of HE use in addressing children. Unfortunately this information is not available in any formal study that I know of. In the absence of this research, I will report here on my own informal observations.

My observations of the environment in which Suzy and Nani were growing up suggest that when a speaker of HE is required to address a child, he or she will choose a style that employs a larger number of creole features than he or she might choose in addressing an adult (even — in some cases — a close friend). It seems, then, that any speech style addressed to children is a very informal one. It is possible that this tendency is in some way connected to the impression that some people have that a pidgin or creole language is simpler and easier to understand than a standard language.[6] Perhaps creole features are chosen to make understanding easier for the child. Whether this is of benefit to children or simply a social custom unrelated to the development of language would be a worthwhile question to investigate. It is not, however, within the scope of the present report.

In any case, the tendency to use a speech style that contains many creole features when speaking to children seems to be less widespread as children become older than four or five. This is no doubt connected to the belief that parents have (and which has traditionally been supported by the schools) that their children will be more successful if they speak a dialect closer to GAE.[7] Among themselves, however, some groups of children favour a variety of speech which contains many creole features. For pre-school children, the impetus to use creole features comes not only from peers but also from older children and from adults.

The tendency to urge children not to use creole features does not seem to inhibit many adults from using these features. In fact, the use of such features has continued as a sign of group membership at least through high school and throughout the lifetimes of many local-born people who are now middle-aged and older. Carr (1972) calls this type of speech 'neo-pidgin' and says that it has 'high peer-group value' (p. 56).

This is the third of her 'types or stations'. Carr fails to suggest that even among peers, style shifts occur. In a continuum situation like Hawaii, style shifting implies the use of varying amounts of creole features. The amount and type of creole features that occur from one social or ethnic group to another are also variables which Carr ignores completely.

A child growing up in an HE-speaking environment is, according to all available descriptions of HE, exposed to a range of style shifting in which the informal to formal continuum is realised as a changing proportion of creole to non-creole features. The child's exposure includes the speech that she overhears as well as the speech that is directed towards her. Furthermore, the adult-child and child-child styles of HE tend to have as many or more creole features as any other style that a given individual normally uses. I do not know if some creole features are more likely to occur in informal adult-adult interaction than in child-child interaction or the reverse. In any case, I cannot imagine an environment in which a child acquires a first language in the absence of style shifting of all sorts.[8] Nevertheless, this question is ignored in the literature. The results which Brown obtained seemed not to be influenced in any way by style shifting in the environments in which Adam, Eve and Sarah grew up. As in the case of possible deviance from a single dialect, Brown does not mention variations in style in adult speech.

I realised at the time I was transcribing the data for this study that HCE features were occurring regularly, but I simply did not know what use to make of this fact. It seemed natural at the time that Suzy and Nani should use these features because I heard adults and other children using them in conversation with the girls.[9] I did not realise how different this situation was from the situations in other descriptions of children's language until I tried to compare my data with Brown's. Researchers have not considered language acquisition in a continuum situation, although Forman, Peters and Scollon (1975) proposed that such a study be undertaken.

While some recent work has been done on the total effect of certain kinds of input data (Nelson, 1973, 1975; Newport, 1976; Berko-Gleason, 1975), I know of no work which discusses whether, and at what point, language acquisition is affected by adult style shifting. We know, of course, that the child will eventually master all the language to which she is exposed. She will learn which forms are to be used in casual speech (and which situations are considered casual) and which forms are reserved for other situations. Previous studies seem to assume that some kind of basic grammar is learned before a child learns rules of usage that depend on social relationships. Most researchers assume that this basic grammar is a homogeneous entity which corresponds to some general description of the native language. For example, when Brown (1973) determined the acquisition of grammatical forms such as question formation or the use of fourteen grammatical morphemes on the basis of whether they occur in an 'obligatory context', he assumed that the contexts in which each of these might occur in adult speech are categorically obligatory. He supported this assumption with a check on the speech of the children's mothers, which he treated as monostylistic and as belonging to the same dialect. Even if one accepts Brown's reasoning in this area, the same assumption cannot be made in the case of language acquisition in the HE continuum. Analysis of HE has shown that a speaker chooses to use a form on the basis of the point on the continuum from which he draws his speech in any given situation (Odo, 1972). In a given speaker, the same feature in the same grammatical context might be obligatorily used in one speech situation, optionally used in a second situation, and obligatorily omitted in a third situation. Perlman illustrated this in his discussion of the expression of indefiniteness which may be expressed in a form cognate with the GAE article *a* or in the creole form *wan* ('one') or the creole feature, ∅.[10] Perlman reported that in the most formal of three situations, speakers tended to use *a* more than *wan* or ∅. In the least formal situation, they used ∅ more often than *wan* or *a*. Use of *wan* and ∅ was more likely than *a* in a situation which was neither the least nor the most formal (1973, p. 107).

The following are examples of the three ways of expressing indefiniteness:

(1) *a*   She had a baby (Watson-Gegeo and Boggs, 1977, p. 71).
(2) *wan* She was walking like she had one egg (ibid., same speaker).
(3) ∅   Stephanie the fat girl with million bucks (K. Watson, 1972; Story 3, p. 4).
(4) ∅   I had to eat liquid diet (field notes).

Not all of the types of variation that Perlman discusses can be definitely identified as related to style shifting. In the case of variation in the expression of forms of the verb *to be*, Perlman (p. 117) recorded these sentences from the same speaker:

Full	*Contracted*	*∅*
You know what is	What's 2,000 pounds?	What his name?

contract?

> You know what's a
> popolo?[11]
>
> You know who's giving   You know who
> you bread and butter?   Johnny Walker?

Although Perlman does not provide enough information to determine whether style shifting accounted for this variation, this example is typical of the kind of variation a child growing up in Hawaii might be exposed to. Whatever the cause of this type of variation in adult speech, the child who is learning this language must start somewhere.[12] If the example from Perlman is typical of one kind of speech to which Suzy and Nani were exposed, and I think it is (Example 4 above of expressions of indefiniteness was spoken in Nani's presence), we should not be surprised to find the following in the girls' speech:

Full	*Contracted*	ϕ
This is mine too. (S4/9)[13]	What's that? (S4/9)	
You think that that is your dolly? (N29/8)	What's this? (29/8)	School there. (S14/9).
What are you doing? (N2/10)		I gon have candy. (N14/9)

The comparison between adult and child speech in Hawaii differs significantly from the comparison Brown made in his study (1973). After choosing fourteen grammatical morphemes to look for in the child's developing language, Brown set the point of acquisition of each morpheme by counting the percentage of times a morpheme was used 'correctly'. Correctness was determined by the grammatical contexts in which an adult would be obliged to use the morpheme. Among the fourteen, Brown listed copula twice (Number 7, contractible copula, and 13, uncontractible copula). As the example from Perlman shows, [14] we have not yet determined which (if any) grammatical contexts are obligatory for adult speakers of HE for various forms of the verb *to be*, including the copula. It is also the case that many of the other fourteen morphemes are used variably by speakers of HE.

In addition to problems in defining obligatory grammatical contexts in adult HE for Brown's fourteen morphemes, it is also difficult to define 'correct' sentence structure in some cases. The structure of questions is a case in point. Brown says that even before a child learns to invert subjects and verbs to make yes-no questions, she learns an intonation pattern that approximates adult question intonation. In comparing two features of GAE question structure (intonation and subject-verb inversion) with HE, we find that equivalent creole features are totally different. The intonation pattern of GAE questions includes an upward movement at the end of the question. One creole feature is downward movement at the end of a question. Carr supplies these examples (1972, p. 53):

American (Central Midland)   Are you / Bill Jones? ⟋

Hawaii's dialect (Type III)   Ey, you Bill \ Jones? ⟍

As with other non-GAE features of HE, there is variability among adult speakers. Within the same sample, Carr records (52):

What time the party goin' be? ⟋

What kind this party goin' be? ⟍

Variation in question intonation is not unusual, according to what I have observed. Variation in the use and non-use of subject-verb inversion and DO-insertion also seems to be common. Examples of lack of subject-verb inversion and DO-insertion appear in the data from Perlman and in the data from Carr which I cited above. These features in addition to intonation are prominent creole features of HE. They are often among the first that a newly arrived GAE speaker notices. Like other creole features, they are variable. Because they are the inverse of GAE features as well as variable, it is sometimes difficult to determine whether a given sentence is a question or a statement. I found this to be the case when I transcribed Suzy and Nani's speech. Since grammatical indications — intonation and subject-verb inversion — were variable, I had to depend on the response of the second child in order to interpret what the first child had said.[15] On the basis of contextual clues as well as grammatical form, the following are typical of Suzy and Nani's questions:

Intonation	*Yes-no questions with subject-verb inversion and Do-insertion*	
HE	Can you ask your mommy? ↘	(S29/8)
HE	Do you wan', eat grapes? ↘	(S29/8)
GAE	Are you going back to my home? ↗	(S4/9)

	Yes-no questions without subject-verb inversion and Do-insertion	
HE	You wan' to, home at my house little while? ↘	(S29/8)
GAE	Your mommy eat the cracker? ↗	(S29/8)
GAE	You think that that is your dolly? ↗	(N 29/8)

	WH-questions[16]	
HE	Mommy, what's that?↘	(N4/9)
GAE	What's that?↗	(S4/9)

The variability of intonation patterns is especially noticeable when rising and falling patterns occur consecutively:

GAE	Suzy coming to our house? ↗
HE	Suzy going to my house? ↘

Variability of question formation also occurred in sequences like this:

(A) 1. N: Are you come to our house, Suzy?

2. Do you come to our house?→

3. S: No.

4. N: Does Suzy come to our house, Mommy?

5. Is Suzy come to our house? ↘

6. D: Yes . . . .

And also this:[17]

(B)   1.   Are you tired?↗

2.   Are you tired?↘

3.   Are you tired?↗   (N4/9)

In illustration A, Sentences 2 and 4 are approximately GAE sentences. I am not sure how to characterise 1 and 5. The correct form of *to be* is not only present, but it is also in the right place for GAE question structure. The only GAE element that is not found is the *-ing* on *come*. Bickerton and Odo (1976) in their list of features coded for the analysis of HE speech samples, do not list *-ing* as a feature but as a context for the occurrence of other features such as forms of the verb *to be*. This seems to indicate that *-ing* is more likely the auxiliary verb, but I cannot find any direct treatment of *-ing* in the literature on HE. The absence of *-ing* in Questions 1 and 5 in Example A may be developmental or may be a creole feature.[18]

In trying to compare my data with Brown's, I often had to conclude, as I did above, that the absence of such features as one of the fourteen morphemes and rising intonation, subject-verb inversion and DO-insertion on questions could be the result of *either* the influence of creole features in the speech Suzy and Nani heard *or* developmental immaturity. Furthermore, I found it difficult to use the presence or absence of the fourteen morphemes as a measure of complexity because the speech situation which I recorded was an intimate interaction. This is exactly the kind of interaction which Brown said would be less likely to contain grammatical morphemes: 'In a face-to-face conversation between well-acquainted persons, the meanings signalled by grammatical morphemes are largely guessable from linguistic and non-linguistic context' (1973, p. 399). Brown concluded that these morphemes were therefore 'dispensable in child speech and in non-literate adult speech in a way that content words and word-order are not'. HCE may be an example of what Brown meant by 'non-literate adult speech'. In any case, he did not entertain the possibility that both children and 'non-literate' adults leave out morphemes intentionally rather than because they do not know how to use them. Children, 'non-literate' adults and 'well-acquainted persons' may use the presence or absence of certain features as markers of style. Grammatical morphemes may be among these features. If this is the case, and I believe it is, the presence of features is revealing, but their absence is inconclusive evidence.

A further difficulty with the use of Brown's fourteen morphemes as a means of measuring linguistic complexity is that some of these morphemes only occur when certain subjects or certain aspects of topics are discussed. If these topics simply do not come up in the conversation, the investigator has no opportunity to observe whether the child knows how to use relevant grammatical morphemes. If, for example, the child never discusses events that occurred in the past or activities that involve a third person, at least four of the fourteen morphemes — past tense (Numbers 3 and 9), third person (Numbers 10 and 11) — cannot be expected to occur. Suzy and Nani seldom discussed past events or third persons during sessions of data collection for this study, although they often discussed the future and used many imperative sentences. Neither of these latter accomplishments can be scored in terms of Brown's fourteen grammatical morphemes.

I found that measures of sentence complexity such as those in Brown and Hanlon (1970) were more useful than the techniques in Brown (1973) in comparing Suzy and Nani's speech to Adam's, Eve's and Sarah's. Adam, Eve and Sarah were in or beyond Stage V when they mastered the complex structures that Brown and Hanlon looked for. Since Suzy and Nani had also mastered these structures, they were presumably also in or beyond Stage V. Brown (1973) believed that measures of MLU and the acquisition of the fourteen grammatical morphemes are less salient towards the end of Stage V. This may be a major reason why it was easier for me to compare Brown's and Hanlon's data with my own.

The purpose of the following discussion is to show that in the first nine sessions (at ages 3;0 to 3;1 and 2;9 to 2;10, respectively), Suzy and Nani were employing some of the same structures that Adam, Eve and Sarah were using at Stage V as described by Brown and Hanlon. Brown's and Hanlon's work cannot be separated from other studies of Adam, Eve and Sarah. The five developmental stages which Brown and his colleagues set up for the three children were based on Mean Length of Utterance (MLU). The rates of acquisition of the fourteen grammatical morphemes were used as corroborating evidence. Because of difficulties I had in comparing my data and theirs as outlined above, I did not attempt to set up analogous stages for Suzy and Nani. In any case, as the following will show, Suzy and Nani seem to have been well into Stage V when I collected my data for this study.

Brown and Hanlon looked for seven sentence types in the first 700 utterances at each of the five stages and used larger samples — up to 2,100 utterances — in the case of rarer sentence types. Since I had not established stages for Suzy and Nani, I simply started with the earliest data and looked through the transcription of each session until I found no new structures or until Brown's and Hanlon's criterion (six instances for each type) was reached. I stopped after nine sessions (about two hours of recorded data) which had taken place over a period of 44 days. In these first nine sessions, Suzy and Nani had each used four of the seven sentence types at least six times. The three types on which Suzy and Nani had not yet reached criterion were apparently late in developing in Sarah (Stage V at 40 months) and in Adam (Stage VI, sometime after 34 months). Suzy was 37 months old by the ninth session, and Nani was 34 months. Table 3 summarises the data.

Table 3: Nani and Suzy Compared with Adam, Eve and Sarah

	Stages at which criterion was reached for seven sentence types						
	N^a	Q	Tr	TrN	TrQ	NQ	TrNQ
Adam	III	V	V	IV			VI
Sarah	II	IV	III	II	V		V
Eve	III	V	V				

	Criterion reached in the first nine sessions				
Nani	x	x	x	(4)	(3)	
Suzy	x	x	x	x	(1)	

a. N = Negative; e.g. *We didn't have a ball.*
   Q = Question; e.g. *Did we have a ball?*
   Tr = Truncated; e.g. *We did.*
   TrN = Truncated negative; e.g. *We didn't.*
   TrQ = Truncated question; e.g. *Did we?*
   NQ = Negative question; e.g. *Didn't we have a ball?*
   TrNQ = Truncated negative question; e.g. *Didn't we?*

As Table 3 shows, Suzy and Nani controlled types of sentences which Adam, Eve and Sarah had acquired by Stage V except for TrN in which Nani was short of criterion by two instances and TrQ and TrNQ which only Sarah had acquired by the end of Stage V. I therefore concluded that Suzy and Nani were approximately at Stage V — at least as far as the limited set of structures investigated by Brown and Hanlon are concerned.

2.3 Analysis of the Data

When the object of study is children's speech, the researcher has the additional challenge of examining a system which is very different from her own. The differences between the linguist's system and that of the child are not only due to the stability of the adult system as opposed to the child system, but also due to diachronic changes which occur continuously. Diachronic changes mean that even within the same speech community people of different ages will be exposed to different environments at the time they are acquiring language for the first time. Nevertheless, the researcher must reach a preliminary level of interpretation before she can select aspects of the data to examine closely. A first step towards reaching this preliminary level is an understanding of the difference between an adult system and that of a child. The child's system is changing rapidly; some areas will approximate the adult system more closely than others at any given time. A child is absorbing, with varying degrees of efficiency, a constantly changing flow of linguistic information. The rate of change and the variations in the amount and type of new material taken in are enough to create a high degree of uncertainty with regard to interpretation of surface output in children's speech.

Using data from child-child interaction reduced the uncertainty about how to interpret what each child was saying. Although I could not assume that the systems of the two children were identical, at least I was able to compare my own adult reaction with a child's reaction to the same bit of child language. I also believe that the children encouraged each other to explore more fully aspects of their abilities to manipulate language. Suzy and Nani's systems were probably more alike than either system was to an adult system. Factors of social and physical equality (as children they were of lesser status and smaller size than adults) may also have made their verbal interaction a positive, exploring activity. Observing the reactions of the girls to each other's speech provided the necessary understanding of what the girls meant by what they said and it also drew my attention to those areas of communication which required the greatest co-operation between the children.

Using the intensity of Suzy and Nani's interactions as a guide, I was able to identify sections of their conversation that they seemed to treat as units. By 'unit' I mean a section of their conversation which the children reacted to differently than they did to the general flow of talk. Their reactions to a unit of conversation included anger, tears, giggles and intensity or duration of interest (when they talked about something for a long time). Some of these units coincided with chains of adjacency pairs such as questions and answers,[19] others were larger sections of talk; all were constrained by what each child expected the other to say. These constraints identified such units as routines; that is, as standardised forms of speech which could occur in a variety of conversational contexts. Some of these routines developed additional constraints when they recurred frequently. As I mentioned above, I call these routines 'ritualised routines'. (See above, p. 28.) 'Ritualised' here refers to those routines which came to be used as rituals within Suzy and Nani's society of two. Among the chains of adjacency pairs that the girls treated as separate from the ongoing conversation, some seemed more like routines than others. When chains which were very similar occurred several times, standardised elements in these chains could be identified.[20] At this point, I felt justified in calling these similar chains 'short routines'. I will define this term further in the following chapter (3). I will not attempt to identify the point at which similar chains became a routine or the exact moment when a routine became ritualised. The differences between chains of adjacency pairs, routines and ritualised routines are differences of degree rather than kind. Furthermore, I am most interested in the transitional stages which reveal some of the changes which Suzy and Nani made that resulted in chains of adjacency pairs becoming routines and routines becoming ritualised.

My study of the transitional stages between the units I found in the data began with the discovery of the most complex ritualised routine, the Hiding Game. Although I will not discuss this routine in detail until Chapter 7, it was my examination of this popular routine that drew my attention to Suzy and Nani's skill in the use of rules of grammar and rules of conversation to identify, construct and develop routines. I then noticed that they interacted in similar ways in other routines. As I began to put my findings into written form I found that it was easier to discuss the Hiding Game after I had described the kinds of skill and co-operation that occurred to a lesser degree in less complex routines. Chapters 3 to 6 will describe these routines and the ways in which Suzy and Nani developed and expanded them.

The changes which Suzy and Nani made were related to the kinds of constraints that influence the form of all conversation. Goffman (1976) identifies three types of constraint: grammatical, system and ritual. Grammatical constraints are apparent throughout the flow of conversation. 'Each participating utterance[21] is constrained by rules of sentence grammar' (p. 258). Although ellipsis can occur in conversation, grammatical constraints limit the degree of abbreviation that can occur.[22] System and ritual constraints make conversation possible; they keep the conversational channel open.[23] Goffman's division of rules of usage into system constraints and ritual constraints will be useful here if I change the definitions slightly.

Although Goffman's use of the word 'system' is confusing because 'system' can also refer to a person's entire linguistic knowledge, his delineation of three types of constraints is insightful. I will adapt them to the discussion here. In a footnote (Chapter 1, footnote 2), 'system' was defined as including everything one knows about one's language. At various points throughout the discussion which preceded and followed that footnote, I referred to 'rules of grammar' and 'rules of usage', to 'rules of grammar' and 'rules of interaction', and to the relationship between 'grammatical elements' and 'social interaction'. Some of these terms came from sources such as Slobin (1975). I believe all of these terms overlap almost completely, if not exactly, Goffman's intentions when he discussed his three types of constraint. He and the other researchers I have referred to assume that there are two types of sets of rules or patterns in a linguistic system: rules of grammatical construction and rules of social usage. Rules of grammar concern the surface patterns of the system and are phonological, morphological and syntactic realisations of underlying meanings. Goffman called these 'rules of sentence grammar' or 'grammatical constraints' (1976, p. 258). The second set of rules, rules of social interaction or rules of usage, is subdivided by Goffman into 'system constraints' and 'ritual constraints'. Since his use of 'system' is not the same as mine, I will call these constraints 'conventional constraints'. By these, I mean constraints on the structure and use of dialogic discourse which most adult speakers of American English would accept. By 'ritual constraints', I mean those which are specific to the society made up of Suzy and Nani. I considered calling the latter 'private', but this word does not seem to connote the regularity with which the girls responded to the rules which they imposed on themselves and each other.

In tracking the changes in some of Suzy and Nani's routines, I found that developmental progress in the subsequent occurrences of a routine was a major source of information about the relationship between grammatical construction, social expectations (conversational constraints) and interpersonal expectations (ritual constraints). Several routines underwent this process, which I call ritualisation. In my view, a routine became ritualised when it acquired a sense of historical perspective for the children because they had shared it and the history of this sharing was acknowledged by both of them. This acknowledgement was often manifested in acquiescence to or discussion of each other's suggestions about when a routine should occur or what changes should be made in its form. Often the structure of a routine became abbreviated in consecutive occurrences because the girls simply lost the need to explain to each other something — in this case a familiar routine — that they both knew increasingly well. Such familiarity was in itself a statement about Suzy and Nani's close friendship. An unexpected change in a ritualised routine was often treated as a threat to their friendship. If one girl tried to change a ritualised routine, the other might become offended by the introduction of the unfamiliar element. It then became the obligation of the first girl to either drop the proposed change or show how it was related to the familiar parts of the routine.

The structural changes which occurred as a routine and became ritualised provide information about the relationship between rules of grammar and rules of usage (both conversational and ritual constraints). Suzy and Nani's need to explain their expectations to each other decreased as a routine became more familiar during successive occurrences. This meant that when one of them wanted to begin a familiar routine, she could use an abbreviated form of whatever had begun the routine when it had been introduced originally. This movement towards shorter forms is one aspect of what Joos (1961) described as movement from consultative style to casual and even intimate style. While Joos did not attempt to draw rigid lines between styles, he made it clear that the less explanation needed between parties, the less formal and the more intimate the style is. Suzy and Nani never discussed the basic structure of ritualised routines, although they did discuss the structure of new, developing routines. These discussions provide data for a description of the process by which they accomplished many of the adjustments in their routines: metalinguistic monitoring, feedback and self-correction. In ritualised games, what Joos called 'jargon' developed in some cases. In these routines, certain words and phrases that the girls used came to have special meanings. Suzy and Nani used these specialised phrases as signals of a jointly-agreed-upon requirement to behave in specific ways without conventional instructions or explanations. Innovation, however, required explanation. Some of the innovation then, in turn, became part of the ritual and did not need to be discussed thereafter.

Throughout the development of any routine, changes were limited by the girls' knowledge of grammatical rules. Nothing was ever shortened to the extent that it lost all connection with grammatical rules or with conversational constraints. Changes or new routines that could be connected in some way to older routines were begun more quickly and accepted more easily by both girls. In this way, all three types of constraints — grammatical, conversational (or social), and ritual (or dyadic) — were influential in determining the shape of Suzy and Nani's conversation as they rode back and forth between pre-school and home.

In the following chapters, I will discuss some of the sections of the girls' ongoing conversation in which they were especially interested and which they constructed and manipulated as a co-operative activity. I will focus on the process by which they achieved this level of co-operation. This process included metalinguistic monitoring, feedback and self-correction, and was always constrained by grammatical, conversational and ritual rules. Most of what follows will treat small sections of the data that were collected during the 66 ten-to-fifteen-minute sessions; transcriptions of two complete sessions, along with explanatory notes, are given in Appendix B.

Notes

1. This is an important aspect of the data, and I will discuss it in some detail below (see section 2.2).

2. 'Routines' were defined above (p. 29) as 'standardized forms of speech that have a particular function and can be differently combined in a more encompassing discourse' (Boggs, 1975, p. 8).

3. According to Goffman (1976, p. 264), 'conversation' in sociolinguistic practice is used in a loose way as the equivalent of talk or spoken encounter. I will adopt this usage.

4. Superficial examination of some creole features discloses that they seem to make speech less explicit than varieties of HE that do not contain them. Speakers who use those creole features may therefore need more shared information in the circumstances where those features are appropriately used in order to communicate adequately. This would support Joos's theory about informal styles (see above, p. 22). I would not, however, speculate as to whether informal HE speech which includes creole features employs more ellipsis than informal GAE.

5. At least as early as age four, children become aware of the need to change styles when speaking to younger children (Shatz and Gelman, 1973).

6. Forman, Peters and Scollon (1975).

7. This prejudice against creole features is not restricted to local-born parents. Chou-Allender reports that the immigrant parents of a child she studied were very concerned that he was learning 'bad English' from his Hawaii-born playmates (1976, p. 36).

8. For the purpose of the point being discussed here, I am treating as a whole changes that occur along the formal-informal continuum and changes that occur when adults speak to children of different ages and to other adults.

9. I am not myself a native speaker of HCE, having come to Hawaii as an adult a year before Nani was born.

10. I use italics to indicate stress and also to identify certain lexical items which may fit into some theoretical framework or are the focus of discussion at some point.

11. Small dark berry; epithet for blacks, or, more generally, dark-skinned people.

12. Perlman (p. 243) wonders how newly arrived adults learn to use the features of the local dialect: 'How do they learn it? And where do they belong in the continuum?' And where, I would add, do children belong at various stages of their development?

13. The information in parentheses indicates the speaker (S = Suzy; N = Nani) and the date of the recording.

14. I do not believe that the samples from Perlman and from my data are exactly parallel in structure, but I think they illustrate the nature of the problem.

15. Goffman (1976, p. 257) pointed out that question-answer format is some-what independent of *what* is being talked about. Because an answer refers back-ward to what has just been said, analysis of interactive data allows judgements that could not be made if only isolated sentences are considered. This is especially true when the features which are variable are the ones which make major distinctions such as which sentences are intended to *provide* information and which are *requests* for information.

16. The examples I give here of HE and GAE intonation for WH-questions are greatly over-simplified. It is difficult to explain what happens in WH-questions for several reasons. One likely source of difficulty is the perception of the interaction between pitch, stress and volume and the question of which of these elements (or which combination of them) carries the morphological burden of marking some utterances as questions and others as non-questions.

Although the intonation pattern for GAE WH-questions is usually considered to go down at the end (↘), I have shown the arrow going up to symbolise the contrast between HE and GAE which I hear in my data. This is intended to show a first approximation since I have not yet determined which element or combina-tion of elements (pitch, stress, etc.) results in the impression that a contrast exists. Furthermore, as Susan Fischer suggests (personal communication), the difference in intonation may also have to do with old and new information. In a series of questions, all of which are 'What's that?', the first one will have more of a rising intonation, while all the others will have more contrastive stress on 'that'.

17. This may indicate a searching for an effective intonation pattern. The degree to which such searching is inspired by models or is nearly random cannot be known from the present data.

18. The similarity between pidgins and creoles and children's speech has received some attention in the literature, although the process of language acquisition in a pidgin-standard continuum has not. Givón (1976) says, 'Both child language and Pidgins/Creoles share one condition in common: They develop under heavy *communicative stress*' (p. 156; emphasis his). In pidgin situations, children 'speak with much greater fluency than adults. Children, exposed to adult variability, tend to make new (shorter, more concise) forms obligatory and regular' (Slobin, 1975, pp. 23-4). Givón believes that school systems are respon-sible for extinguishing such 'natural tendencies' with the result that these tenden-cies 'survive longest in the language of the less educated or illiterate' (Givón, ibid.). In a continuum situation where children need not wait to achieve school age to be exposed to less 'natural' (but more standard) forms, how can we charac-terise the language the children are acquiring? When creole features exist side by side with standard features in the speech community, do children preserve relics of their developmental past and add standard (non-creole) features or do they acquire creole features at about the same time as standard features and learn to mix them appropriately at various points along the continuum?

19. An adjacency pair was defined by Schegloff and Sacks (1973, pp. 275-6) as a unit within conversation that is made up of two utterances (one spoken by each of two participants) that follow each other as parts of the pair and are related

because the participants expect them to follow each other. Goffman (1976) called questions and answers 'one example, perhaps the canonical one' of 'first pair part' followed by a 'second pair part' (p. 257). (See also Chapter 1, footnote 9.)

20. Boggs (1975) uses the element of contradiction of one speaker by another to identify what he calls the 'contradicting routine' in the verbal exchanges of part-Hawaiian children (p. 8). Many of Suzy and Nani's routines had a similar element of contradiction. Although I believe I use the notion of 'routine' as Boggs does, I am interested in what routines can reveal about the development of language while Boggs is interested in the role of routines in establishing 'key cultural values' (p. 1).

21. The term 'utterance' in the context of discourse dates back at least to Harris. He defined it as 'a stretch of talk, by one person, before and after which there is silence on the part of the person' (1951, p. 14). 'Utterance' defined in this way suits my purposes here. Even though Goffman prefers 'turn at talk' to 'utterance' as a minimal unit in analysis of conversation, he falls back on 'utterance' when he defines other units of conversation. Schegloff and Sacks also use 'utterance' in defining such terms as 'adjacency pairs' (see footnote 19). I will use 'utterance' as Harris defined it.

22. Slobin (1975) expresses this relationship as the tension between compactness, processibility, clarity and expressiveness.

23. Goffman believes that system constraints are pan-cultural, but he does not say whether he means that all cultures have them or that all cultures share the same ones. Reisman (1974) identifies system constraints in an Antiguan village that are very different from any that I am familiar with.

3   SHORT ROUTINES

3.1 Introduction

In this chapter, I will begin the discussion of sections of conversation during which Suzy and Nani exhibited the greatest co-operation and in which they appeared to be the most interested. For the purposes of this discussion, I sorted these sections into four general types: routine-like chains of adjacency pairs, correction activities, routines and ritualised routines (see pp. 49-50). These four sets are by no means discretely bounded but will be useful in explaining some of the dimensions of sections of the girls' conversations.

A routine is defined as a 'standardised speech form' (see above, p. 29) that might occur in different conversational contexts. Chains of adjacency pairs occurred throughout conversation within and outside routines. I found that in Suzy and Nani's conversation some chains of adjacency pairs were somewhat like routines because they contained elements in common (similar to contradiction in Boggs's contradicting routine) (see Chapter 2, footnote 20). These chains did not, however, seem like full routines because the structure of the chains did not seem transferable to other conversational contexts. That is, the elements that were transferable seemed more superficial than those of a full routine. Although these routine-like adjacency pairs were not full routines, neither were they merely ongoing conversation. I decided to call them 'short routines' rather than invent a new term.

Short routines, then, were chains of adjacency pairs which Suzy and Nani treated as separate from ongoing conversation. The elements in these short routines which were similar from one instance to the next were suprasegmental elements such as stress, volume and intonation. While such elements were important parts of full routines, only in short routines were suprasegmental elements the major unifying factor. That is, the beginning and ending of full routines were indicated by less superficial factors such as manipulating word meaning, while the beginning and ending of short routines were indicated primarily by alternating volume, intonation, voice quality and other suprasegmental factors. When suprasegmental factors were transferred to full routines, they remained superficial elements in relation to the girls' major interests, such as playing with antonyms (Antonym Games, Chapter 5) or inventing a story (the Hiding Game, Chapter 7).

3.2 Repetition and Imitation

The examples of short routines which follow illustrate how the girls were able to manipulate grammatical structure in response to the interactive situation. The referential meaning of what was being said was often not an issue in these exchanges. Suzy and Nani were expressing feelings and ideas that were not always connected directly to the referential meaning of what they were saying. In some chains of adjacency pairs the girls were not interested in referential meaning at all. They were primarily interested in manipulating grammatical elements in response to conversational and/or dyadic needs. In 'grammatical', I include suprasegmental, segmental, morphological, syntactic and semantic structures and patterns. The grammatical elements which the girls manipulated in response to interactive conditions in these short routines were primarily suprasegmental patterns (stress, volume, intonation). In the longer, more complex routines and in correction activities which included both long and short routines, phonetic and syntactic patterns were also important. These will be discussed in subsequent chapters.

Many of the short routines were characterised by a great deal of repeated linguistic material. This material can be divided into two types: 'repetition', the consecutive use of the same form by one speaker, and 'imitation', the same phenomenon created by two speakers. (These definitions are from R. Scollon, 1976.) In the short routines which included either imitation or repetition, Suzy and Nani did not seem to be interested in the referential meanings of the repeated material past the initial three or four utterances. The grammatical structures that they manipulated did, however, seem to be the focus of their attention. (See especially Example 4, 'here/there', discussed below.)

The girls' lack of interest in the meaningfulness of their conversation at these times should not suggest that they failed to communicate. On the contrary, they communicated very efficiently because they co-operated well in devising short routines that depended on mutual acceptance of social and dyadic constraints. Some of these short routines seemed to demand less co-operation than others. That is, the need to respond to each other's personal expectations seemed less strong. The best examples of this type of short routine were those that contained a great deal of repetition and imitation.

Repetition and imitation differ in terms of the complexity of the interaction in which they occur. Repetition — the consecutive use of the same form by one person — does not necessarily involve a second speaker. Imitation, on the other hand, *requires* two speakers.[1] Repetition is less complex than imitation because if one speaker repeats linguistic material without intending to elicit a response, the interaction is minimally complex. Repetition can be more complex if the speaker repeats herself with the intention of eliciting a response because the second speaker is needed to complete the interaction. Imitation is more complex than repetition because the participants directly affect the form of each other's speech. In imitation, the superficial form of the repeated material is determined by what each participant makes available for the other to imitate and by what each chooses to imitate in the other's speech.

Although repetition and imitation have long been considered characteristic of children's speech, these phenomena have received limited attention in the literature. Many studies have ignored repetition since researchers have argued that it seems to be either meaningless or direct imitation of an adult speaker and therefore not part of the child's spontaneous repertoire. Furthermore, repetition in the form of what Piaget calls 'echolalia' has been seen as an indication that the child is unable to 'decentre'; that is, to take the perspective of anyone other than herself (Piaget, 1926). Although there are arguments for studying repetition even when it does not appear to be social (see, for example, Weir, 1961), I am interested here in children's use of repetition as a means of facilitating or even intensifying communication between themselves (Keenan, 1974b; Scollon, 1974). In Suzy and Nani's conversations, this use of repetition functioned as one type of short routine. As such, it required decentring. In Piaget's theory, decentring is a developmental trend towards cognitive and social extroversion (Flavell, 1977, pp. 30-1). Through this process, the child gradually becomes aware of the difference between herself and another. The child gains a more objective view of reality (including other people's points of view) and a more subjective view of herself. In the course of its development, the child's language reflects the process of decentring.

Suzy and Nani's highly social use of repetition seems to contradict Piaget's view that repetition reveals a failure to decentre. In their interactions, each was aware that the other was co-operating in the repetition of words and phrases. Repetition in this case became a form of language that they used to manipulate each other and thus can be considered extroverted, non-egocentric behaviour.

The girls were also aware that language can be used for reasons other than the transfer of information. In their social use of repetition, Suzy and Nani knew that they were using the repeated words as the focus of the interaction. As the following examples will illustrate, the girls intentionally ignored the information-transmitting potential of the words they used. They did not do so out of ignorance of referential meaning, nor because they were unable to decentre. Indeed, the opposite seemed to be the case. They understood each other so well that they could suspend the need to exchange concrete ideas (to talk about a topic). They could manipulate the grammatical elements of their conversation in a way that did not diminish their dependence on or acceptance of system constraints (e.g. taking turns). It seems to me that this indicates that repetition was not simply simultaneous monologue during which the girls had some vague notion of companionship, but that it was an activity which used language as the object to be played with in the sense that a ball or a doll is a plaything.

In the following examination of short routines, we will see illustrations of how repetition can require perception of another person's point of view. Such perception not only indicates that social rather than egocentric communication is achieved, but it also indicates that the communication fulfils Slobin's (1975) requirement for expressiveness.

The more clearly Suzy and Nani were able to understand each other's point of view, the more expressive their communication became. Of the various types of routine that occurred in Suzy and Nani's conversation, the short routines required the least understanding by one girl of the other's 'inner state of mind'. The girls' long routines, which will be discussed in the following chapters, were based on even greater ability to understand each other's perspective. This seems to indicate that at least these children (and probably many others) are not as slow in meeting the challenge of expressivity as Slobin believed. Perhaps they have achieved more than Slobin would give them credit for in areas which he said must precede the ability to be expressive — clarity and processibility. In order to reach the stage at which language could become an expressive tool, each girl needed to accomplish at least two goals: (1) control the possibilities of her own linguistic system; and (2) account for her partner's perspective. Complexity can be seen to increase with the growth of these two factors.

The factors of linguistic control and interactive sensitivity were involved in imitation and in some kinds of repetition. Linguistic control can be expressed in the answer to the question, 'What forms are being repeated or imitated?' Interactive complexity can be described in two questions: 'What does each speaker choose to repeat or imitate from the material available for repetition or imitation?' and 'What effect does her choice have on her partner?'

While imitation necessarily involves two speakers, repetition is more difficult to classify as interactive or non-interactive (monologue). When one speaker repeats a statement in response to questioning by another, the interactive purpose is clear: the first speaker is repeating in order to get her meaning across. This kind of activity has been called a 'repair sequence' (Sacks *et al.*, 1974). Goffman (1976, p. 269) pointed out that conversational and ritual constraints are unlike grammatical ones in that they 'open up the possibility of corrective action as part of' their operations as constraints. Grammatical structures can be the object of corrective action. In such a case, metalinguistic correction can occur. Suzy and Nani spent quite a lot of time correcting each other's behaviour — both verbal and non-verbal. Their correction activities are among the most complex of the short routines because corrective action requires not only the knowledge of grammatical, conversational and ritual constraints, but also the ability to refer to these constraints, and the ability to change one's speech in response to criticism. Some correction activity occurred in repetitive and imitative short routines. This is a major difference between short routines, in which listener reaction shaped only the suprasegmental elements of the speaker output (and sometimes not even that) and correction activities, in which each speaker tried to change significant parts of the other's speech. This was also indicative of the competitive aspect of Suzy and Nani's relationship. I will discuss correction activities fully in the chapter which follows this one.

Although one person does not need another to engage in repetitive speech, the presence of another person and the desire to get her to respond can trigger the repetition of sentences. In this case, the speaker might continue to repeat until the listener responded. When Suzy and Nani did this most of the preceding sentence or phrase was repeated, but sentences often changed shape to some extent with each repetition. The *form* of successive changes was not directly influenced by the listener, although the *number* of repetitions might depend on how long it took for the listener to respond. The following two examples illustrate that listener response was sometimes the only way to stop the speaker from continuing to repeat. The repetition was not exact. When the speaker repeated some parts of her previous sentence and changed others, she may have designed these changes to get the listener's attention. The choice of which parts to alter and which to repeat in successive utterances was entirely the speaker's. She received no input from the listener — except lack of response — that could influence the shape of each sentence.

Example 1

4 Sept. p.m.[a] (The children had just been told that Suzy would come home with Nani and the driver and that her parents would pick her up later. Nani asked for confirmation of this announcement several times. The following was the longest of Nani's requests.)

1. N: Are you come to *our* house, Suzy? (pause 1.1 seconds)
    Do you come to [b] $\{$ *our* house?
2. S: $\{$ No.
3. N: (after pause 2.1 seconds)
    Does Suzy come to *our* house, Mommy?
    Is Suzy come to *our* house?
4. D: Yes.

a. A.m. or p.m. is indicated after the date of a recording to show if a trip was a morning trip to the pre-school or a return (afternoon) trip home.
b. Brackets like this indicate that one speaker started speaking before the previous speaker finished.

Example 2

7 June p.m. (The children received balloons at the pre-school.)

1. N: I got some balloons in here. That you, that you could blow up and it won't pop.[a]

    This kind[b]   cannot[c] pop.
    Mommy   these kind kind[d]   cannot *pop.*
    (slower, louder)
    Mommy,   *this* kind   cannot *pop.*
2. D: I hope not.

a. Nani had a recent memory of a very large balloon that had 'popped' when she hugged it.
b. When I intend to discuss patterns that are repeated in a series of utterances, I will align the data in columns. Such alignment is intended to guide the reader towards the relationships relevant to the discussion.
c. 'Cannot' is used by adult speakers of HCE in place of 'can't'. Although it is not considered a GAE feature, neither is it as close to the creole end of the continuum as 'no can' (Perlman, 1973, p. 184).
d. The use of 'kind' in Hawaii is very complex. A probable gloss is 'this type of thing'.

In the above example, Nani changed the shape of her sentences only slightly as she sought an appropriate response. I attempted to measure the length of pauses in both excerpts with a stop watch. Only two of the inter-sentence pauses were measurable by this means. The speed with which Nani went from one sentence to the next seemed to indicate how eager she was to get a response. In the series of four questions that Nani asked in Example 1, the first two (addressed to Suzy) are separated by a pause of 1.1 seconds. Suzy did not answer the first question in that period of time so Nani began to repeat the question. Before she finished, Suzy answered. Suzy's answer was, however, contrary to what the driver had said previously when she told them that Suzy would come home with Nani. Nani, therefore, after pausing for 2.1 seconds, addressed her question to the driver. In her second utterance,[2] she made the correct adjustment for person, changing 'you' to 'Suzy' and 'do' to 'does'. This time she did not pause or hesitate until she received the response she sought. This discrepancy between what the driver said and what Suzy said apparently bothered Nani enough to cause her to ask the driver to repeat what she had said earlier. This was a simple corrective action. Nani made appropriate grammatical adjustments and repeated her question until the adult, who was the authority on the topic, resolved the discrepancy. The adjacency pairs form a pattern of questions and answers. The question of what motivated Nani to make syntactic adjustments as she repeated her question is intriguing. In Utterance 1, she moved from a less adult-like question to a more adult-like question. When she addressed the driver, however, the second question was less mature than the first. I can see nothing in the data that suggests why she chose to make the changes she made. In short routines, factors which motivated grammatical alterations were not apparent. As we will see in the next chapter, such factors were clear when Suzy and Nani engaged in correction activities.

Nani had a different worry in Example 2. This time, she was anxious about the possibility of the balloon popping after it had been blown up and she sought reassurance from her mother. She did not pause between sentences but kept repeating slightly different forms of her question. By the time she reached the third repetition, her voice had an impatient edge as she spoke louder, enunciated the words more carefully, and addressed the driver directly as 'Mommy'.

By providing the requested reassurance in both excerpts, the listener, in this case the driver, ended the repetition and thus controlled the number but not the shape of the repeated sentences. The speaker's choice of changes in the repeated pattern was not determined by advance knowledge of what would make the listener respond. The speaker, Nani, knew that she would eventually get a response if she continued to request the assurance she wanted. Nani did not need to understand the listener's point of view beyond the fact that repetition is monotonous and the listener is likely to want to stop it.

In the above examples of repetition, the speaker (Nani) made two allowances for the listener's viewpoint. First, she addressed the listener directly either by adjusting the pronouns appropriately, as in Example 1, or by calling the listener's name, as in Example 2. In addition, the speaker knew that the listener was likely to want to stop the monotonous repetition.

In the short routines which involve imitation, there is comparatively greater co-operation between speaker and listener. Indeed, the line between listener and speaker becomes less clear when imitation is taking place because both partners must attend to the linguistic structures that are being imitated. The speaker limits what the listener (the imitator) will say while the listener chooses which parts of the available speech to imitate and which parts to ignore. Imitation is, however, less complex than interactions which involve non-imitated, novel linguistic structures. I will discuss the latter in subsequent sections.

In this data, imitation often occurred as a series of utterances in which each girl imitated some of the other's immediately preceding utterance. This produced an echo effect. However, a series of utterances which consisted of imitated material was usually more than just reciprocal echoing because Suzy and Nani co-operatively added features which gave such a series a kind of external structure. This external structure was made up of contrasting grammatical elements — usually some kind of suprasegmental contrast. When Suzy and Nani combined imitation and suprasegmental contrast, they succeeded in constructing a short routine which they treated as separate from their ongoing conversation. When, for example, a contrast in voice quality was initiated, such a routine could be considered to have begun. The routine was over when the girls used their normal voices again. When the end of the routine was indicated by a return to normal suprasegmental patterns, the other features of the routine — such as imitation — were usually no longer present. Occasionally, the repeated material and the suprasegmental contrast in a given routine did not end at the same time. An example of this will be discussed below (Example 6).

Types of suprasegmental contrast that occurred with series of imitated utterances included contrasting intonational contours (questions/answers), contrasting voice quality (normal/gruff), contrastive stress (degrees of emphasis), and volume (loud/soft). The last of these, volume,[3] was used frequently when the girls were shouting goodbye to the people at the pre-school as they sat in the departing, homeward-bound car. Although there was little substantial difference in what each was saying, the girls were, in fact, engaged in a shouting match until the pre-school was out of view. While competition on the basis of volume was not a sophisticated game, it did mark the boundaries of a routine which existed because the participants recognised when it started, how it continued, and when it ended. They acknowledged that the end of the routine had been reached by introducing a new topic. This was true even when such a routine consisted of nothing more than imitated or repeated phrases. Although the goodbye routine was usually composed only of shouting 'goodbye', variations such as the following did sometimes occur. Notice that the echo effect is maintained by the similarity of the shapes of each successive sentence and by the same pitch and stress patterns resulting in a kind of calling 'tune'.

Example 3

30 Oct. p.m. (Both girls have been shouting 'B'bye' out of the window. All utterances are shouted. Syllables at the end of utterances are long and high-pitched.)

1. N:	Bye,	Tsukamoto-o.[a]
2. S:	Do you have fun,	Miz Tsukamoto-o?
3. N:	We	have fun Miz Tsukamoto-o.
4. S:	We	have fun Miz Tsukamoto-o.
5. N:	We	have fun
6. S:		when I go ho-ome.
7. N:		when I go ho-ome.
8. S:		with my mom-me-e.
9. N:		with my mom-me-e.
10 S:		with a roachi-ie.
11. N:		with a roachi-ie.

a. Mrs Tsukamoto was the director of the pre-school.

In this shouting match, the first four utterances ended with the same four syllables. Utterances 6-11 are a chain of adjacency pairs while the first three words in 3-5 are repeated without change. Because the semantic content of all eleven utterances is not very complex, the relationship between pairs of sentences seem to be an echo created by the imitation of parts of preceding sentences. The ideas could have been expressed in fewer sentences if the ideas were all that the children were interested in. The exchange could be analysed in terms of phrases as follows:

		Subject	Verb-Object	Vocative	Temporal & Locative	Comitative
2.	S:	Do you	have fun	Miz T.		
3.	N:	we	have fun	Miz T.		
4.	S:	we	have fun	Miz T.		
5.	N:	we	have fun			
6.	S:				when I go home	
7.	N:				when I go home	
8.	S:					with my mommy
9.	N:					with my mommy
10.	S:					with a roachie
11.	N:					with a roachie

As this analysis shows, Suzy and Nani took turns changing the last phrase of what seems to be an underlying sentence. The form of the sentence might be expressed as follows:

'We have fun,
$$\left\{ \begin{array}{l} \text{Miz Tsukamoto'} \\ \text{when I go home'} \\ \text{with my mommy'} \\ \text{with a roachie'} \end{array} \right\}$$

Other phrases such as 'with my friend' might also have been possible. In any case, the routine was enjoyed as a follow-the-leader game for as long as it lasted (until the school was out of sight and/or the girls ran out of breath or ideas).

The 'goodbye' example seems more like a full routine than other short routines because several aspects of it could be considered 'standardised'. That is, they could occur in other conversational contexts. The standardisation in this case, however, is at least partly related to the girls' awareness of how leave-taking events are supposed to be acted out. The shouting and sing-song 'tune' that the girls used is in a way a parody or caricature of leave-taking as a generalised or standardised speech event. The girls seemed to be conscious of the system constraints of leave-taking and they co-operated in distorting them to suit the constraints of their own dyad. They tacitly agreed to limit their changes to those that would make sense after 'We have fun, Miz Tsukamoto . . .' The girls clearly understood both the underlying pat-

tern that they shared and the expressive use of shouting and the calling
'tune'. Within these constraints, they developed a chain of adjacency
pairs that set this piece of conversation apart from the conversation
which preceded and followed it. The intention of saying goodbye to
Mrs Tsukamoto was forgotten after they began to construct this chain.
Once the pre-school was out of sight, only their interest in the chain of
adjacency pairs kept the routine going.

In other short routines, as well as in the 'goodbye' routine, Suzy and
Nani were interested in manipulating suprasegmental elements. In some
cases, they manipulated several suprasegmental elements in the same
routine. Occasionally this was accompanied by the manipulation of
other grammatical elements. An example of this occurred on 12 September.

Example 4

12 Sept. a.m. (The following occurred after Suzy had joined Nani and
the driver in the car and they started driving to the pre-school.)

1. N: Eh, where's your *mom*my? (pause) Where's your *mom*my?
2. S: Right *there*?
3. N: Over *there*.
4. S: Over *there*?
5. N: Over *here*.
6. S: Over *there*.
7. N: No, over *the-ere*.
8. S: Over *there*.
9. N: No, over *here*.
10. S: (gruffly) No, over *here*.
11. N: Over *there*?
12. S: No, over there. ('there' is less stressed than elsewhere)
13. N: Over *here*?
14. S: Yeah.
15. N: Oh-h-h.

Suprasegmental elements in this example included intonational contrast (questions/answers: Utterances 1-5 and 11-14), contrastive stress
(Utterances 1-15), and contrasting voice quality (normal/gruff: Utterances 9 and 10). The girls also manipulated semantic and lexical elements
even though most of the utterances were made up of nearly the same
words. Semantic differences between utterances involved very few fea-

tures. For example, the difference between Utterances 7 and 8 was the word 'No' and the meaning of 'there' which referred to a different place in each of these utterances.[4] In any case, referential meaning was of diminishing importance because Suzy's mommy had been left behind and was no longer in view. The girls were less interested in where Suzy's mother actually was than in playing with 'over here/there'.

Like previous examples of short routines, Example 4 required co-operative intention to have fun v 'th talk, not necessarily to use talk to communicate information. The beginning and end of the routine was marked by contrasts in lexical and semantic choices. Lexical choice involves the choice between words of the same or nearly the same meaning. Semantic choice is the choice between meanings when more than one meaning is possible. In the case of Example 4, 'there' can refer to a variety of locations (semantic choice) while 'here' and 'there' can refer to the same place (lexical choice). Although children seem not to understand formal verbal play like riddles until age five (S. Fischer, personal communication), Suzy and Nani enjoyed the kind of word play that depends on knowing that words have more than one possible meaning and that more than one word can be used to express an idea.

In Example 4, the girls focused on the relationship between 'here' and 'there' as soon as Nani said 'over *there*' (Utterance 3). Although they seemed to be contradicting each other, the audio-recording alone cannot provide the information needed to determine whether they were talking about the same location or different locations. In any case, they were interested in what Halliday called 'verbal pointing' (1976, p. 570). Their manipulation of the demonstrative adverbs 'here' and 'there' ended when Suzy stopped disagreeing and said 'Yeah' (14). Nani acknowledged the end of the routine by saying 'Oh-h-h' (15).

At the same time as Suzy and Nani contrasted 'here' with 'there', they also manipulated suprasegmental elements. One of these elements was intonational contour: question intonation (2, 4, 11, 13) contrasted with statement intonation (3, 5, 12). This gave the routine a contradicting quality[5] and also served to mark the beginning and the end of the routine. Other types of suprasegmental contrast kept the focus of the game on 'here' and 'there'. In the routine, these key words were not only stressed within each utterance (except in 12 where 'there' received normal stress), but also received another kind of special treatment in 7 where 'there' was lengthened. The normal stress which 'there' received in 12 contrasted with the heavily stressed realisations of this word in other utterances. Suzy added further contrast, this time in voice quality, when she made her voice gruff (10) as she repeated Nani's words.

The 'here/there' example illustrated that the girls could manipulate a variety of elements (stress, intonation, voice quality) at the same time. It also showed how contrasting suprasegmental elements could affect the delivery of material. Shouting matches and other imitation routines which involved contrast between degrees of loudness often reflected Suzy and Nani's strong feelings about certain important issues. One area about which they (and probably most other American children) were sensitive was name-calling. On one occasion, Nani was able to infuriate Suzy not only by calling her names but also by continuing to speak softly while Suzy, in her anger, started to shout.

Example 5

13 May p.m.

1. N: Hey *don*key, *don*key.
2. S: I'm not *don*key, *don*key.
3. N: Yes, you *are*.
4. S: No, I'm *not*.
5. N: Yes.
6. S: *Lani*[a] I'm not *don*key, *don*key.
7. N: (softly) You *mu*shi, *mu*shi.[b]
8. S: (loud) Lani.
9. N: You mushi, mushi.
10. S: (loud) Lani.
11. N: (giggle) You mushi, mushi.
12. S: I'm not *mu*shi, *mu*shi. (tearful) I not goin' play with you.
13. N: I'm not (noises, giggles)
(pause before new topic)

a. Suzy used 'Nani' and 'Lani' interchangeably. 'Leilani', the full form of Nani's name, also occurred. I could find no pattern in these variations.
b. [muʃi] is a Japanese word which, according to Hawaii-born informants, means 'worm', and is used to refer to children who cannot sit still.

For Suzy, this exchange was not fun. Even though this name-calling episode was not enjoyable to both partners, they used the same expressive techniques that they used in routines that were fun for both of them. The contrast between loud and soft volume and between normal and heavy stress allowed the girls to show how they felt about the words they were speaking.

Suzy and Nani also used suprasegmental elements when they disagreed about other topics. One such disagreement occurred on the same day as the name-calling episode. In this case Suzy shouted again because she was angry that Nani disagreed with her. This time, however, Nani began to agree with Suzy rather than to continue the argument as she had when she kept calling Suzy names. In spite of Nani being more agreeable this time, Suzy continued to shout. Although the subject of the dispute was important to both of them, the suprasegmental element of volume continued independently of the fact that agreement might be considered to have been reached. As in other short routines, suprasegmental elements — in this case, Suzy's shouting — was the factor the girls attended to most closely.

Example 6

13 May p.m. (at a traffic light)

1. N: Say *cross*. It's red, red, red, red.
2. S: *No. Green* say *go*.
3. N: I sawed red.
4. S: (chants) Green says go and red says stop.
5. N: (softly) I sawed red said stop, Suzy.
6. S: (tearful, loud) No, our grandma know, our grandma knows my *grandma* knows because it (fades)

Utterances 1 and 2 constituted a semantic disagreement which was resolved when Nani changed her claim (5). Suzy was so involved in the initial disagreement that she was unable to pay attention to the semantic agreement that was reached in 4 and 5. Evidently she figured it out at the end of 6 because her voice faded after she tried to justify her claim on the basis of authority (grandma). The girls then started to giggle.

Although Suzy and Nani appeared to be seriously interested in whether red means 'stop' or 'go', they did not seem to be interested in the contradiction between the meaning symbolised by a red light and the meaning symbolised by a green light. They both wanted to determine a fact about the real world. They used the same techniques that they used in playful short routines to dispute the issue of whether red means 'go' or 'stop'. The use of contrastive stress occurred in playful exchanges like the 'here/there' routine (Example 4). The use of a tune, in this case a chant that seemed to be a mnemonic device, occurred for a different reason in the 'goodbye' routine (Example 3). The fact under discussion — colour symbols used in traffic lights — was undisputed by the end of Utterance 5. The dispute, however, did not end there if suprasegmental features are taken into account. In Utterance 6, Suzy was still involved in the dispute as her use of stress (on 'grandma'), volume (loud) and voice quality (tearful) indicated. In this way, Suzy expressed her emotions even after Nani agreed with her. The upset caused by the dispute ended only at the point at which Suzy's voice faded. She apparently had not understood immediately what Nani had said in Utterance 5. Suzy's loudness in contrast with Nani's soft speech indicated that Suzy was still involved in the dispute. This contrast between Suzy's loudness and Nani's softness began as early as Utterance 3 when Nani failed to stress 'red' in response to Suzy's stress on 'green' and 'go' in 2. Suzy's continued loudness seems to indicate a lag which suggests that mental processes involved in speech do not operate simultaneously at all times. Suzy's involvement in defending her point of view may have slowed her comprehension of the meaning of Nani's Utterance 5, while her understanding of the use of suprasegmental features in a dispute dictated the delivery of Utterance 6. Suzy's emotional involvement probably contributed to her problems in construction as witnessed by her self-corrections.

Both the name-calling and the red light/green light examples illustrate that the girls contrasted suprasegmental elements in serious or semi-serious disputes as well as in routines that were only play.[6] In both of these examples, Suzy tried to make Nani retract or alter what she had said. In the first case, she wanted Nani to stop calling her 'donkey' and 'mushi'. In the second case, she corrected Nani's erroneous statement that one should cross when a traffic light is red. Although the girls were interested in the real-world significance of red and green in traffic lights, they were caught up in the kind of manipulation of suprasegmental elements that characterised short routines. The girls did not explore the possibilities of contrasting meanings in this case (stop *v.* go) although they explored such contrasts in other routines. This kind of exploration occurred in the 'here/there' routine (Example 4) and in a number of other routines. (See Chapter 5, 'Antonym Games'.)

The referential meaning of the words and phrases used in these short routines was of varying importance to Suzy and Nani. Manipulation of suprasegmental elements was, on the other hand, always important. As Table 4 shows, the use of stress included emphasis on the point of information desired (Examples 1, 2, 6), the source of the dispute (5,

Table 4: SSE: Suprasegmental Elements Used in Short Routines

Examples	1	2	3	4	5	6
	N asks if S is coming to our house	N says balloon won't pop	'goodbye'	'here/there'	name-calling	red light/green light
Stress	Key word: our (point of information)	Key word: pop (source of anxiety)		Key words: 'here', 'there' (focus of interest)	Key words: 'donkey', 'mushi' (source of dispute)	Key words: 'cross', 'green', 'go' (point of information)
Volume		Loud (N): to get driver's attention	Shouting match		Loud (S): anger Soft (N): to annoy S	Soft (N): to annoy S Loud (S) to outshout N
Tune			Leave-taking			
Voice Quality				Gruff/ normal		Tearful
Intonation				Questions and answers		Mnemonic

name-calling), and focus of interest (4, 'here/there'). Loudness expressed anger while lower volume was used to annoy (5, 6). Question and answer intonation (4) seemed to amuse the girls while they pondered the meaning of 'here' in relation to 'there'. Suzy and Nani used special tunes in their leave-taking routine (3), and Suzy seemed to use a chant as a mnemonic to remember that 'Green says go and red says stop.'

In all of these examples, Suzy and Nani were able to manipulate the suprasegmental dimension of their linguistic systems to express ideas that were not included — and possibly could not be included — in the referential or content meaning of what they were saying. At times, they were simply not interested in referential meaning. At other times, referential meaning was extremely important (Was Suzy really a donkey? Does red really mean cross?). At all times they manipulated suprasegmental elements in response to social needs (saying goodbye) and dyadic needs (insulting another and defending oneself). As Labov has pointed out (1971, p. 72), 'grammar is busy with emphasis, focus, down-shifting and up-grading; it is a way of organizing information and taking alternative points of view.' Suzy and Nani used grammar for exactly this purpose when they stressed key words, organised their conversation into a chain of question-and-answer adjacency pairs, and used volume to annoy each other or to express anger.

Notes

1. Imitation as I am using it is limited to the repetition of immediately preceding speech and excludes role play (pretending to be someone else) or reported speech.

2. 'Utterance' was defined in Chapter 2 (p. 55) as a stretch of speech by one speaker followed by silence by that person. Note that in Example 1, Nani's second question was interrupted by Suzy, but Nani continued to speak until she finished her second question. Although no one spoke between the time Nani finished her second question and began her third question, the silent pause was so long (2.1. seconds) that I considered it an utterance boundary. When Nani paused earlier (1.1. seconds), she seemed to be waiting for a response. This might also be considered an utterance boundary. The shorter pause seemed less significant not only because it was half the length of the longer pause but also because Nani merely rephrased her question superficially. I therefore did not give the second question a separate utterance number. This example illustrates one of the reasons I prefer 'utterance' to 'turn'. Although Nani did not relinquish her turn until she received the response she sought, she did begin a new approach in Utterance 3 when she began to address the driver after a relatively long period of silence.

3. Brennis and Lein (1976, p. 8) pointed out that, in their study of first, third and fourth graders' acting out of role assignments, volume escalation was the 'single most popular stylistic strategy with younger children'. Apparently, children's appreciation of volume starts much before age six.

4. This assumes that each odd-numbered utterance after 1 and up to 13 (3, 5, 7, 9, 11) contradicted the even-numbered utterances even though 'No' occurred explicitly only four times.

5. This one of Suzy and Nani's routines that seems similar to the contradicting routine described by Boggs (1975). (See Chapter 2, footnote 20.)

6. Boggs (1975) described verbal disputes among part-Hawaiian children which were seen as a means of practising needed social skills.

4 CORRECTION ACTIVITIES

4.1 Introduction

This chapter is divided into sections according to the forms that correction activities take in these data. Like Fromkin, I do not intend to 'treat the errors in the corpus as a random sample of all errors made, but to attempt an explanation for the errors which were recorded' (Fromkin, 1971, p. 28). My definition of error is error as perceived by and mentioned (or in some way noted) by at least one of the children. The eighteen correction activities that I found in Suzy and Nani's conversations therefore determined the subdivisions of this chapter. This approach focuses on the interactions between the children and attempts to avoid as much as possible misinterpretation on the part of the researcher as to what should be classified as error.

In the discussion of short routines, we saw that Suzy and Nani could successfully manipulate suprasegmental elements in their speech and that they could co-operate in developing chains of adjacency pairs even when they were not interested in exchanging concrete information. In some cases, such as the 'here/there' example (Example 4 in Chapter 3), Suzy and Nani did not discuss their understanding of how the chain should progress; they simply built one pair after the other. In other cases, such as the red light/green light example (Example 6 in Chapter 3), the discussion was triggered by the desire to reach a 'correct' understanding of a real-world fact. Such corrective action is, according to Goffman (1976), a function of conversational and ritual constraints, but not of grammatical constraints. This, however, does not mean that we can learn nothing about grammatical constraints by looking at corrective action. On the contrary, Fromkin (1971) has shown that errors (some of which might trigger corrective action) provide valuable information about the psychological reality of grammatical units, rules, and about the relationship between 'performance' and 'competence' (1971, p. 27).

'Error' in studies of children's speech, however, has traditionally meant divergence from the adult system. This notion was challenged in comparing my data with Brown's (1973; see above, section 2.2). One problem is that the adult system to which a child may be exposed can vary greatly even with limited social and geographic boundaries. Furthermore, it is not always possible to determine when a child has reached criteria of acquisition of a given feature because we do not know how a child perceives surface forms, especially when these forms vary within similar (adult) grammatical contexts. The discrepancy between perception and production in a child's speech is generally acknowledged (e.g. Brown and Berko, 1960; Metcalfe, 1962). This discrepancy is, of course, related to the problem of whether a child's grammar is made up of adult surface structures or adult deep structures (see pp. 19/20 above, also Fischer, 1976). I have been interested in this problem, and the related problem of how to handle production data, for some time. In a paper (Iwamura, 1972), I pointed out that many studies of the acquisition of phonology failed to distinguish between the development of sound production and the development of phonologically meaningful segments. In these studies, a child was credited with acquiring a phoneme as soon as she produced a sound that the (adult) researcher could understand in terms of her own (adult) system.

At the time I wrote that paper, I had access to a draft of Moskowitz' dissertation (1972) in which she discussed 'phonological idioms'. She defined 'idioms' as 'entire units which are handled as such by the child' (n.d., Chapter 3, p. 25). That is, units which the child reproduces without analysing them into smaller parts. I was intrigued by her use of 'idiom', although I interpreted it more broadly than she did. It seemed to me that the notion of 'idiom' centred on the problem of when and how a child analyses any unit into smaller parts — not only in the area of phonology (phrase, word, segment, feature) but also syntax (sentence, NP, noun, affix, VP, verb, tense) and lexicon (word, grammatical class, semantic feature). If 'error' in a child's speech is interpreted as whatever does not sound 'correct' to an adult, how will we learn which of these smaller parts is psychologically real to the child at a given point in time? How can we study the progress of the child's analysis of idioms?

Fromkin (1971, pp. 29-30) suggested that one way to substantiate the psychological reality of discrete units is to study errors in speech production. In a child's speech, however, we (as adults) know which production data violate *our* system, but we do not know which data violate the *child's* system. One way to determine what violates the child's system is to listen to children correcting each other. It is especially helpful if the children happen to be very critical of each other. Suzy and Nani were exactly that. As the examples in Chapter 3 illustrate, they were very competitive and seized every opportunity to engage in what Goffman (1976) calls 'corrective action' (p. 269).

'Corrective action', in Goffman's terms, means anything that one or more persons do to adjust the flow of interaction. Error — or what speakers perceive as error — stands as it is until it is replaced by another bit of speech. If that replacement is intended as a correction, then we can say that the error is corrected. Since such replacement is done in the course of discourse (replacement always occurs *after* the error itself), only conversational and ritual constraints can effect corrective action. Any element in an interaction can potentially be replaced or corrected. The range of replacements includes articulation of a segment (Fromkin (1971) showed that even subsegment distinctive features can be rearranged), intonational contours, morphemes, lexical items, parts of sentences, whole sentences, and even strings of sentences. In Suzy and Nani's conversation, corrective action could range from a short 'repair sequence'[1] to a routine that involved discussions of who should say what and in what order. Some of this range is included in this chapter. The routine during which the girls gave each other instructions about what to say is covered in Chapter 6, the You Say routine.

Correction activities involved several aspects of Suzy and Nani's speech. In a correction activity there were always at least two grammatical forms that were competing for a 'correctness' judgement. Competition existed between (1) different phonetic realisations of the same word, (2) different syntactic patterns and (3) different lexical items. There was, of course, overlap between these three types of grammatical structures. In classifying what I found in the data, my goal was to weigh most heavily the particular error that the girls had noticed.

On some occasions, the girls corrected each other indirectly by repeating competing forms until one form ceased to be used or until both children settled on a third form (see Example 8 below). In other examples, they told each other exactly what to say and the sequence in which to say it (see Example 7 below). In all cases, correction activities required at least three steps or procedures. First, the children had to monitor; that is, attend to each other's speech in a critical way. On occasion they seemed to believe that *what* you say is not as important as *how* you say it. Second, one child had to challenge — directly or indirectly — whatever form she was critical of. And third, the first child had to respond either by removing or replacing the questionable form in her speech or by insisting on keeping the form. Sometimes, one of the girls would monitor, criticise and change her own speech without any input from the second girl. This was also an example of a child's perception of error since the speaker judged her own speech as incorrect or in need of alteration.[2] To execute these three steps, Suzy and Nani had to have an awareness of language as an object in itself. They had to have metalinguistic awareness that allowed them to separate language from its communicative function.

Some of the judgements that Suzy and Nani made seemed to be judgements of appropriateness, while others seemed to be judgements of grammaticality. Sometimes, the girls noticed that something one of them said did not fit into the context of the conversation because a routine was in progress and someone said something that did not fit into the routine. At other times, the girls were concerned about how something should be said either because one girl was sure she knew the best way to say it (for reasons which may have had to do with grammaticality, appropriateness or simple bossiness) or because communication could not succeed without adjustment. The only time that any utterance or part of an utterance was marked as less than grammatical or appropriate was when it occurred as the focus of a correction activity. This does not mean that all other sentences succeeded in fulfilling the speaker's intentions (in so far as the speaker's intentions were clear), but that other failures were not marked by the girls as inappropriate or ungrammatical, and may have been due to factors such as lack of co-operation between the children.

A child receives 'positive data' from the speech to which he is exposed in normal interchange (although his perception of such data may be different at different stages of his development), and 'negative data' when he is corrected, laughed at or misunderstood (McCawley, 1976). Correction activities provided Suzy and Nani with a means of giving each other metalinguistic feedback in the form of negative data whenever one child found fault with the other's speech and positive data whenever a 'correct' form was agreed upon.

I classified the correction activities I found in terms of the errors that were perceived rather than the form that each activity took. I found eighteen examples of correction activities in my data. Of these, five concerned phonetic or phonological errors, five concerned syntactic errors, and eight concerned lexical errors. This is, of course, a much smaller corpus than the one Fromkin (1971) had. Since she was working with data from adults only, she was not concerned with whether or not an error was perceived. She assumed that her own perceptions of error could accurately reflect the state of the speaker's system. Nevertheless, the categories she set up are somewhat similar to mine. Her categories included: segment or phone, phonetic features, phonological and morphophonemic constraints, word classes and syntactic phrases, and semantic features.

Some of the eighteen correction activities I found could be considered candidates for more than one of the categories I set up. The

distribution of correction activities in these categories did not follow
any pattern that I have found, and I have not been able to discover
why some points were even chosen by one of the girls for correction.
The apparently random distribution of correction activities may have
resulted from changes in the children's moods and interests from day
to day. It may also have been due to the rapid development of their
linguistic systems, which may have caused them to pay more attention to some features than to others at a given point in time. They may
also have been unaware of some elements or some difficulties at certain
stages of development.[3] In the case of the interaction between the
rapidly developing systems of the children in this study, there may have
been considerable lack of 'match' between the systems.[4] The following
discussion of correction activities will show that the girls' need to
communicate, not only about information but about the state of their
relationship, was urgent at times and the ability to construct correction
activities was a valuable way of talking about talk.

4.2 Correction of Pronunciation

Correction activities that focused on pronunciation concerned (1) alternative articulations of some items, and (2) misunderstandings about the
phonetic shape of others. Examples of (1), articulatory alternatives, did
not interrupt the flow of communication because both Suzy and Nani
knew what the other was talking about. Their disagreement was about
how a given word or words should be articulated. Instances of (2),
however, presented more serious problems because each girl had a
different word in mind — not merely a different pronunciation of the
same word. As a result, one did not know what the other was talking
about.

4.2.1 Articulatory Alternatives

Overt discussion of the correct pronunciation of several words occurred
in the data. They discussed the pronunciation of 'please', 'permission',
'mainland',[5] and 'cheek'. In their discussion of 'cheek', both girls had
so much difficulty trying to articulate this word that they asked the
driver for help. They were garbling it so badly that the driver could not
understand what they were trying to say. When the driver turned to
look at the girls, they pointed to their cheeks. In spite of adult coaching,
Suzy gave up the efforts, saying she could not articulate the word to
her own satisfaction. Of the words Suzy and Nani discussed, their
discussion of 'please' (Example 7) is the best illustration of a correction
activity that involved the adjustment of articulation in response to
metalinguistic criticism.

Example 7

8 Oct. a.m.

#	Speaker	Utterance	Coding	Symbol
1.	N:	(wants S to help her roll down her window) [pi:z]		N
2.	S:	[pli:z]	*Step 1* Correction activity starts. Model provided (S_1). Error repeated (N_1).	S_1
3.	N:	[pi:z]		N_1
4.	S:	No, *no*, not like that, [pəli:z]	*Step 2* Fact of error noted (S_2). Adjustment attempted (N_2).	$S_{1,2}$
5.	N:	[pli:z]		N_2
6.	S:	Nani, don't say like that. [pli:z]		$S_{1,2}$
7.	N:	[pi:z]		N_1
8.	S:	No like that, no. No, no.		S_2
9.	N:	Yes.	*Step 3* Criticism rejected (N_3).	N_3
10.	S:	No, no		S_2
11.	N:	Yes. We say [pli:z] like *that*, yeah? we say [pli:z] like that, year? We say [pli:z] like *that*.	*Step 4* Authority appealed to (N_4).	$N_{3,4}$
12.	S:	[pli:z]		S_1
13.	N:	Mommy we say [pli:z] like that, yeah?		N_4
14.	S:	[pli:z]		S_1
15.	D:	Like that, yeah (laughs)	Authority responds (D_4).	D_4
16.	S:	(?) Not like that. Not like that. [pəli:z]		S_1

(arrive at school)

Questions and answers can be seen as the first and second pair parts of adjacency pairs (Goffman, 1976; Merritt, 1976). The first pair part establishes conditional relevance for the second pair part. That is, once the first pair part (a question) is spoken, the pair would be incomplete without the second pair part (an answer) (Merritt, pp. 328-9). The conditional relevance which exists between a question and an answer is similar to the conditional relevance which existed between perceived error, correction and response to correction in Suzy and Nani's correction activities. Relevance between utterances in the girls' discussion of 'please' was apparent as soon as Suzy noticed what she considered to be a mistake in Nani's speech.

The 'please' correction activity can be seen as having four steps during which Suzy and Nani discussed competing phonetic shapes of the word 'please'. They did not resolve the issue in this case, but the form which their discussion took is similar to the form of other correction activities that involved chains of adjacency pairs.

Step 1. The correction activity started when Suzy offered Nani a model for the word that Suzy thought Nani had pronounced incorrectly. Nani repeated the offending pronunciation (3).

Step 2. Suzy explicitly told Nani that she had made a mistake. Suzy repeated the model changing it by adding a schwa. Nani responded (5) by changing her version of 'please' to include an [l]. It is not clear whether she was simply repeating the word or consciously trying to insert the [l] that was missing in Utterances 1 and 3 (since she drops [1] again in 7). It is also not clear whether Suzy thought [pəli:z] was better than [pli:z]. Even when Nani managed to pronounce the [l], Suzy failed to acknowledge Nani's version as correct.

Step 3. Nani rejected Suzy's criticism. Suzy continued to tell Nani that she was wrong.

Step 4. Nani appealed to authority ('we' in Utterance 11; 'mommy' in Utterance 13). The authority supported Nani, but Suzy repeated her own version of the correct pronunciation of 'please'.

Example 7 above shows that Suzy and Nani were able to discuss alternative ways of articulating the same sound. Their dispute was unresolved in the end (as far as can be inferred from the data). Each had taken a side and continued to produce utterances which required a response from the other. Conditional relevance of the chain of responses could be seen in each girl's refusal to compromise. Suzy continued to either repeat her version of 'please' or tell Nani she was wrong. In spite of the limited variety of her replies, Suzy's contributions were relevant in that they kept the debate going.

The 'please' example revealed that Suzy and Nani were able to talk about language — in this case alternative ways of saying 'please'. They were also aware that not all of the alternatives had equal value. We do not have data on what measure or measures they used to judge the value of one alternative against another. Nani's method of corroborating a judgement was to appeal to the driver. Suzy, however, did not accept the adult's judgement. When Suzy first decided that Nani's [pi:z] was incorrect, she may have noticed that the [l] was missing. Nani inserted the [l] in her attempts to say 'please' in Utterances 11 and 13. Suzy may have heard the [l] in Nani's 'please' in these utterances and, in order to be able to continue to criticise, may have changed her pronunciation of the model to [pəli:z]. The fact that both girls inserted [l] in every example from Utterance 11 on suggests that [l] was a psychologically real segment for them at least in the environment after [p] and before [i:]. Though a very tentative claim, this illustrates one way of analysing a child's language in terms of the child's system rather than in terms of an adult's system.

4.2.2 Resolving Miscommunication

While Suzy and Nani were involved in the debate on the pronunciation of 'please', they never lost sight of the thread of their discussion. That is, each girl always understood what the other was talking about. On at least one occasion, however, they became confused because each girl pronounced a certain word so differently from the other that they failed to communicate. In this case, they were not merely discussing alternate ways to pronounce the same word; the meaning was totally obscured by a failure to agree on which phonetic shape realised which meaning. Even the context of the conversation and attempts at non-verbal communication failed to untangle the confused message at first.

The reader will need some background information in order to understand Example 8 below. It was traditional at the pre-school that parents of children who celebrated birthdays send a birthday cake and packages (usually small paper bags) filled with candy and favours for the other children. One day, Suzy and Nani got into the car at the school after a birthday party. They were very interested in the 'packages'[6] they were bringing home.

Example 8

7 June p.m.

1. S: (obscured, may be [pɔkɪts])
2. N: I don't have any [*pɔkɪts*].
3. S: But *I* have.
4. N: So? I have *these*.
5. S: Put it in you [pɔkɪts].
6. N: I couldn' *find* it. I don'
7. S: In your [pakɪts].
8. N: I cannot *find* any [pɔkɪts].
9. S: No, put in your [pʌkɪč]. In your [pækɪǰ].
10. N: No I just wannu hold it. And my mommy's goin' hold my [pækɪǰ]. And I'm *hold*ing this.

(N describes the contents of her 'package'.)

In this example, Suzy and Nani were encountering difficulty in communicating. The crux of the problem was that Suzy pronounced 'package' in a way that sounded like 'pockets' to Nani. This led immediately to Nani's confusion because Nani had no pockets in the clothes she was wearing as she explained in Utterance 2. Since she heard 'pockets' when Suzy meant 'package', Nani could not understand what Suzy was trying to tell her to do. It was only when Suzy changed her pronunciation of 'package' to a phonetic shape less like what Nani heard as 'pockets' that communication was finally successful. Although the quality of the recording is not good enough to describe accurately all the steps she took to change her pronunciation of 'package', it is clear that Suzy adjusted the first vowel and the final consonant cluster in three steps. The phonetic symbols used here are intended to approximate the steps which occurred between the obscured form of [pɔkɪts] which did not communicate the idea of 'package' to Nani and the final form [pækɪǰ] which did.

In her first attempt (7), Suzy produced [pakɪts] in which she adjusted only the first vowel. When Nani continued to hear 'pockets', Suzy tried again. Her second two attempts occurred in Utterance 9. In the first of these, Suzy changed both the vowel and the final consonant and produced [pvkɪč]. At that point she was somewhat closer to her goal. She finally hit her target when she changed the vowel to [æ] and the voiceless affricate [č] to the voiced affricate [ǰ]. These changes yielded [pækɪǰ].

Not only did Suzy realise that she was not getting the message across, but she also understood that the problem concerned her pronunciation of 'package'. When the distinctions between [ɔ], [a] and [æ] and between [ts], [č] and [ǰ] was called to her attention by Nani's misunderstanding of her, Suzy had the skill to dredge up and articulate distinctions which she had previously ignored but which she must have stored somewhere so that she could retrieve them when necessary. Suzy appeared to be aware in some psychologically real way that [ɔ], [a], [ʌ] and [æ] are different; that [ts] is different from [c] and that voicing differentiates [č] from [ǰ].

This example illustrates the interplay between the context of the conversation and the girls' manipulation of grammatical forms. Nani and Suzy's skill in using language was intricately tied to their ability to construct cohesive text over several utterances. Without this skill, they would not have been able to carry on the conversation long enough (that is, construct a discourse of adequate length) to achieve the communication that had become blocked by problems in the area of phonology. It was the negative feedback which Suzy received from Nani which first prompted her to isolate the problem – the phonetic shape that represented the meaning 'package' – and then suggested to her how to make the necessary adjustments. The dialogue, made possible by the girls' knowledge of conversational and ritual constraints, provided the setting for the corrective action that led to adjustment of grammatical constraints.

Correction activities that involved the correction of pronunciation were of two types. Suzy and Nani discussed the articulation of a word in the first type. In the second type, they used what they knew about constructing cohesive dialogue to resolve a communication block. The block had been created by the fact that each girl pronounced two words slightly differently. By examining the correction of pronunciation, we have been able to suggest that certain segments or phones, such as [l] and certain features such as [+voice] seemed to be real units in the girls' linguistic systems.

4.3 Syntactic Correction Activities

Correction of syntax was more likely to involve self-correction than the interactive type of correction that took place in correction activities in which the girls were concerned with the pronunciation of words. The impetus to change the syntax of a sentence was the (often urgent) desire to communicate an idea or get a response. The first examples (Examples 9 and 10 below) will illustrate one way in which Suzy and Nani co-operated in constructing sentences. These examples are similar

to Example 3 in which the girls constructed an underlying sentence:
'We have fun Tsukamoto

$$\left\{ \begin{array}{l} \text{when I go home.'} \\ \text{with my mommy.'} \\ \text{with a roachie.'} \end{array} \right\}$$

The challenge (Step 2) in the correction activity format (see p. 76) was implied in Examples 9 and 10 when Suzy used question intonation in proposing additions to Nani's sentence (Utterances 3 and 6).

Example 9

21 May p.m.

1. S: Then   don'   hit.   People with it.
2. N: I not goin'   hit   peopl $\left\{ \begin{array}{l} \text{e} \\ \\ \end{array} \right.$
3. S: With it?
4. N: No I'm not.
                Not goin'   hit   'em   with it.
(The following day, Nani repeated a similar sentence with a different object pronoun.)

Example 10

22 May p.m.

5. N: Not goin' hit you with this.
6. S: *Again*?

The underlying sentence is something like this:

$$I'm \left\{ \begin{array}{l} \text{don'} \\ \text{not goin'} \end{array} \right\} hit \left\{ \begin{array}{l} \text{people} \\ \text{'em} \\ \text{you} \end{array} \right\} with \left\{ \begin{array}{l} \text{it} \\ \text{this} \end{array} \right\}$$

The fullest form of the sentence was never expressed. However, both girls seemed to be repeating parts of it at different times. When Suzy inserted 'With it?' (3), she seemed to be asking Nani whether Nani had forgotten to finish the sentence in Utterance 2. Apparently Nani thought that 'with it' belonged on the sentence because she added it in 4 and 5. I included 5 and 6 from this data collected on the day after 1-4 were recorded because 5 and 6 seemed to be a continuation of the previous day's topic. Suzy seemed especially amused when she said 'A*gain*?' (6). I think she recognised that Nani's sentence had originated the day before. Nani did not seem about to hit anyone with anything. The girls simply enjoyed talking about it. This was one place where the girls seemed to recognise that a sentence was part of their past experience. It is therefore likely that 5 was related to the long sentence that was never produced in full on 21 May (Example 9 above). If so, this is an example of a ritual constraint operating to influence grammatical constraints. The basic grammatical meaning of *to hit someone with something* is a negative, unpleasant one. In the context of Suzy and Nani's society of two, the negative meaning was modified by a mutual understanding that no one intended to hit anyone with anything. Suzy and Nani had established a ritual constraint that modified the meaning of *to hit someone with something*. Suzy's use of question intonation in 3 and 6 challenged the completeness of what Nani had just said. This suggested that Suzy was interested in the form of what Nani was saying as well as the content. For this reason, I consider 9 and 10 above to be examples of correction activities as well as examples of co-operative sentence-building.

Another topic the girls enjoyed talking about was the clothes they were wearing. When Example 11 below was recorded, Suzy was wearing a poncho and Nani was wearing a shawl. Both articles were knitted with thick yarn so that they looked similar except for their shape and the way they were worn. The first seven utterances are provided as context. Utterances 8-12 will be discussed in detail below.

Example 11

22 May p.m.

1. S: My poncho's *big*ger now.
2. N: My pon', my. My sh', my shaw', my shawl is *big*ger *now*.
3. S: My, my poncho's bigger now. Your poncho is bigger now. Just like mine.
4. N: (upset) No, this is not a poncho.
    Mines ⎧ is
5. S: ⎨ Just pretend to have a poncho.
6. N: This is not a poncho. This is a *shawl*.
7. S: Just pre*tend* to have a poncho.
8. N: No, I wan' to. No I don' wanna. I wanna be it, a, shawl.
9. S: Sha'
10. N: I wan' it to be a *shawl*.   I wa ⎧ n'
11. S: ⎨ Sha', sha'
12. N: (shouts) No, I say it my*self*. (giggles)

Utterances 8, 9, and 10 can be diagrammed this way:

8	N:	No I		
8'	N:	No I don	wan to	
8"	N:	I	wanna	
9	S:		wanna be it,	a shawl
10	N:	I		sha'
			wan it to be	a shawl.

In Utterance 8, Nani was upset and spoke quickly. She had trouble forming the sentence that she wanted and paused after 'it' and 'a', finally finishing the sentence with the word 'shawl'. Suzy was ready to help her remember the word she wanted, but that only made Nani more angry. By comparing 8 and 10, the target Nani finally achieved, it is clear that one aspect of the target sentence that Nani found difficult was the problem of dividing 'wanna' into its components 'wan' and 'to' and inserting 'it' between them. She managed to separate the components at the beginning of Utterance 8 but was not able to take the next step of inserting 'it'. She then tried to construct a negative (8') but was not satisfied with that. Her last attempt in Utterance 8 consisted of all the correct components but in the wrong order (8"). Although Suzy continued to contribute the final word in Nani's sentence (9), Nani herself had a target sentence in mind and reaching her target was a matter of pride for her ('No, I say it my*self*' (12)). Nani's giggle at the end of 12 showed that she was no longer upset (as she had been in 4 by Suzy's initial proposal that Nani *pretend* that her shawl was a poncho). The argument over whether to pretend that Nani's shawl was a poncho provided a specific point of conflict. When Nani expressed her views clearly, the topic was dropped. In the course of the dispute Nani was forced to resolve problems of syntax in the sentence that she wanted to use to express her feelings.

Nani's syntactic difficulty centred on *wanna*. *Wanna* (like *gimme*) is among the unanalysed forms which children learn early and which they must later re-analyse and 'unpack'. 'Very early, without any evidence that they have dative movement, children produce forms such as *gimme* and one often hears children saying *gimme it* in, as it were, one breath' (Fischer, 1976, p. 93). *Wanna* occurs very early in the typical child's vocabulary. Indeed, it is likely that *wanna* enters a child's vocabulary well before any other kind of complement verb (Gruber, 1967). In her paper, Fischer, borrowing from my data, used the sentences I analysed above (Utterances 8-10) to illustrate how unanalysed wholes like *wanna* 'may break apart before your very eyes' (p. 93). Fischer also suggested that the child may have in her vocabulary at the same time forms such as *pick it up* and *gimme* (but not *give it to me*) (R. Scollon, 1974, cited by Fischer). This may reveal an intermediate stage between the unanalysed form and the 'correct' adult form. In Nani's struggle to break *wanna* into its constituents, we can see that she seemed to be working out a conflict between her less mature, unanalysed *wanna* which could not be used to express VP + NP + VP and the more mature *want to* which can be used to express *want it to be*. Fischer warned that the apparent existence of transitional stages such as the one Nani appeared to be in at this point is one reason to be cautious about deciding whether what children produce reflects the total complexity of their deep structure (p. 101).

Unanalysed wholes such as *wanna* may be seen as syntactic (or lexical) 'idioms' in the sense in which Moskowitz applied this term to phonological forms (1972). The process of learning new items and then fitting them into the existing grammatical system is probably accomplished by the child at varying speeds depending on many factors. In the case of *wanna*, Nani had probably used it for a long time in sentences such as 'I wanna cookie.' and 'I wanna come too.' She would have had to learn the difference between *wanna* meaning 'want a' and *wanna* meaning 'want to' before she could approach the construction of *want* + NP + VP. This construction, however, must have existed in some form in her deep structure before she could attempt the analysis of *wanna* that she produced in Utterance 10. Throughout the history of her use of *wanna*, the relationship between deep structures and surface structures must have been changing constantly. As Fischer pointed out, we have as yet no empirical evidence on the nature of this relationship. I believe we might find such evidence by examining what children say when they are under pressure to communicate. During correction activities, Suzy and Nani were under this kind of pressure. The expression of *want* + NP + VP involves, of course, a more complex understanding of the structure of English than simply the unpacking of *wanna*. One aspect of this complexity is the embedding of a subordinate sentence into a superordinate sentence that contains *want*. This aspect is illustrated by the following example which occurred about one month after the girls discussed the shawl and the poncho (Example 11 above). In Example 12 below, however, the problem was not with the verb or the order of constituents but with the form of the NP that separates *want* from the following VP. This NP is the subject of the embedded subordinate sentence.

Example 12

17 June (Nani is upset and angry.)

1. N: I don' *wan she*. I don' *wan she* to talk to me.
   I don't wan *him, she* to talk to *me*. Don' wan' Suzy to talk to *me*.
2. S: Nani   ⎰ (?)
3. N: ⎱ I don' wan' you to talk to me.
4. S: Whose friend you are?
5. N: I'm not your *friend*. I'm not going to talk to *you*. Don' wan'. Don't talk to *me*.
6. S: (?)
   Who's your friend (?) not talk to you any more.
7. N: My *mom*my goin' be my friend.

Utterances 1, 3, 5 can be diagrammed as follows:

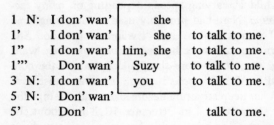

1 N:	I don' wan'	she	
1'	I don' wan'	she	to talk to me.
1"	I don' wan'	him, she	to talk to me.
1"'	Don' wan'	Suzy	to talk to me.
3 N:	I don' wan'	you	to talk to me.
5 N:	Don' wan'		
5'	Don'		talk to me.

A critical difference between Nani's target in Example 11, 'I want it to be a shawl' and her apparent target in Example 12, 'I don't want her to talk to me' is the surface form of the subject of the embedded sentence. Once she had unpacked *wanna* in Example 11, she did not need to change the subject of the embedded sentence because the surface form of *it* was the same as the underlying form as this tree shows:

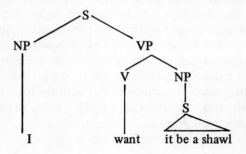

Nani's problems in Example 12 were more complex because she had to change the deep structure *she* to get the correct surface form *her*.

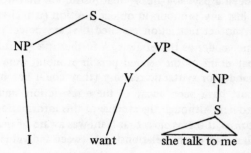

In Utterance 1 of Example 12 above, Nani constructed a sentence which had acceptable word order except that she could not find the right pronoun to use as the NP between *want* and *to talk*. Her efforts to find an NP she was satisfied with suggest the way in which she analysed the pronouns and the complement structure of the sentence. The first one she tried was *she* which fitted Suzy because it was [+ female] (1 and 1'). We will assume that Nani was working with a deep structure in which the NP following *want* was the embedded sentence, *she talk to me*. If so, Nani had already appropriately transformed the verb into the infinitive form, *to talk*, but had not yet changed the subject form of the deep structure pronoun, *she*, to object form of the (adult) surface structure, *her*. In Utterance 1'', Nani chose the object pronoun *him*. Although *him* was correct syntactically, Nani recognised that it could not refer to Suzy because it was [- female]. In 1'' ', Nani gave up trying to find a suitable pronoun and used a proper noun which was acceptable in both deep and surface structures. In 3, she also chose a form that was suitable in both deep and surface structures, the pronoun *you*. In 5, Nani seemed to be attempting the same difficult sentence, but she stopped after 'Don' wan' ', eliminated the word *want*, and changed the sentence into a negative imperative which eliminated all of the problems she had had with pronouns and complement structure (5').[7]

The corrections Nani imposed on herself in her own speech indicate that she understood the sentence grammar constraints on individual words in terms of grammatical class and semantic features. Nooteboom (1969, p. 130) found that 'a mistakenly selected word always or nearly always belongs to the same word class as the intended word [indicating] that the grammatical structure of the phrase under construction imposes imperative restrictions on the selection of words' (quoted in Fromkin, 1971, p. 44). This is apparently what happened to Nani, There must have been a psychologically real restriction that would not allow her to put just any pronoun in object position (it had to be an object pronoun). Another restriction required that any object pronoun must have the same gender as its referent. A further rule (or rules) dictated that a proper noun or the second person pronoun were neutral with respect to gender or syntactic relation (they could be objects or subjects). Nani must have been aware of these restrictions and/or the options available to her. Although the storage of this information might take a variety of forms, it seems clear that Nani was aware of the reality of grammatical class and of the relationship between individual words and syntactic relations.

The relationship between words and syntactic relations involves lexical as well as syntactic rules. The next section of this chapter will deal more specifically with word choice when syntax seems to exert little or no pressure on that choice. The following example involved the choice of a phrase which became abbreviated, thereby losing some of its surface syntactic complexity.

When Example 13 was recorded, both girls were wearing long muumuus, a favourite kind of apparel. With reference to their clothes, Nani asked the same question in three different ways:

Example 13

14 June

1. N: Is it a long dress?
2. S: Yes.
3. N: I'm wearing a long dress.
4. S: I   ⎰ too.
5. N: ⎱ Is that one is a down-to-the-floor dress?
6. S: Uh-huh.
7 N: Is it a down-floor dress?
8. S: Uh-huh, mines down.[8]

Utterances 1, 5, and 7 can be diagrammed as follows:

1. N: Is it	a long	dress?
5. N: Is that one is	a down-to-the-floor	
7. N: Is it	a down-floor	

In this example, Nani was trying different ways to express a single question. Utterance 1 was straightforward. Utterance 5 seemed to be a rephrasing of 1, but it was longer because 'it' became 'that one' and 'long' became 'down-to-the-floor'. The second 'is' in 5 is redundant and may indicate that the sentence Nani had constructed had more components than she was able to handle comfortably. In 7, she reduced 'that one' to 'it' and 'down-to-the-floor' to 'down-floor'. Thus, the last question in the series was exactly like the first, except that 'long' was expressed as 'down-floor'. Nani lexicalised a syntactic unit by removing the functor words *to* and *the*, thus eliminating the surface prepositional phrase, and ended up with a single lexical unit. *Down-floor* was pronounced as a unit (like *pants-suit* or *after-dinner drink*) and was interchangeable with 'long'.

Suzy and Nani had discussed down-to-the-floor dresses two days before this excerpt occurred. (I discuss this in detail in the analysis of the 12 June session in Appendix B.) Example 13 provides enough history of *down-floor* as a lexical unit to suggest that such shortened[9] forms in children's speech are not always the result of their inability to deal with complex forms. Nani was able not only to construct a complete prepositional phrase, but also to use it as an adjective to modify *dress*. We know that the prepositional phrase was not an unanalysed idiom because it was original with the girls – they invented it – and because Nani would not have known which words to delete unless she had a deep structure of the form Adj → Adv + Prep + Art + N. Utterance 7 looks like examples of the speech of very young children which contain only content words and no functors. As the example of *wanna* becoming *want to* (Example 11) illustrates, the child must control the necessary deep structure before she can successfully break down unanalysed wholes. The *down-floor* example suggests that a step which can follow the analysis of a whole into its parts may be the deletion of appropriate (i.e. deletable) parts.

In syntactic correction activities, Suzy and Nani were responding to their need to communicate and to their growing ability to manipulate syntax to answer this need. Their speech during these activities suggested that both deep and surface structures were developing and that there may have been intermediate stages where similar forms existed only on the surface (*wanna* before re-analysis) or only at a deeper level (*want* + NP + VP before the re-analysis of *wanna*).

4.4 Lexical Correction Activities

As I discuss the form of the lexicon, lexical entries, lexical retrieval and related theory, I will use the model proposed by Chomsky (1965). In this model, the lexicon is the component of the grammar which stores lexical entries. Each entry contains all of the information needed to insert the lexical item into a syntactic structure. Lexical retrieval and insertion occur when the syntactic component has generated a structure which includes the information needed to retrieve the correct lexical item from the lexicon and insert it into the syntactic structure.

The examples that I have chosen to discuss as lexical correction activities are only a small set of the examples in the data which might yield information about the girls' lexicons. I divided some of the others into two sets: associated terms and Antonym Games. Associated terms occur throughout the data and suggest some of the ways the girls organised lexical information. I listed examples of these in the Tables of Contrasting Words and Phrases (Appendix A) under the subheading, Associated Words and Phrases. I included under this subheading all of the words and phrases that occurred when the girls were talking seriously to each other and/or were manipulating words in such a way that associations became clear in the course of the dialogue. The exact meanings of the associations cannot always be specified on the basis of context. This list is intended to suggest some of the ways in which Suzy and Nani seemed to think about words and phrases as belonging to sets. The girls also used a number of words as antonyms. The direct opposition between a pair of words seemed to intrigue the girls. Their interest was so great that they developed their play with antonyms into a full routine which I call the Antonym Game (see Chapter 5).

4.4.1 Word Associations

In looking at correction activities in which one or both girls substituted one lexical item for another, I will be primarily interested in what might be inferred about the state of the girls' lexicons from the ways in which they manipulated lexical items. I will also be interested in how examining lexical correction activities helps in the interpretation of the data. When a set of lexical items occurred in a correction activity, it was often easier to understand what Suzy and Nani meant than it was to understand the same words when they used them in other contexts than in correction activities.

In this section, I will discuss inferences about ways in which Suzy and Nani associated words. The data which are included in this section fall between Antonym Games and associated terms with respect to what can be inferred from them about what Suzy and Nani meant when they used certain words. Antonym Games were based on a narrow association. That is, within a pair of antonyms the possible kinds of association are limited to the single feature which differentiates the two words. Antonyms are associated because of that one feature. When this limitation is absent, however, a wide range of possible associations is available. Lexical correction activities provided context that limited this range to a certain extent. On the other hand, the words and phrases which I listed in the Table of Associated Words and Phrases can only be interpreted broadly. Claims about the exact nature of associations imply claims about the specific content of lexical entries. Such claims are possible when associations were made within the context of a correction activity. This is because such a sequence was focused either partly or fully on the association itself. The idea suggested by one term would lead to the introduction of another because of the way in which the girls associated the terms.

The amount of information that an excerpt can provide depends on the number and type of associations the girls introduced. Example 14 is a minimally interactive exchange. It is similar to the type of repetition I discussed in section 3.2. In this type of repetition one child continued to repeat a sentence until the listener responded.

Example 14

4 Oct.

S: Last night I go to the library and (?) books.

Wanna	*hear*	my book?
Wanna	*see*	my book?
	Read	my *book*.

N: Oh yeah. Read the book.

This dialogue gives very little information about what 'hear', 'see' and 'read' actually mean to the children.[10] Although Nani responded only to the last sentence, she herself was noted to have said, 'Read me a story' when she wanted someone to make up a story for her when there was no book[11] (field notes). This indicates that the activity which is labelled as 'reading' in adult speech was associated with telling a story. Perhaps a pre-literate child does not know that reading can be accomplished without speaking or that reading is a way of getting a story from a written record rather than from memory or spontaneous

invention. If this is the case, such a child could have a complex notion
that related the word *read* to all the activities that are involved in story-
telling with or without a book. A possible description of the lexical
entry for *read* might include: [12]

$$
\left[
\begin{array}{l}
+ \underline{\hspace{3cm}} \text{ story} \\
+ \underline{\hspace{3cm}} \text{ book} \\
+ \text{ use eyes} \\
+ \text{ can be heard (involves speaking)} \\
+ \text{ Vb}
\end{array}
\right]
$$

Even though Example 14 above yields no conclusive evidence about
the specific feature composition of the lexical entries *see, hear* and *read*,
it does suggest that these are all associated with books and it shows that
Suzy and Nani changed lexical items in successive sentences just as they
did phonetic shapes and other forms in correction activities. One of
their strategies seemed to be 'if it doesn't work the first time, change it
a bit and try again.'

In Example 15 below, the referential meaning was quite clear. Nani
used 'heads' instead of 'hands' when 'hands' were the objects out of the
window.

Example 15

30 Oct. p.m. (Suzy and Nani have their hands — all four of them — out
of the car window. Nani imitates Suzy's intonation and pitch almost
exactly.)

S: I can put my *hands* inna window.
N: I can put my *heads* inna window.
S: *Hands*.
N: *Hands*.
S: See this four little *hands*?
N: And this four little *hands*?

The association of 'heads' and 'hands' may have simply been that of
parts of the body. If so, Nani might as likely have used any other body
part — or at least a body part that could be put out the window. However, similarities in the phonetic shapes of [hɛdz] and [hædz] may also
have been involved in Nani's confusing 'heads' and 'hands'. On the basis
of his work with children's spelling, Michael Forman (personal commu-

nication) suggests that contrasts among vowels of the set [æ, æ̃, ɛ̃, ɛ] may not be evident to children in the same way that such distinctions are clear to adults. Vowel similarity combined with the same initial and final consonants, [h] and [dz] in 'heads' and 'hands' may have added fuzziness in phonetic discrimination to Nani's difficulty in finding the right name for the body part that was out the window. In any case, Nani quickly accepted Suzy's correction and provided no more information about how she associated 'hands' and 'heads'.

In some situations, however, the referent was not as clear as 'hands' in Example 15 above. Sometimes the children themselves were not sure of what it really was. In these cases, the correction activity was really a discussion of language use. Example 16 below illustrates this point. The girls were interested in a large red plastic container which they found in the back seat. They recognised that the container had some connection with the mechanical functioning of the car. (In fact, it was filled with water in case the car's cooling system, which had not been working properly, overheated.) The girls incorporated the container into several of their conversations during the week that it was in the car. It was rectangular and heavy for the girls to move. Usually they pretended that it was a door. 'It' in the following discussion refers to the container.

Example 16

18 June p.m.

1. N: Share. Share that. Kay? Share it inna car.
2. S: 's gas. This is gas.
3. N: No, this is, belongs to me for g, and that's for, and that's *wat*er for *put*ting in the *car*.
4. D: That's right. That's what it is.
5. N: It's water, yeah?
6. D: (?)
(N and D discuss the fact that it is dirty water that is for the car.)
7. N: Yes, see, ⌠my mommy says it's water. ⌠
8: S: ⌊Makes[a]fill ⌊Makes filled up.
9. N: Not make it fill, all filled up.
   S: (giggle)
   N: (giggle)

a. The use of *make* as a causative was not unusual in Suzy and Nani's speech and has been noted in HCE by Forman (1971) and Bickerton (1971).

Although Suzy did not know what was in the container, she was able to guess that it was a liquid and that it was needed for the car's engine or at least that it was in some way connected with the mechanical operation of the car. In Utterance 2 she called this liquid 'gas'. In the process of correcting Suzy in 5, Nani appealed to the adult for corroboration of her claim that the substance was water. Suzy understood the technical description of the liquid and its purpose as stated by Nani in Utterance 3, waited while Nani had further discussion with the driver on the subject, fitted her new information into her familiarity with cars, and concluded that the water could cause the car to become 'filled up' (8). Because 'gas', 'water', and 'car' were associated due to the girls' familiarity with cars, it is reasonable to assume that information on the subject was stored somewhere in their lexicons.

In the examples given above of correction activities involving lexical choice, Nani and Suzy were concerned with accurately naming physical objects according to attributes which they could observe by sight, sound or touch. Correction activities also occurred when lexical choices involved abstract or non-physical features. The following example shows how the children discussed abstract terms, such as time, and also how lexical correction activities sometimes revealed sets of associated terms.

Example 17

21 May p.m. (This was an afternoon trip. Nani had been explaining to Suzy how her slippers should be arranged on the floor of the car. Nani had been bossy and Suzy continued to challenge her. Suzy started to go down to the floor of the car.)

1. N: Don' go in there because it's dirty.
2. S: Oh, let's hide in here.
3. N: Huh?
4. S: Let's hide.
5. N: Hide in there? No, no it's dir*ty*.
6. S: Last *night* we did. Last night you told me want, to hide up there.
7. N: Hum?
8. S: Last night you said you want to hide over *there*, with me.
9. N: So, last *time*, last time you said, put your, uh, sweater *here* and your slippers *here* and your sweater *here*. Last time you *tell*.[a] This morning when I was hiding, last time.
10. S: Long *time* ago (?) Long, long time ago.
11. N: And last time, we hide yeah, under it.
12. S: Huh?
13. N: Last time, we hide. Last time, last time, that we hide. Last time we hide under, the, last time we hide under, the bag, last time.

Last, when you was here.
(short pause followed by Nani singing.)

a. *Tell* was synonymous with *say* in Nani's speech at this time and for a long time thereafter (at least until 5;1). *Tell* as a synonym for *say* is also a common creole feature of HE (Carr, 1972, p. 152). For more *tell/say*, see discussion of the Name Game (section 6.2.3) and related work by C. Chomsky (1969) (Chapter 6, footnotes 5 and 6).

The discussion in Example 17 above had a serious tone. There was no giggling or use of contrasting voice quality. Throughout the exchange, Suzy tried to convince Nani to play on the floor, but Nani did not want to because 'it's dirty' (5). The phrase 'let's hide' (2, 4) was part of the Hiding Game and always referred to getting down on the floor (see Chapter 7). In Utterance 6, Suzy appealed to past experience to strengthen her request. That is, she tried to get Nani to co-operate by reminding Nani that she herself had played on the floor before. Suzy's ploy did not work. Nani rejected the argument that past behaviour binds present actions (N: 'So . . .' (9)). Nani pointed out that this time Suzy was not being co-operative about what Nani wanted to do (i.e. arrange slippers and sweaters) even though, according to Nani, Suzy had done so in the past. Nani was referring in Utterance 9 to a sequence which preceded the data given here in which Suzy had agreed to arrange the slippers and sweaters.

References to past time were used by the girls to strengthen their challenges to each other. They both seemed to think that if they could establish the fact that a person had done something in the past, then that fact would obligate that person to do it again. The various expressions they used to indicate past time included: 'last night' (S: 6, 8); 'last time' (N: 9, 11, 13); 'this morning' (N: 9); and 'long time ago' (S: 10). The meanings of these expressions did not seem to be different except for the last one, 'long time ago'. Nani's 'last time' (9) seemed to refer to the same point in time as Suzy's 'last night' (8) and as her own 'this morning' (9). Suzy then (10) disputed the events described by Nani (putting slippers and sweater *here*) by challenging Nani with 'long, long time ago', which seemed to antedate 'last time' for Suzy. Nani's last attempt to defend her position (which at Utterance 13 appeared to have become the same as Suzy's initial goal at Utterance 2) consisted of another way of referring to 'last time': 'when you was here'.

The association of phrases which express past time was clear within the context of the correction activity. For Nani at least, 'last night', 'last time' and 'this morning' were synonyms for a time in the past 'when you was here'. Suzy was also interested in specifying past time, but she wanted to refer to an event which occurred before 'last time'. To do this, she chose the phrase 'long, long time ago'. From an analysis of this excerpt, it can be seen that the children have at least two degrees of past time: the recent past and the time which came before the recent past. They have at least three phrases to discuss recent past and one for more distant past.[13] They were able to maintain communication in this instance because they shared similar concepts and similar enough lexical items to express these concepts. In some interchanges, however, they were unable to communicate because of idiosyncratic use of lexical items and semantic realisations.

4.4.2 Idiosyncratic Use of Words

Idiosyncratic use of words sometimes led to sequences in which some kind of correction was crucial to communication. That is, the establishment of common understanding of the use of a word or the replacement of an idiosyncratic term by one that was understood by both participants was a prerequisite for getting the message through. One example of the correction of the idiosyncratic use of a word occurred on 13 June. Nani was in the habit of using 'mean' and 'mad' to mean 'angry'. In Nani's speech, the expression 'She's mean at me' was as common as 'She's mad at me' (field notes). On 13 June, Nani was unhappy about something the driver had said and she told Suzy in a confidential tone, 'We mean at her.' Suzy did not understand what Nani meant so Nani corrected herself and said, 'We mad at her.' If Nani had not realised that her term 'mean' failed to convey the meaning 'angry' to Suzy, she would not have been able to get the message through. Nani replaced 'mean' with 'mad' because she was able to understand Suzy's perspective. Nani understood that 'mean' was her own private realisation of 'angry' — not one that Suzy shared.

Idiosyncratic use of words, if uncorrected, could lead to complete failure of communication. An example of such a communication breakdown occurred on 12 June (Example 18 below). Nani had made up an expression 'happy dress' to refer to dresses made out of a fabric that had smiling faces in the printed design. (In fact, the name of the design is 'Happy Faces'.) This design was very popular at the time and both girls had such dresses. Suzy, however, did not know what Nani meant by 'happy dress'.

Example 18

12 June (This excerpt is also in the full transcription of the 12 June

session given in Appendix B.)

10. N: This is my, happy dress. I got happy dress like you. I got happy dress like you.
11. S: I don't have happy dress.

Nani did not attempt to explain her private term for the kind of dress she was referring to. The girls continued to discuss dresses, but Suzy probably never figured out what Nani meant by 'happy dress'. McCawley (1975) claimed that the specific history of personal language acquisition determines morpheme identification. If private morphemes are different from public ones, then the acquisition process must enable the speaker to acquire rules which differentiate between private and public usages (as Nani did with 'mean' and 'mad' and which she failed to do with 'happy dress'). Rules must also be learned which transform private identification to public. An intermediate step might be learning to establish intimate and casual levels which make all levels of speech (phonological and syntactic as well as lexical) more public and less private or at least restrict public usage to a small group. Public usage within a restricted group comes under control of what Goffman (1977) called ritual constraints. It is permissible – and sometimes imperative – to ignore some conversational and grammatical constraints when establishing intimacy. Ritual constraints can dictate which constraints may be suspended. If neither ritual, conversational nor grammatical constraints operate, then communication fails. Suzy used conversational constraints to let Nani know she did not understand 'mean' in the first case and 'happy dress' in the second. In the first case, Nani understood that she had broken all constraints: grammatical constraints do not allow 'mean' to indicate 'angry'; conversational constraints could not provide the context in which 'mean' could be used in this way; ritual constraints – those specific to Suzy and Nani's private shared language – also did not support Nani's use of 'mean' because this usage was known only to her (and the ubiquitous investigator) and was not shared by Suzy. Whatever Nani may or may not have known about the grammatical constraints that applied, she was obliged to explain 'mean' by her knowledge of what she had shared with Suzy or what she knew about the lexicon of English in general. When Nani accepted this obligation, she was able to communicate with Suzy. By not accepting this obligation in the 'happy dress' example, Nani failed to communicate. This time, Nani was unable or unwilling to take Suzy's perspective. Nani simply did not account for the difference between her point of view and Suzy's.

In addition to difficulties encountered because of private use of words as illustrated in the two examples above, the children also had trouble communicating when they both attached the same meaning to a lexical item but applied the word to different specific instances. In Example 19, Suzy was talking about 'Jason', who was apparently a person in a book or story, while Nani was talking about a friend named 'Jason' who had recently slept at her home (until his parents came to pick him up). Both girls understood that 'Jason' was the proper name of a male person, but they failed to acknowledge each other's point of view to the extent that they could talk about the *same* male person with that name.

Example 19

21 June a.m.

1. S: Do you remember Jason?
2. N: Huh?
3. S: Remember Jason (?) the mountain?
4. N: No, *mines*.[a] I have a Jason. You 'member *my* Jason-um-he was sleeping in my, my mommy and daddy's *bed*. That's what, yeah. That *my* Jason just come down but he didn'. Somebody did { pick him up.
5. S: { Mountain.
6. N: Huh?
7. S: Jason in the mountains.
8. N: What?
9. S: Jason at the moun*tains*. Jason, at the, moun*tains*.
(Both start to make noises)

a. Brown (1973) listed *mines* as an over-generalisation. It is, however, a very common feature of HE. See Chapter 4, footnote 8.

The girls' use of stress is revealing in this excerpt. When Nani stressed '*mines*' and '*my*' in Utterance 7, she indicated that she knew that *her* Jason was not the same as Suzy's Jason. Nani did not want to talk about the character in a story; she wanted to talk about her friend. Suzy, however, had never met Nani's friend. Suzy and Nani probably had heard a story about 'Jason at the mountains' at the pre-school at the same time. Suzy expected Nani to 'remember Jason' (the one at the mountains). When Suzy brought up the hero of the story as a topic of conversation, however, Nani remembered a different Jason (her friend) and wanted to explain what *her* Jason ('I have a Jason' (4)) had done. But Suzy did not want to talk about any Jason other than the one in the mountains. She repeated the reference to the story every time she spoke, emphasising the second syllable of 'moun*tain*' as a parting shot, as it were, before the girls started a new activity. Throughout this exchange, each girl continued to refer to her own specific instance of 'Jason'. Both girls stubbornly refused to compromise. Neither was willing to respond to conversational constraints which demand that participants maintain a minimal level of understanding. 'Huh?' and 'What?' (N: 2, 6, 8) are common requests for what Goffman calls 're-runs' (Sacks *et al.*, 1974, call such requests 'repair mechanisms'). (See Chapter 1, footnote 4.) This kind of request can be used to indicate that references are unclear, especially when identicality is involved (Goffman, 1976, p. 261). Since Suzy and Nani refused to talk about the identical 'Jason', their exchange did not meet a minimal level of understanding. As previous examples have shown, they were certainly capable of achieving and maintaining this minimal level if they chose to do so. In this case, they preferred to abandon the dialogue completely.

While the girls' failure to talk about the same Jason could be attributed to sheer stubbornness on their parts, it is important that they could have handled the exchange differently if they chose to do so. Utterances 1-9 appear at first to violate Halliday's claim that 'cohesion lies in continuity of reference' (1976, p. 31). By refusing to discuss the identical Jason, Suzy and Nani apparently failed to establish continuity of reference. Nevertheless, there was a sense in which these nine utterances cohere. In this case, cohesion lay not in the continuity of reference (both Jasons being the same person), but in the girls' awareness that a lexical item, *Jason*, could have the same semantic features [+ proper name, + male], but different referents. Cohesion may also have derived from the fact that the girls could have chosen to talk about the same Jason but did not want to. Their refusal to account for each other's point of view on this specific issue may itself have contributed to the cohesion of this exchange.

4.4.3 Semantic Features

In the 'Jason' example (19), the girls chose not to talk about the identical instance of the same lexical item. In other examples, lexical items they used differed by a small number of features. In Example 20 below, the features which differentiated these items were specific and were the focus of the interaction. In this case, Suzy and Nani could not agree on who should play which role in a make-believe game.

Example 20

30 August

1. N: I'm grandpa, you *fa*ther. I am grandpa.
2. S: No.
3. N: I'm grandma, you mommy, kay?
4. S: No, I'm grandpa.
5. N: Yes, you *are mom*my.

The features in focus here are sex and generation. Suzy did not want to be [-female, +parent]. Nani changed the sex feature in Utterance 3, suggesting that Suzy be [+female, +parent]. Suzy rejected that idea, too, because it was not the sex of the role that interested her. Suzy wanted to be [+parents' parent]. The dispute over who would play which role provided evidence that the girls were aware that the terms *mommy, father, grandpa* and *grandma* can be divided into classes in two ways, depending on whether sex or generation is used to classify them. Although other items in the Table of Associated Words and Phrases (see Appendix A) suggest similar kinds of cross-classification, i.e. terms that differ by a small number of features, this example shows especially clearly that Nani and Suzy were able to distinguish lexical items solely on the basis of two features. The interaction isolated the issues of the dispute and made the conflicting features, sex and generation, available for analysis.

The ways in which Suzy and Nani used words in lexical correction activities suggest what information may be stored in their lexicons. In these activities, the girls provided each other with metalinguistic feedback and consequently made adjustments that enabled them to continue their conversation. If they chose not to make adjustments, communication between them broke down. Lexical correction activities were similar to other kinds of correction activities in that a series of alternate forms occurred in the dialogue. One of these may have become the final form. Choice of a final form may have involved the semantic feature distinctions between alternatives ('grandpa-father/grandma-mommy' in Example 20) or the semantic representation (influenced perhaps by similar phonological shapes) associated with the term ('heads/hands' in Example 15). Several words or phrases could also be used interchangeably as referents to the same point in time ('last night/last time/this morning' in Example 17). Idiosyncratic use of a word could inhibit communication or could be explained and thus made part of the girls' shared vocabulary. The three types of constraints suggested by Goffman (1976) — grammatical, conversational and ritual — seemed to influence the various forms that these correction activities took.

This chapter has looked at ways in which Suzy and Nani adjusted their speech in response to metalinguistic feedback. Sometimes they provided each other with this feedback while at other times one girl changed parts of a phrase while she repeated it either for her own private reasons or because she seemed to be trying to improve communication. Areas in which correction activities occurred were pronunciation, syntax and lexicon. Correction was guided by conversational and ritual constraints.

Throughout the foregoing discussion, I discussed the meaning that the girls gave to the words they used. In so far as possible, I tried to justify my own interpretation of the data by noticing what the girls said and did rather than by comparing my linguistic system with theirs. Looking at correction activities provided three major kinds of information. First, we were able to observe how the girls' understanding of conversational and ritual constraints made correction possible by enabling Suzy and Nani to construct cohesive discourse. Second, we were able to observe aspects of the girls' linguistic systems, including the storage of lexical information and the development of syntax, through transitional stages such as the reanalysis of *wanna* into *want* and *to*. Third, we were able to see the effect of their ability or willingness to take each other's perspective on the success of their communication. In the following chapters, we will see how Suzy and Nani's abilities to construct discourse, to handle a number of linguistic patterns, and to take each other's point of view into account enabled them to develop their own private game-like routines.

Notes

1. 'Repair sequences' are adjacency pairs which consist of a repair mechanism (the first pair part), such as 'Huh?' which requests repetition or clarification, plus the requested repair (the second pair part) (Sacks *et al*., 1974). Goffman calls the requested repairs 're-runs'. See also p. 22 and p. 101.

2. In these cases, I do not attempt to draw a clear line between self-correction and mutual or reciprocal correction. Because my primary interest here is the effect the girls had on each other's speech, I have included mainly those correction activities which involved the three steps described here. That is, one of the children had to perceive some bit of speech as an error and either replace it with

another bit of speech or request that her partner replace the perceived error with something else.

Co-operative sentence-building such as occurred in Example 3 (Chapter 3) was, of course, closely related to mutual correction. The difference between the two activities was the omission of an explicit challenge (Step 2) in co-operative sentence-building. See Examples 9 and 10 for co-operative sentence-building that included explicit challenge.

3. McCawley (1976, p. 12) calls this 'shifts of awareness'.

4. For example, the failure to work out a shared understanding of idiosyncratic use of words could prevent communication. See section 4.4.2.

5. According to general use in Hawaii, 'Mainland' refers to the continental US. Both girls had grandparents living there.

6. 'Package' in Hawaii can mean paper bag or sack as well as the GAE meaning, a box wrapped in paper. Suzy may have been more familiar with the local usage than Nani was. If so, the adjustment of the pronunciation of the key words was only part of their problem; Suzy also had to persuade Nani to extend her notion of 'package' to include paper bags.

7. Ferguson and Farwell (1975) found that children avoid sounds they find difficult. In Example 12, Nani had difficulty handling both case and semantic features of the pronoun which followed *want*. Like the children in Ferguson and Farwell's study, Nani avoided what she had trouble with; she did this by choosing 'Suzy' and 'you'. Unlike the children in Ferguson and Farwell's study who were much younger (just over 1;0), Nani was able to work out her problem in the context of discourse.

8. There seems to be no categorical interpretation of Suzy's Utterance 8. *Mines* in both an HCE feature having the same function as GAE 'mine' and an over-generalisation typical of children's speech (Brown, 1973). Suzy was also likely to have heard the contraction *mine's*. Since the data do not permit a clear choice among these alternatives, there is no way to specify what was elided or left out. Here are some possible interpretations. (Following Merritt (1976), broken lines surround the material that may have been left out.)

a. Mines   ⌐is a⌐   down   ⌐floor dress⌐ .

b. Mines   ⌐is⌐   down.

c. Mine's   down.

d. Mine's   ⌐a⌐   down   ⌐floor dress⌐ .

See p. 100 for another example of the use of *mines*.

9. See Gleitman and Gleitman (1970) for more on innovative uses of shortened forms. In my examples here, I am ignoring the issue of contrasting stress patterns and other aspects of compounding

10. There is, however, a fascinating area that could be developed based on the kinds of lexical relations that Suzy and Nani used here and in the terms listed in Appendix A. Unfortunately, time and space do not permit investigation of what Halliday and Hasan (1976) call 'lexical cohesion' (Chapter 6). Some of the cohesive patterns that occur in discourse are built on relations between lexical items. One lexical relation which pertains to Example 14 is collocation. This relation among *see, hear* and *read* is evident in their regular co-occurrence with *book*.

This and similar ideas were suggested to me by an excellent handout prepared by Jim Martin for Susan Ervin-Tripp's course on Child Discourse in July and August 1977.

11. Halliday and Hasan said that 'In general, any two lexical items having similar patterns of collocation – that is, tending to appear in similar contexts – will generate a cohesive force if they occur in adjacent sentences' (1976, p. 286). The collocation relation in this case is between *hear* and *read* with relation to *book* and *story*.

12. This lexical entry is clearly over-simplified. For example, it does not take into account the fact that *read* in 'Read me a story' when said in the absence of written material is [-use eyes]. An adequate handling of detailed formalisation of lexical entries and lexical rules is beyond the scope of the present work.

13. Other terms referring to time also occurred in the data. A dialogue on 3 June included a series of utterances which provided a context for time terms 'now', 'already' and 'tomorrow'. 'Now' and 'already' referred to events that had occurred earlier in the day. 'Tomorrow' referred to the immediate future. See Appendix B, analysis of 3 June, Utterances 19, 21, 26, 27, 34; and Appendix A, Table VI, Associated Words and Phrases.

5 ANTONYM GAMES

5.1 Introduction

When Goffman looked for answers to the 'embarrassing question of units', he first rejected sentences, then 'turn at talk' which can contain more than one sentence, then he considered 'move' which can be made up of more than one turn, and finally decided that a chain of adjacency pairs can have a 'unitary, bounded character' (1976, p. 272). The short routines and correction activities that we have looked at so far were such chains. In the case of short routines, the chains were bounded by Suzy and Nani's manipulation of suprasegmental elements. In correction activities, the girls devised chains for the purpose of exploring alternative ways of saying the same thing. In Antonym Games, however, the girls developed chains of what Goffman calls 'neat packagings of aggression' (p. 274). Goffman considers children mature practitioners of this form because they are 'given to making open jibes'[1] (ibid.). He credits Lewis Carroll with providing 'Englishry with linguistic models to follow in the pursuit of bickering as an art form' (ibid.). While Lewis Carroll had no influence on Suzy and Nani's Antonym Games as far as I can tell, the Antonym Games which will be discussed in this chapter do make up 'neat packagings of aggression'.

Although adjacency pairs that we have looked at so far did contain elements of disagreement, only Antonym Games seemed to exist mainly for the purpose of giving the girls an opportunity for bickering. This gave Antonym Games a 'unitary, bounded character' that allowed them to be events in themselves (full routines) or to be readily embedded into other conversational contexts (including other full routines). Since the bickering that was involved in the Antonym Game focused on polar oppositions between words, Antonym Games provide a view of Suzy and Nani's use of rules of grammar which is mainly limited to their lexicons. This routine also provides information about how they manipulated conversational and ritual constraints. Their ability to control each other's speech on the basis of dyadic expectations can be seen in the Antonym Game and in the You Say routine which will be discussed in the following chapter. The need to watch simultaneously what children do with grammar and what they do with conversation is, I think, what Halliday had in mind when he wrote:

Since children are simultaneously both interacting and constructing the system that underlies text [their interactions belong to the set of] certain types of social context [which] typically engender text in which the coding process, and the congruence relation, tend to be foregrounded and brought under attention (1976, p. 581).

As I mentioned in the section on lexical correction activities, my task of assigning meanings was easier when the words or phrases in question occurred as pairs of antonyms, i.e. words having the same features with opposite values. Fortunately for my purpose, Suzy and Nani liked to put together antonym pairs. In my data, I found 29 different words and phrases that occurred as pairs with opposite meanings. All instances of the use of these pairs added up to 47. (All these instances are listed in the tables in Appendix A under Table I, Opposites.) These pairs are useful not only in helping to interpret the data but also in adding to the information about the girls' lexicons.

In Suzy and Nani's interactions, antonym pairs occasionally occurred within correction activities, although this was not always the case. In the development of the routine which I call the Antonym Game, the girls often corrected each other according to their expectations of how the routine should proceed. Such correction decreased after each knew what the other expected. Once mutual expectations were established with respect to the Antonym Game, it could be considered a 'standardised speech form',[2] that is, a full routine rather than a short routine. As a full routine, the Antonym Game occurred in a variety of conversational contexts, including other routines. Whether or not antonym pairs were part of a correction activity or embedded into other interaction, they had the potential to yield the kind of information that Fromkin found in adult errors which involve the substitution of one word by its antonym. She believed that 'such errors provide important evidence as to the storage of vocabulary and the generation of speech' (1971, p. 46).

In this chapter I will discuss how the Antonym Game developed first into a full routine and then into a ritualised routine. The terms 'full routine' and 'ritualised routine' are intended to indicate signposts rather than final products of the processes I will discuss. My entire data collection is a record of only a small portion of the verbal activity involved in these processes. I use the terms 'short routine', 'full routine' and 'ritualised routine' to indicate that changes occurred which resulted in differences between earlier and later instances of the same routine over a period of time. One difference between short routines and full routines was that the latter were more likely to be embedded in larger routines. Only full routines could have another routine embedded in them. As full routines Antonym Games occurred as part of the Hiding Game (see Chapter 7). The types of correction activity that I discussed in Chapter 4 were short routines. They were never embedded in larger routines.[3] Another distinction between short routines and full routines was that in many short routines each girl had personal feelings about her set of the pair parts of the adjacency pairs in a chain.[4] When the pronunciation of 'please' was the topic (Example 7 above), Suzy seemed to really *care* whether 'please' |was pronounced [pi:z], [pli:z] or (pəli:z]. Nani seemed interested mainly in disagreeing with Suzy. In Antonym Games, neither girl seemed to care who said which word of the opposition in question. All that was important was that the opposition between the antonym be maintained regardless of who said what. Correction that occurred in connection with Antonym Games was concerned with maintaining this opposition, not with finding the best pronunciation of a word or the most suitable word for a given syntactic context or even with establishing a real-world truth (as in the red light/green light exchange, Example 6 above). Suzy and Nani's giggles, which frequently accompanied full routines, indicated that they felt that language was fun to manipulate as a shared activity. The girls were able to use their understanding of the semantic relationship between opposites to set up Antonym Games. They were further able to communicate to each other that this relationship was the focus of a routine and that a routine such as the Antonym Game was fun to do.

5.2 Development of Antonym Games

Pairs of antonyms occurred in three basic patterns or in combinations of these patterns. I have given each pattern a number and a name. The names are intended to be mnemonic devices to help remember the characteristics of the patterns. Because combinations contained elements of more than one pattern, there is no clear way of saying where one pattern ended and another began. I do not intend to imply that these patterns were rigid, but that the girls had a variety of ways of keeping in focus the opposition between antonyms. In identifying these three patterns, I am attempting to loosely characterise the way the girls set up and continued their Antonym Games.

Pattern 1: Oppose: each child said the opposite of what the other child said.

Pattern 2: Echo: one child was the leader. The second child was the follower. The leader said one part of the antonym pair and the follower repeated it. The leader then said the opposite and the follower repeated that.

Pattern 3: Switch: this pattern was a combination of the other two. If Pattern 1 was in progress, one child could break the pattern by repeating what the other had said (instead of saying the opposite). On the contrary, if Pattern 2 was in progress, one child could break the pattern by saying the opposite (instead of echoing).

Length of exchange was a function of pattern identification. The longer the Antonym Game went on, the more possibilities there were for Pattern 3 to occur. Whereas Pattern 1 could be established in two turns, Pattern 2 required at least four turns. A pattern could be called 3 if the Antonym Game lasted for more than two turns and if opposition turned into echo or vice versa.

The three patterns can be illustrated schematically: (A and B are the two children; 1 and 2 are antonyms)

Pattern 1 Oppose	Pattern 2 Echo	Pattern 3 Switch	
A_1	A_1	A_1	A_1
B_2	B_1	B_2	B_1
		or	
A_1	A_2	A_2	A_1
B_2	B_2	B_1	B_2
			A_1

The patterns often occurred in combination. The following is an example of a very popular Antonym Game. This game was based on the opposition between 'hot' and 'not hot'. It was recorded nine times, the first time (Example 21) during the third recording session. When it first occurred, the object which was either 'hot' or 'not hot' was the seat of the car. Subsequent occurrences may have been related to the seat, but others clearly had no real-world significance to Suzy and Nani. After the 'hot/not hot' game had occurred five times, it became part of a larger routine, the Hiding Game which will be discussed in Chapter 7.

Example 21

30 August

```
                    (Patterns:   1 = hot,   2 = not hot)
1. N:  Hot        A₁ ⎤
                      ⎥ oppose ⎤
2. S:  Not hot.   B₂ ⎦         ⎥
                               ⎥ switch
3. N:  Not hot.   A₂ ⎤         ⎦
4. S:  Hot.       B₁ ⎦
5. N:  Hot.       A₁ ⎤
6. S:  Hot.       B₁ ⎥ echo    ⎤
                      ⎥         ⎥ switch
7. N:  Hot.       A₁ ⎤ oppose  ⎦
8. S:  Not hot.   B₂ ⎦
(giggles)
```

This example is typical of the kind of word play that made Suzy and Nani giggle. It illustrates the girls' interest in opposite meanings and their ability to continue to contrast opposites over a series of utterances. Example 22 also involves antonyms.

Example 22

2 Nov.

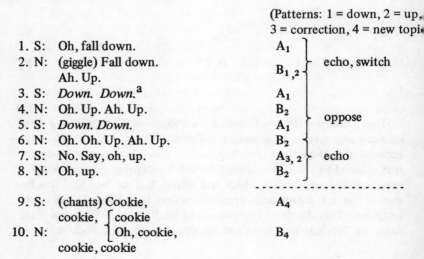

```
                                      (Patterns:  1 = down, 2 = up,
                                       3 = correction, 4 = new topi⟨
 1. S:  Oh, fall down.                 A₁  ⎤
 2. N:  (giggle) Fall down.                ⎥ echo, switch
        Ah. Up.                        B₁,₂ ⎦
 3. S:  Down. Down.ᵃ                    A₁
 4. N:  Oh. Up. Ah. Up.                 B₂ ⎤
 5. S:  Down. Down.                     A₁ ⎥ oppose
 6. N:  Oh. Oh. Up. Ah. Up.             B₂ ⎦
 7. S:  No. Say, oh, up.               A₃,₂  echo
 8. N:  Oh, up.                         B₂
------------------------------------------------
 9. S:  (chants) Cookie,                A₄
        cookie, ⎧ cookie
10. N:          ⎨ Oh, cookie,           B₄
        cookie, cookie
```

a. The word 'down' was pronounced with a long vowel and falling pitch. This created the impression of contrastive stress.

This Antonym Game contained a new element — correction. The correction which occurred here was more explicit than in any of the examples I discussed in Chapter 4. In the correction activities that I discussed there, neither girl used the word 'say'. All correction was indirect in those examples. In Example 22 above, however, Suzy gave Nani precise instructions, 'Say, oh up' in 7 when she rejected Nani's previous utterances. Suzy expressed explicitly the metalinguistic awareness that seemed to underlie the correction activities that were discussed in Chapter IV. When Nani said 'Ah. Up' (6), Suzy was not satisfied. Although Nani had said the appropriate antonym, Suzy also wanted her to preface the antonym with what Suzy considered the appropriate interjection. Suzy was not talking about the referential meaning of 'up' or even about whether 'up' was the opposite of 'down'. She was telling Nani how to talk. During the course of this study, both girls showed that they were adept at telling each other what to say and when to say it. In fact, they were so good at doing this that they developed a routine which I call the You Say routine. This routine will be discussed in the following chapter (6).

In Example 22 above, Suzy's command 'Say, oh, up' indicated that she assumed that there was a format which had to be followed and that Nani was aware of it or at least might be willing to comply when told about it. This format, or procedure to be followed over a series of utterances, is one of the characteristics of full routines in Suzy and Nani's interactions. As Goffman said, a chain of adjacency pairs can have a unitary, bounded character (1976, pp. 270-2). Suzy and Nani seemed to recognise this characteristic in their routines. This was especially evident when they told each other what to say. In giving each other explicit instructions about what to say and when to say it, they acknowledged that they expected to co-operatively create a series of utterances which must be 'said' in a certain way and in a certain order.

In Example 22, Suzy's command and Nani's compliance (8) indicate that both accepted for themselves and expected of each other a kind of behaviour-limiting part or role[5] in certain routines. In this particular exchange, Suzy was the one who forced these assignments. I can think of no grammatical or conversational constraint that might be responsible for Suzy's feeling that Nani needed to be corrected or for Nani's compliance. No breakdown in communication would have resulted whether Nani said, 'Ah. Up' or 'Oh. Up.' Suzy, however, seemed to feel that a constraint on the form of the chain of adjacency pairs was a ritual that existed within her and Nani's society of two and this would make the correction acceptable. Nani's compliance indicated that she did not dispute Suzy's expectation. She also followed Suzy's lead in chanting 'cookie, cookie, cookie', which had no apparent relationship to the preceding dialogue. Even though there is no logical relationship between 'up/down' and 'cookie, cookie, cookie', Suzy and Nani may have simply wanted to continue playing with words, and chanting 'cookie, cookie, cookie' may have been as much fun for them as the preceding Antonym Game.

'Up/down' and 'hot/not hot' were typical examples of the oppositions that Suzy and Nani incorporated into their conversation. I have listed other examples in Appendix A. The girls used many of these in fully developed Antonym Games such as Examples 21 and 22 above. Others were used in short exchanges (two to four utterances). In short exchanges, it often was not clear whether the girls were using contrasting words and phrases in serious dialogues or were playing with them. In serious dialogue, the referential meaning was important to Suzy and Nani. In the discussion of the red light/green light (Example 6), the girls were concerned about the symbolic values of traffic lights. They really wanted to know which light 'says' go and which 'says' stop. They did not focus on the opposition of 'stop' and 'go'. In play, referential meaning had more limited importance. In the 'up/down' Antonym Game (Example 22), for example, the only semantic features that mattered to the girls were those that identified 'up' as the opposite of 'down'. This suggests that these features were represented in some way in the girls' lexicons.

The 'hot/not hot' Antonym Game (Example 21) had a long history in the context of Suzy and Nani's conversation. The referential meaning of 'hot' was important when it was used to describe the condition of the car seat. Usually, however, the girls did not seem to care whether the seat was hot. What interested them was the contrast for them between the positive and negative values of their semantic feature [+hot]. To explore their interest in this contrast, they established between themselves three patterns of exchanges. These patterns comprise the routine which I call the Antonym Game. This routine was standardised so that the girls could explore any semantic opposition they chose by making their conversation fit one or more of the three Antonym Game patterns. By examining which oppositions they chose to treat in this way, we can discover what semantic features were real parts of the girls' lexicons. We will see in the following chapters (6 and 7) that parts of other routines were Antonym Games which followed one of these three patterns. In the following chapters, we will also examine the development of Suzy and Nani's tendency to use language as an object of play.

As they manipulated language for fun, they moved away from semantic transparency towards rhetorical expressiveness. The nature of their relationship appeared to foster the kind of expansion that Slobin (1973) said is required of all fully developed linguistic systems. (See above, p. 26).

Notes

1. Antonym Games were by no means the only chains that included open jibes. See, for example, the name-calling exchange in Example 5.

2. See p. 29 for definition of 'routine'.

3. As mentioned on p. 76, a routine which was composed of the girls' instructions to each other about what to say will be discussed in Chapter 6.

4. This terminology is borrowed from Schegloff and Sacks (1973). See Chapter 2, footnote 19.

5. The term 'role' is used to indicate communicative role or posture within a conversation, not the kind of play in which miming takes place. Halliday (1973) discussed this with respect to the acquisition of language (see above, p. 21).

6 THE YOU SAY ROUTINE

6.1 Introduction

Some contrasting words and phrases such as 'hot/not hot' occurred many times in Suzy and Nani's conversation. As this happened, the girls developed expectations about how an exchange which contained a familiar opposition would progress. Their ability to talk about talk led to exchanges in which they explicitly told each other what to say. As a result, some Antonym Games became part of a larger routine which I call the You Say routine. This new routine gained a history of its own as Suzy and Nani discussed who should say what and developed expectations about what each of them would say while the routine was in progress. Talking about saying was another expression of the girls' metalinguistic awareness. Their expectations about what each would say functioned as ritual constraints; they determined those aspects of the routine which were not controlled by grammatical or conversational constraints. The form of the You Say routine changed as Suzy and Nani established ritual constraints to govern it. Therefore, I call this process 'ritualisation' and I call the eventual forms of those routines which underwent this process 'ritualised routines'. In this book I will discuss two ritualised routines. In addition to the You Say routine, which occurred six times over a period of five weeks, I will devote the following chapter to the Hiding Game, which occurred twenty times over a period of ten months.

Ritual constraints were the result of the experiences that Suzy and Nani shared. By accepting these constraints, each girl showed that she also accepted the intimate friendship that had led to, and was part of, the sharing of experience. Once a routine became ritualised the routine seemed to get under way faster for at least two reasons. First, the girls no longer had to explain to each other how they expected the routine to proceed; each girl could predict what the other should do and what she herself would do. Second, the routine became an indication of how the girls felt about each other. In its abbreviated form (without explanation or introduction) the ritualised routine became even more exclusively their property; others would be less likely to understand it. Furthermore, once it had the power to express their intimacy, it also gained importance as a way they could control each other. That is, if either child refused to respond to a ritualised routine, the refusal was construed as saying that their intimacy was in question. This was not something they would do lightly, as witness their frequent conversations about being friends. (See Example 12 above, Appendix A and Appendix B: Analysis of 3 June session.) A ritualised routine, therefore, was one which the girls started quickly and which they did not take time to introduce or to explain to one another.

The theme of the You Say routine was telling someone what to say. The routine developed in a direction that seemed to be influenced by Suzy and Nani's competitiveness and by their notions about how adults monitor and correct children's speech.[1]

Children are first taught to say the right thing at the right time regardless of whether they understand the meaning of what they are saying. They learn many if not all of the ritualised social formulae: 'polite' children must know by being told 'Say thank you,' 'Say please,' 'Say fine' (when someone asks you how you are). This social use of language may appear as early or earlier than the 'referential use of language and must be considered in any theory that attempts to deal with the child's acquisition of language as means of human communication' (Gleason and Weintaub 1976, p. 95). Suzy and Nani's interest in telling each other what to say may be one effect of having been told to 'say' expressions that they did not understand. The kind of metalinguistic awareness they exhibited when they opposed antonyms and made up other word games may have been stimulated by the knowledge that people talk about language even as they are using it.

Talking about talk is like looking into a mirror while another mirror is positioned behind your head. There seems to be no end to the reflected images even though you know there is only one flesh-and-blood face. Metalinguistic awareness requires the ability to keep the 'real' meaning of language in mind while you talk about the symbol for that meaning. In ritualised routines, Suzy and Nani were always aware of the 'real' meaning of the words they used, but often they did not use these words to refer to anything in the real world. In effect, they used the words as entities separate from their value as meaningful symbols much as an adult might say, 'How are you?' and continue talking or walking by without waiting for an answer. In a ritualised routine, the use of a word without attention to its reference in the real world was very useful in these respects: (1) ritualised routines could be initiated at any time (no non-linguistic variable was needed); (2) players' responses could be reversed (as far as the structure of the routine was concerned, it did not matter who said 'hot' and who said 'not hot' or who said 'you say . . .'); and (3) inertia (a compulsion to participate in the routine) derived from (1) and (2). Indeed, a ritualised routine existed independent of anything but the girls' interest in playing it. Not to play was a failure to interact and Nani and Suzy wanted to interact with each other. Their routines were similar to saying 'please,' 'thank you,' 'How are you? I'm fine,' etc., because reference to non-linguistic factors was less important to them (in fact, non-existent) than the interaction which took the form of a ritualised routine.

Factors outside the verbal interaction had no direct bearing on the You Say routine. Throughout examples of this routine, Suzy and Nani were giving and accepting or rejecting instructions about verbal behaviour (saying and singing) as the routine became ritualised. In many instances, this activity was an end in itself — something they apparently liked to do. As the routine became more familiar, they used it for other purposes, such as to resolve a communicative impasse. (See Example 28 below.)

6.2 Development of the You Say Routine

The first recorded instance of either girl telling the other to 'say' something took place in November (the 'up/down' Antonym Game, Example 22 above). Nevertheless, no You Say routines were recorded until May. It is possible that this routine occurred during the period (December-April) when no recordings were made. Even if this were the case, the first recorded You Say routine was not fully developed. As the girls continued to use it, they changed it to conform with changes in the ritual constraints that affected this particular routine. One such change was the diminished need to explain or discuss mutual expectations. Another change was the diminished need to relate what they were doing with language to reference points in the real world. Since they spent less time explaining the routine to each other and no longer needed non-linguistic referents, they jumped into the routine more quickly and with little or no resistance from either participant.

In the first two of the six recorded instances of the You Say routine, the newer routine seemed to be based on an older routine — the Antonym Game. The focus of the girls' interest began to change, however. The opposition between the antonyms (in this case 'no' and 'yes') became less important to them than the fun of telling someone else what to say. In order to trace the changes, I will present a chart for each of the six examples of the You Say routine. The conclusion to this chapter will include a chart which shows the totals from the six individual charts.

6.2.1 The First Two Examples

The first You Say routine started with a genuine disagreement between
Suzy and Nani. Several Antonym Games also started in this way. The
best example was 'hot/not hot', which referred to the temperature of
the car seat at first, but later lost that reference when it was incorporated into the Hiding Game (see Chapter 7). In the case of the first You
Say routine, the girls disagreed about whether Nani should do what she
was doing. The You Say routine started at Utterance 14.

Example 23

13 May p.m. (antecedent for 'it' not known)

1. S: No. Leave it there.
2. N: I'm pushing it in.
3, 5, 7, 9. S: No.⎫
4, 6, 8, 10. N: Yes.⎬ (repeated 4 times, getting louder)
11. S: [lá:ni:]
12. N: (giggle) Yes.
13. S: Don't do it.
14. N: Yes.
15. S: No.
16, 18. N: (giggle)⎫
17, 19. S: No. ⎬ (repeated twice)
20. N: (giggle) Yes, yes,⎧ yes, yes, yes.
21. S: ⎩ No-o-o-o-o-o-o
22. N: I say no and you say no. Ah, bump your head.[a]
23. S: (giggle)
24. N: (giggle) You say yes and I say no.
25. S: (giggle)
26. N: Now, you say yes. No. No.⎧ No.
27. S: ⎩ No.
28. N: Now you say yes. Yes, no.⎧ No.
29. S: ⎩ No.
30. N: (giggle) Yes, no. Yes, no. (noises)
(pause before driver introduces new topic)

a. The phrase 'bump your head' was sometimes used when the girls were jostled
by the movement of the car. They always giggled when one said, 'Bump your
(or my) head.'

Table 5: YS1: You Say 13 May 'No/Yes'

Speaker	Utterances		Totals	
	N	S	N	S
Instruction[a]	22,24,26,28		4	
Refusal[b]		21,27,29		3
Giggle[c]	22,30	23,25	2	2
Game Play[d]				
with instruc-tions	26,28		2	
without instructions				

a. Instruction: any kind of direct attempt to dictate what the other person should say; e.g. correction, explanation, interruption.
b. Refusal: any kind of resistance to the instruction, e.g. counter-challenge.
c. Giggle: any kind of apparently intentional nonsense. It is not always clear whether this is a kind of resistance or a sign that the game is being enjoyed.
d. Game Play: the execution of the game according to the instructions. Utterances often include both instructions and game play. This is represented on the table as 'with instructions'. Utterances which are part of the game but do not include instructions are in the row 'without instructions'. The total number of categories that occur in a game may exceed the total number of utterances given in the data.

Table 5 divides the utterances from the above data into categories. Since the word *say* did not occur until 14, only Utterances 14-22 are shown on the table.

In the course of the exchange shown in Example 23 above, Nani stopped Suzy from telling her what to do by involving Suzy first in an Antonym Game and then in the You Say routine. Suzy seemed very serious when she told Nani to 'leave it there'. Nevertheless, Nani insisted on 'pushing it in'. They continued to disagree. Their repetition of 'no' and 'yes' falls into a Pattern 1 (Oppose) Antonym Game. Suzy tried to continue to sound serious by saying 'Lani' (a variant of 'Nani') in a scolding tone. Nani giggled and said, 'Yes' — not in agreement, of course, but in response to being called by name. From this point (12), Nani looked for a way to stop Suzy from being serious. She giggled several times and then said 'yes' five times in a row (20). This expanded the Antonym Game in a new way. Antonym Games never before included repetition of an antonym by one speaker. Then Nani finally managed to make Suzy giggle by telling her to 'say no' and by saying a phrase that always made them giggle: 'Bump your head' (22). (I never figured out why they thought it was funny.) Between utterances 22 and and 30, Nani tried to make Suzy say 'yes', but she would only say 'no'. While Nani was focusing on the contrast between 'yes' and 'no', Suzy seemed to remember the origin of the exchange and refused to give up her original negation. Nani at least succeeded in stopping Suzy from telling her what to do.

Suzy's lack of interest in participating in the You Say routine and her insistence on maintaining the original meaning of 'no' indicate that You Say was a new routine at this point. It is, of course, possible that this routine had already occurred when no recording was made. I do not think this was the case, however. Suzy's behaviour in Example 23 above indicates that the ritualisation of the You Say routine had not yet begun. If the routine had been ritualised already at this time, Suzy would have ignored the original meaning of 'no' and not only would have responded to Nani's instructions but also would have told Nani what to say. Indeed, this is exactly what happened five days later during the next recorded session. In the following example, note that the driver's initial question and Suzy and Nani's response seemed to fit a general ritual of an adult asking questions that children themselves are not particularly interested in. I did not count the number of times one of the drivers asked the girls how their day had been, but I expect it happened often.

Example 24

20 May p.m.

1.	D:	Have a nice day, girls?
2.	S&N:	(unison) Ye-e-es.
3.	N:	(giggle) No-yes, no-yes, no-yes, no-yes, no-yes. You say no-yes, no-yes.
4.	S:	Say no-yes, no-yes.
5.	N:	No-yes, no-yes, no-yes, no-yes. Say no-yes, no-yes. (short pause)
6.	N:	You say [nowɪs]. You Say, no-yes. |
		[You say
7.	S:	[I 'ready say no-yes.
8.	N:	No you didn', I didn' *hear*.
9.	S:	You say [nowɪs nowɪs].
10.	N:	No, you say no-yes.
11.	S:	I *did*.

(Example 24, continued)

12. N: I didn't *hear* you.
13. S: (faster, more slurred) [nowɪsnowɪsnowɪsnowɪs] . Your
         turn say [nowɪsnowɪs] .
14. N: [nowɪsnowɪs] . Your turn say [nowɪsnowɪs] again.
15. S: [nowɪsnowɪs] . Your turn say [nowɪsnowɪs] .
16. N: [nowɪsnowɪs] . Now
              ⎡ your turn say [nowɪs] .
17. S: ⎣ [nowɪsnowɪs] . Your turn say [nowɪs] .
18. N: [nowɪsnowɪs] . Your turn say ⎰ [nowɪsnowɪs] .
19. S: ⎱ (sings)
20. N: No-yes, no-yes. You turn say no-yes. Your turn say
         no-yes. (sings) 'you turn say no-yes.'
         (shouts) You say no-yes, no-yes, no-yes.
21. S: You say [nowɪsnowɪs] .
22. N: No I said did say [nowɪsnowɪs] .
23. S: [nowɪs] . You say [nowɪsnowɪs] .
24. N: I did say [nowɪsnowɪs] ⎡ I
25. S: ⎣ No I didn't hear you say
26. N: I did say (fast) [nowɪsnowɪs] . I did already
         [nowɪsnowɪs] .
27. S: [nowɪsnowɪs] .
28. N: [nowɪsnowɪs] .
29. S: [nowɪsnowɪs] .
30. N: No, no. No-yes, no-yes, no-yes.
31. S: No-yes, no-yes, no-yes.
32,34. N: No-yes, no-yes
33,35. S: No-yes, no-yes.   (twice)

Table 6: YS2: You Say 20 May 'No/Yes'

Speaker	Utterances		Totals	
	N	S	N	S
Instruction	3,5,6,8,10,12, 14,16,18,20	4,9,13,15, 17,21,23, 25	10	8
Refusal	10,22,24,26	7,11	4	2
Giggle		10		1
Game Play				
with instructions	3,5,14,16,18, 20,26	13,15,17,23	7	4
without instructions	28,30,32,34	27,29,31,33 35	4	5

Example 14 illustrates several of the steps that occurred as a routine became ritualised. First the point of reference in the real world (the answer to the driver's question) was forgotten immediately. Then the girls focused on the opposition between 'no' and 'yes'. This time, however, they did not take up one of the three patterns of the Antonym Game. In Antonym Games, each girl usually said the opposite of what the other had said. This time the poles were combined into a single unit. The first form of this unit, 'no-yes', preserved the normal pronunciation of the two antonyms (Utterances 3-6). This form was further reduced to form a second unit [nowɪs] which seems from an adult point of view to be complete nonsense (Utterance 6). When Nani first said [nowɪs], the girls discussed what was being said. In this discussion (7 and 8), they expanded the You Say format to include 'I 'ready say' (7) and 'I didn' *hear*' (8). Suzy used the You Say format to bring [nowɪs] into the exchange where it was fully accepted by both girls.

The development of a distorted form like [nowɪs] as a kind of word play that Suzy and Nani could share was the result of their shared expectations. Each knew that the other liked to play with antonyms and each knew she was expected to participate when the other introduced antonyms. They both knew that these antonyms need not have any point of reference in the real world at the time they were the focus of the girls' word play. The distortion of the pronunciation of a pair of antonyms therefore did not break the ritual constraints that Suzy and Nani accepted even though [nowɪs] would be seen as a distorted form by a third participant (if it were understood at all). The girls therefore could never use [nowɪs] if they wanted to communicate with anyone but each other. A further aid to the acceptance of [nowɪs] was the You Say routine in which the 'no/yes' Antonym Game was embedded. Since the girls already had experience telling each other what to say, they could incorporate a new item simply by telling each other to say it. The fact that the new item was one of their own invention probably made it even more interesting to them.

[Nowɪs] existed as a special code word. Suzy and Nani knew that it was a reduction of 'no-yes'. It functioned as jargon; i.e. a kind of elliptical language which (according to Joos, 1961; see pp. 13-23) can only occur in the most intimate speech style. Suzy and Nani invented [nowɪs] as part of a private language which they shared only with each other. As such, it indicated the closeness of their relationship and the history of the experiences they shared. It was not as elaborate as the jargon they shared in the Hiding Game (see Chapter 7) but was an off-shoot of their interest in manipulating language for fun, just to pass the time.

6.2.2 Additional Uses

In the following example (25), Suzy and Nani stopped saying [nowɪs] and 'no-yes', but continued to give each other orders about verbal behaviour. Instead of telling each other, 'Your turn to say [nowɪs]' (Utterances 13-20 above), they told each other, 'Your turn to sing.' Example 25 below came immediately after Example 24 above and may be considered a continuation of the same You Say routine. I have divided it for the purpose of this discussion but have numbered the utterances consecutively. Since the words and nonsense syllables that were sung did not appear to affect the interaction, I will not give these data. Instead, I will indicate the length of time — in minutes and seconds — that each 'turn' lasted.

Example 25

20 May p.m.

36. N: Daddy I'm gonna sing a song.
37. D: OK.
38. N: (sings a song which she makes up; time 2 min. 8.5 sec.) Now it's your turn to sing.
39. S: (sings 2 min.) Your turn to sing.
40. N: Kay (sings 1 min. 42 sec.)
41. S: (interrupts after 20 sec.) Now it's my turn to sing. (both sing 1 min. 20 sec.)
42. N: Now it's your turn to sing.
43. S: (sings 20 sec.)
44. N: (interrupts after 10 sec.) No, gotta go.
45. S: (continues singing)
46. N: No, gottu say, do like that. Gottu say (sings 46 sec.) That's how my song goes.
47. S: I going sing my *own song*.

Table 7: YS3: You Say 20 May 'Your turn to sing'

Speaker	Utterances		Totals	
	N	S	N	S
Instruction	38,42,44,46	39,41	4	2
Refusal[a]	40	45,47	1	2
Giggle				
Game Play				
with instruc-tions	38,46	39,41	2	2
without instructions	40	43	1	1

a. Refusal includes refusing to relinquish singing turn as Nani did (40) when Suzy claimed her own turn to sing (41). A singing turn is harder to assign to a category than a usual speaking turn or utterance because the children were often singing at the same time and it is not always clear in listening to the tapes when one or the other started or stopped.

In Utterance 36, Nani told the driver that she was going to sing. The girls subsequently enforced a turn-taking pattern on each other. After one had sung for two to three minutes, either the singer told the non-singer that it was her turn or the non-singer demanded her turn. In Utterance 44, Nani changed the content of her instructions from talking about when to change turns to talking about what to sing. She was still giving orders and Suzy was still refusing to comply. After Suzy insisted on singing her own song (47), the girls continued to discuss the proper way of singing a song which the boys at the pre-school had been practising. (These data are not shown.)

Because You Say had become a ritualised routine, it was the only context Suzy and Nani needed to indicate what they expected of each other. Thus the phrase 'you say' became a quick, easy way to direct the course of a conversation. By the third time the girls used the You Say routine, it had become a vehicle for talking about something other than antonyms, namely singing. In the last three recorded instances of the You Say routine, Suzy and Nani found additional uses for it. They used it to reduce the tension between themselves (Example 26 below), to make a tedious conversation more interesting (Example 27), and as a corrective action to solve a communicative impasse (Example 28). In Example 26 below, the girls used the You Say routine to sustain inter-action after they had unsuccessfully tried to find a topic of mutual interest. Earlier in the session, Nani had delivered a long monologue about a paper cup. Suzy had then talked about someone whom Nani did not know. Nani expressed her dissatisfaction with Suzy's choice of topic by taunting her with 'So?' (the first utterance shown here).

Example 26

10 June p.m. (Utterances 6, 7 and 9 are chanted rhythmically.)

```
1. N:  So?   (pause)  So?
2. S:  So?
                        (Each girl uses a different pitch.
                         The result is a rhythmic pattern.)
3. N:  So?
4. S:  So?
5. N:  So?
6. S:  So, so, so, so, so, so, so, so, so, so, so, so, so, so, so,  so.
7. N:  So. So. So. So. So. Now, now, now, now.                   Now
       you say yes, and I say no. No, no, no, no.
8. S:  Ye-e-es.
```

```
 9. N:  No. ⎧ No. No, no, no, no, no, no, no, no, no.  You say no and
            ⎨ I say yes.            ⎧
10. S:      ⎩ Ye-e-es.             ⎨ No, no.
11. N:  Yes, yes, yes, yes.  Yes.  ⎩ Your[a] home.
```
(arrive at Suzy's home)

a. I transcribed this as 'your' rather than 'you're' because 'Here's your home'
   often occurred at the end of the ride.

Table 8: YS4: You Say 10 June 'No/Yes'

Speaker	Utterances N	S	Totals N	S
Instruction	7,9		2	
Refusal				
Giggle				
Game Play				
with instructions	7,9		2	
without instructions	11	8,10	1	2

When Nani got no reaction to her first taunt, 'So?', she repeated it.
This triggered a series of 'So?' as each girl said it in turn. Each used a
pitch which was different from the one the other had used. The result
was a sing-song rhythm as Utterances 3 to 5 were spoken. Having involved Suzy in the chanting of 'So?', Nani continued to manipulate the
conversation by introducing the You Say routine (7). Suzy responded
by accepting Nani's instructions and following them. The result was a
change from belligerency when neither child would accept the other's
choice of conversational topic to co-operation when both were playing
the familiar 'no/yes' game.

Watson-Gegeo and Boggs (1976, p. 21) pointed out that in their
work with the dialogues of part-Hawaiian children, a contradicting
routine (which seems similar to what I call the Antonym Game) could
be de-escalated as a sign of intimacy between the participants or esca-
lated to the point of fighting. In the case cited by Watson-Gegeo and
Boggs, de-escalation was achieved when one participant repeated the
beginning of a routine. The You Say routine achieved a similar de-

escalation when Suzy and Nani used it to reduce the tension between them. It had this effect because it was a product of the girls' shared experiences and a sign of their intimacy. Each girl seemed compelled to respond to it for this reason. In Example 27 below, the You Say routine had a similar de-escalating effect: it marked the end of an argument over whose grandma and grandpa would watch her at her hula lessons. Elements of previous utterances which occurred just before this excerpt were the phrases that made up the You Say responses.

Example 27

17 June p.m. (Suzy was unhappy about the fact that Nani took hula lessons while she did not. Both girls were aware that Suzy was going to move to New Jersey where her father's parents lived.)

1. S: And my grandma and grandpa in New Jersey, they going watch me make hula *les*sons.
2. N: So. My grandma's going see me watch[a] hula lessons, too. My grandma *and* grandma.[b]
3. S: Not.
4. N: Ye-es, ye-es, ye-es.
5. S: Not, not, not, not, not.
6. N: I have grandma and grandma.
7. S: (quickly) I know, I know, I *know*.
8. N: Is my grandma and grandma and grandma and grandma
        ⎰ (?) and grandma and . . .   ⎱   (Unison continues
9. S: ⎱ I know, I know, I know . . . .   ⎰   until both giggle)
10. N: And grandma and grandma and grandma and grandma and grandma
11. S: (laughs)
12. N: Now you say your *own* grandma and grandma.
13. S: I have a grandma and grandpa, ⎰ and grandma (?)
14. N: ⎱ I, I know, I know, I know I
        know I know. OK I'm gonna do my own grandma and grand-
        pa. Is my grandma ⎰ and grandma and grandma
15. S: ⎱ I know, I know, I know

(Unison continues and volume increases until D asks them to stop. N tries to get S to start again, but S refuses. They discuss the names of their relatives until the end of the session.)

a. I think Nani intended 'see me watch' to have the same meaning as Suzy's 'watch me'.
b. I can think of no reason why Nani continued to repeat 'grandma and grandma' instead of 'grandma and grandpa'.

Table 9: YS5: You Say 17 June 'My grandma/I know'

Speaker	Utterances N	S	Totals N	S
Instruction	12,14[a]		2	
Refusal				
Giggle				
Game Play				
with instructions	12,14		2	
without instructions		13,15		2

a. This was not an instruction from one child to the other, but it was a meta-linguistic explanation. Nani explained what she was going to say.

In Example 27, the contrasting phrases 'grandma' and 'I know' were part of the conversations which preceded the beginning of the You Say routine (Utterance 12). Like 'no' and 'yes' in the first You Say routine (Example 23 below), these phrases developed into a game because the girls became more interested in the phrases (or words) than in whatever reference the phrases had to the real world. By Utterances 8 and 9, Suzy and Nani had abandoned the referential framework they had had at the beginning of this excerpt. Suzy had forgotten her unhappiness about not taking hula lessons and was no longer thinking about her grandparents in New Jersey. They continued to contrast 'grandma' and 'I know' through 10 and 11. In Utterance 12, the You Say routine began when Nani instructed Suzy to exchange responses with her. That is, it became Suzy's turn to say 'grandma' and Nani's turn to say 'I know.' Suzy accepted Nani's demand and said 'grandma and grandma' until Nani told her to change back to 'I know.' The pattern of instructions and exchanges was the same as other You Say routines even though a different pair of responses was being used.

The ritualisation of the You Say routine had within a month (15 May to 17 June) progressed to the point where it was no longer connected either to a referent in the real world or to a grammatical opposition. Antonyms were no longer necessary; any pair of words or phrases could be used. Explicit discussion of turns was not needed; the phrase 'you say' was enough to give the routine its familiar structure. The You Say routine had become a standardised speech form that could incorporate any pair of words or phrases that the girls chose to use. All that was needed was for one girl to say 'you say' at some point in the conversation when they were both repeating different phrases. The routine would then start immediately. This was possible because Suzy and Nani had established between themselves a set of ritual constraints, that is mutual expectations with regard to behaviour in dialogue.

6.2.3 The Name Game

The You Say routine in Example 27 above made the tone of the interaction more co-operative. Suzy had been unhappy at the beginning because she was jealous of Nani's taking hula lessons. By the end of the You Say routine, she had forgotten what was bothering her. In the following example (28), the girls used the You Say routine to explain to each other how to play a game that they were in the process of inventing. I call this game the 'Name Game' because names were a topic they had discussed several times[2] and on this occasion they pretended to have someone else's name. Syntactic problems created difficulty when Suzy and Nani tried to start the game. They could not solve the syntactic puzzle, but they made their ideas clear to each other by using various devices. One of these was the You Say routine.

Example 28

21 June a.m.

  1. S: You say, you say what's my name.
  2. N: Suzy.
  3. S: No. You say what's my *name*.
  4. N: What's your name?
  5. S: Laur-um-Lauren.[a]
  6. N: Say what's *my* name.
  7. S: Your name is Lani.[b]
  8. N: No, no, what's, say 'what's your *name*?' What's *my* name.
  9. S: What's your name?
 10. N: Nan, um, I mean, um, Laurie.[a]
 11. S: Laurie.
 12. N: Laurie.
 13. S: I mean, I mean.
 14. N: What's your *name*?
 15. S: Um, Gwynnie.

(Example 28 continued)

16. N: (laugh)
17. S: What's your name?
18. N: Laurie.
19. D: Girls, ready to ⎰ go. (car is approach pre-school)
20. N: ⎱ My name's Gwynnie.
21. S: Laurie.
22. N: My name's Gwynnie.
23. S: I'm Laurie, Laurie, Laurie, Laurie.

(arrive at pre-school)

a. Names of girls at the pre-school.
b. Suzy used 'Nani' and 'Lani' interchangeably; Nani never noticed.

Table 10: YS6: You Say 21 June Name Game

Speaker	Utterances		Totals	
	N	S	N	S
Instruction	6,8	1,3	2	2
Refusal				
Giggle	16		1	
Game Play with instructions				
without instructions			8	8
error[a]	2	7		
correct[a]	4,10,12,14, 18,20,22	5,9,11,13, 15,17,23		

a. The two errors may have been accidental or intentional. In either case, they were attempts to play the game and Suzy and Nani treated them as errors and corrected them during the course of the exchange. Correct and incorrect responses are added together in the totals here.

The Name Game which occurred in Example 28 brought together role play (pretending to be someone else), the girls' interest in names,[3] and the You Say routine. It also pushed the girls to the limits of their abilities to handle pronoun-antecedent and question-answer relations over several utterances. The problems which Suzy and Nani had indicated some areas of language structure and discourse structure which are more complex than others. Carol Chomsky (1969, p. 5), in her study of the syntax of children from five to ten, pointed out that stages of language learning in which children are at the border of adult competence may be revealing with respect to notions of linguistic complexity. Although Suzy and Nani were younger than Chomsky's subjects, exchanges such as the Name Game suggest that they were trying to master some of the same areas of linguistic complexity as those that Chomsky studied. The Name Game also illustrates techniques the girls used to get around linguistic inadequacies.

Before discussing Suzy and Nani's series of attempts to set up the Name Game, I will describe the final form of the game. The girls agreed that the correct way to play the game was for one girl to say, 'What's your name?' and for the second to say, 'My name is ——,' filling in the blank with the name of someone they both knew (but not the real name of the speaker). They came to this agreement by Utterance 14 and played the game until they arrived at the pre-school.

Suzy seemed to have the 'rules' of a game clearly in mind when she told Nani to ask her her name (1) and when she corrected Nani's first attempt to play the game (2). Suzy was able in Utterance 3 to show Nani what her mistake had been by stressing 'name'. Nani was supposed to *ask* Suzy the question, not *answer* it. Suzy used stress to try to repair the misunderstanding, probably because stress was easier for Suzy to handle than changing 'say' to 'ask' and changing the syntax to 'Ask me what my name is.' Carol Chomsky (1969) found that even older children have difficulty using *ask* and *tell* correctly.[4] Indeed, she even found adults who got tangled in their complement subject assignment following *ask* (1969, p. 102). Some of Suzy and Nani's struggles to set up the Name Game can be traced to problems in this area. Utterances 1-14 consist of their attempts to get around their inability to use 'ask me . . .' instead of 'you say . . .'

Suzy used stress in Utterance 3 apparently because recourse to a syntactic solution was not available to her. She succeeded in telling Nani how she expected the exchange to proceed. Since the You Say routine was already established as a means of initiating a word game, Suzy's use of 'you say' also seemed to help her get around deficiencies in syntax. In Utterance 7, Suzy either forgot how she wanted the game to proceed or was confused by Nani's instruction, 'Say what's my name?' (6). Suzy's confusion may have also been due to difficulties with the syntax of 'Ask me . . .' Nani, however, knew how the game should go and tried to correct Suzy's error. Nani was no more adept than Suzy in using 'ask' so she changed the pronoun 'my' to 'your' and changed the quality of her voice so that 'What's your name?' sounded like a direct quotation. She also stressed the possessive pronouns (8). Suzy finally responded appropriately to the You Say instruction (9), but Nani forgot the second rule, that a player was supposed to pretend to be someone other than herself. Nani corrected herself (10) and the game went on. When the driver told them to get ready to get out of the car (19), Nani quickly reversed the immediately preceding order of names. She pretended to be the person that Suzy had just been ('Gwynnie') and Suzy adopted the identity that Nani had just had ('Laurie').

Although it took some effort to set up the Name Game, the You Say device gave the girls something to work with. They had established a pattern of structuring discourse by telling each other what to say and the game which resulted in this case (the Name Game) was a product of their experience in communicating what behaviour they expected of each other. This co-operative effort was possible in spite of difficulties in the use of anaphoric pronouns. Keenan has suggested (1975b) that young children lack skill in the use of anaphoric pronouns[5] and, as a result, depend on other devices. In the data discussed here, it was clear that Suzy and Nani used many devices to overcome difficulties that might not occur among adult speakers, or, if they did occur, might be resolved by other means. The use of the You Say routine as well as the girls' use of stress and alternation of voice quality are devices which might not be found in the same places in adult speech if at all. (Do adults use routines like You Say?) The girls' use of such devices suggests that they were aware of semantic relations (such as between *say* and *ask*) before they could produce them as they would occur in adult speech[6] and that they were capable of finding ways to express them which are not likely in adult speech.

Because the You Say routine was familiar to the point of being a ritual, it could be used by Suzy and Nani to overcome problems with syntax and anaphora. As Table 10 shows, relatively little time was spent introducing the Name Game (4 utterances) while four times as many (16) were spent playing the game.

6.3 Final Analysis of the You Say Routine

The final step in my analysis of the ritualisation of the You Say routine is shown on Table 11. This table shows in numbers some aspects of the ritualisation process as it affected each of the examples of the routine.

Table 11: You Say Totals for Six Games

Table No.	5		6		7		8		9		10		Totals
Game	no/yes		no/yes		your turn to sing		no/yes		grandma/ I know		Name Game		
Speaker	N	S	N	S	N	S	N	S	N	S	N	S	
Instruction[a]	4		10	8 (18)[b]	4	2 (6)	2		2		2	2	36
Refusal	3		4	2 (6)	1	3 (3)					1		12
Giggle	2	3 (5)	1	(6)	2	2							7
Game Play													
with instructions			7		1	1	2		2		8		
without instructions	(2)		4	4 (17)	(6)		1	2 (5)	2	(4)	8	(16)	52
Proportions Non-Game: Game													
raw	12:2		25:19		9:6		2:5		2:4		5:16		
reduced	6.0		1.25		1.5		0.4		0.5		0.31		

a. See Table 5 for explanation of categories.
b. Subtotals for each category for some of the games are given in parentheses.

The only sign of ritualisation that could not be shown in numbers was the loss of referential meaning of the words and phrases involved in each instance of the routines. This was discussed above with regard to each of the six examples. Table 11 shows the effect of every utterance of each of the examples on the efficiency with which the girls used the You Say routine. There is a decrease in the number of utterances spent in giving instructions or introducing the routine and in the number of utterances spent in refusing to engage in it. At the same time, the number of utterances spent in engaging in the routine (playing the game) increases from the first You Say routine until the last. This shows that Suzy and Nani had developed a set of expectations with regard to the You Say routine. They no longer had to tell each other what those expectations were; therefore fewer utterances were spent giving instructions or explanations. As a result, the girls were able to spend more time in game play.

Table 11 also shows that in the last three You Say routines, neither Nani nor Suzy resisted getting involved in the routine. Each girl responded quickly when the other said, 'you say . . .' The routine seemed to gain a momentum of its own because the girls engaged in it so rapidly. By participating in the You Say routine immediately and without resistance, the girls responded to the ritual constraints which they had developed together that applied to this routine. This acknowledgement was a by-product of and testimony to the closeness of their relationship. They were able to use the You Say routine to maintain co-operation when they could not agree on what to talk about. Their shared experience and desire to co-operate with each other helped them to create a new verbal game — the Name Game. The proportional scores show that the number of utterances involved in game play increased as the number of utterances involved in not playing the You Say game decreased.

The You Say routine is one of the indications in these data that Suzy and Nani were finding ways to handle Slobin's second two requirements for a fully developed language. Number three was: Be quick and easy. Number four was: Be expressive. (See above, p. 26). One of Suzy and Nani's answers to requirement three was the speed with which they engaged in the You Say routine. In the case of the [nowɪs] example (24), the girls sacrificed semantic transparency (Slobin's condition one) for speed. Although the meaning of [nowɪs] would be obscure to anyone else, Suzy and Nani knew exactly how they derived it from 'no-yes'. The meaning of 'no-yes' was also somewhat obscure in that it did not refer to anything in the non-linguistic world although it too could be traced to a semantically clear origin.

The Name Game provides an example of rhetorical expressiveness which Slobin defined as alternative ways of expressing notions. The fact that Suzy and Nani were *forced* to find alternate ways to express *Ask me what my name is* does not detract from the fact that they were able to find the necessary alternatives. When their linguistic systems apparently were not mature enough to express the notion *Ask me what my name is*, they used other, non-syntactic ways to communicate this notion. By using stress, changes in voice quality, and the You Say routine, Suzy and Nani found alternative ways to express the notion. Apparently children do not need to completely master the first two of Slobin's conditions (clarity and processibility) before they can begin to develop the last two. In the case of the You Say routine, however, Suzy and Nani started with clear and processible speech (in Example 23, they began with a real disagreement). Through the process of ritualisation they were able to increase the speed and expressiveness of their speech. Whether they (or other children at the same level of development) could do this outside the intimate relationship that Suzy and Nani shared cannot be answered on the basis of this study. It is, however, an empirical question that must be investigated if we are to expand our understanding of what is involved in the process of language acquisition.

Notes

1. Note should be taken here of the fact that cultural expectations are necessarily a factor here. Boggs (1975) pointed out that part-Hawaiian children in his studies engage in dispute behaviour with the object of allowing no one to win. He also reported that in another study of children in Honolulu (two girls of Japanese ancestry) the subjects were very much concerned about who would have the most power over the other. I will not go into the possible place that Suzy and Nani might fit into in the cultural mosaic that exists in Honolulu because I am interested here in ritual constraints that were specific to their society of two.

2. For example, on another occasion (9 May), the girls reviewed the various names a person could have. They decided that a father had a given name and was also called 'Papa' or 'Daddy'. The girls also often recited lists of names of relatives and friends. The 'Jason' example (19) discussed above occurred earlier in the same session as the Name Game.

3. Boggs reports a great deal of interest in names and in the sounds of names among both adults and children in the part-Hawaiian community he studied (class notes, August 1977).

4. In Chomsky's study, the subject was deleted and the problem was to fill in the missing subject. Suzy and Nani had the additional challenge of distinguishing in some way between direct and indirect speech.

5. C. Chomsky (1969) found that the reference of *he* in the sentence, *He knew that John was going to win the race*, is understood by most children by 5;6 (120).

That is, children know by 5;6 that *he* and *John* are two different people.

6. Inconsistency in the behaviour of children reported by C. Chomsky (1969) might be caused by the partial or gradual acquisition of adult-like rules that produce adult-like surface structures. The re-analysis of *wanna* which I discussed above (section 4.3) was an example of gradual approximation to adult surface structure which cannot occur until the child has learned adult-like deep structure. Sudden acquisition of adult surface forms may actually be the acquisition of unanalysed wholes or idioms. Structures as complex as *Ask me what my name is* may not be learnable as idioms and may not be present until the various underlying structures already have been learned.

7 THE HIDING GAME

7.1 Introduction

The best-developed routine in these data was the one which I call the Hiding Game. It contained elements in common with other routines and with correction activities. Like these units, the Hiding Game was distinct from the ongoing conversation because Suzy and Nani gave it a separate structure by limiting the focus of a series of utterances. They also found it an enjoyable way to pass the time. Like other ritualised routines, the Hiding Game developed an abbreviated form as it became ritualised. Furthermore, it became a quick and easy way for either girl to direct the course of the dialogue because whenever one girl introduced the Hiding Game by saying the short introductory line, 'Let's hide,' the other almost always felt compelled to co-operate in continuing the routine. Thus, the Hiding Game seemed to have a momentum of its own. This momentum was indicated by the immediate response of one child to the other's introduction of the routine.

Although the first of the twenty recorded occurrences of the Hiding Game was separated from the last by ten months, the form of this routine changed very little. The series of utterances which identified the Hiding Game was always accompanied by specific physical activity. Whenever the girls agreed to 'hide', they both got down on the floor of the car and discussed topics which they associated with 'hiding'. The focus of the Hiding Game was not simply the contrast between opposites as in an Antonym Game. In the Hiding Game, the girls concentrated on the idea of 'hiding' and notions which the girls related to this idea. After deciding to 'hide', they talked about getting into and out of a 'house' to escape from the 'monster'. While an Antonym Game was based on the girls' understanding of opposites, the Hiding Game was based on what might be called an underlying narrative which both girls understood and which was realised on the surface as the utterances which make up the data.

Correction activity in the development and maintenance of the Hiding Game functioned in the same way as it did in the development of other routines. It helped to limit the focus of the routine, and it allowed the girls to explain their individual expectations and to reach a consensus on what constraints were acceptable in the routine. The difference between correction activity in the Hiding Game and in other routines can be traced to the area of focus. In some routines, correction activity kept the focus on contrast between elements (questions/answers; loud/soft; stressed/unstressed; opposite meanings, etc.). In Antonym Games, for example, the contrast between words with opposite meanings made up the routine. In the Hiding Game, however, the focus was on the underlying narrative. Correction activity therefore involved discouraging the mention of anything that did not belong to the established story. To achieve this goal, Suzy and Nani responded to grammatical constraints in constructing the basic parts of the routine, to conversational constraints in keeping it in the form of a dialogue, and to ritual constraints in adhering to established procedures and in explaining any changes either of the girls wanted to make.

7.2 Structure

The first of the twenty examples of the Hiding Game was recorded on 11 September and the last was recorded on 28 June. The Hiding Game was made up of a set of phrases or topics[1] and associated actions. Some phrases were more likely to trigger actions than others. Nani and Suzy usually used these to initiate the game. For example, when one of the girls said, 'Let's hide' or 'Let's get in here,' they would both get down on the floor of the car and proceed to play the game by using other phrases which almost always triggered other actions. The most popular topic used in this way was 'monsters'. Escaping from monsters was their reason for moving from one side of the floor and/or seat to the other and for discussing whether to get in or out of the 'house'. The location of the 'house' was usually the floor, although it could also be the seat of the car. All of this was accompanied by squealing and giggling.

The Hiding Game was based on the behaviour that Suzy and Nani expected of each other in certain narrowly defined circumstances. It was a routine in the sense of being a 'standardized form . . . of speech that [has] a particular function'.[2] Furthermore, it became a ritualised routine, changed very little in form and function, and, most importantly, required no explanation outside the ritual constraints of rules of (private) usage of the Hiding Game itself. With this sketch in mind, I will describe in this chapter how Suzy and Nani developed the constraints which applied to the Hiding Game, how they used it, and the innovations they introduced and incorporated into the routine.

The Hiding Game was the first routine that I was able to identify in my preliminary work on these data. The girls' laughter when they moved around the back of the car and talked about houses and monsters forced my attention towards the structure and development of this popular routine. As I began to understand how Suzy and Nani used their knowledge of grammatical and conversational rules to identify, construct and develop this routine, I noticed that they interacted in similar ways with regard to other routines. In presenting my findings here, I found that what I discovered first was most easily discussed last. I believe the reason for this is that the Hiding Game was the most noticeable routine because it required the kinds of skill and co-operation that were required by the routines I have already discussed but to a greater degree. This made the Hiding Game easier to notice but harder to describe than the routines I have discussed so far. In this chapter, we will see Suzy and Nani's skilful and co-operative use of language as an expressive tool manifested in the speed with which they responded to each other and in the accuracy with which they fulfilled each other's expectations when they engaged in the Hiding Game.

The Hiding Game was related to conversational topics which preceded the first recording of the game itself by several days. The first recording of the game was on 11 September (Example 29 below). That instance was triggered by another routine, the Antonym Game, that had been played several days earlier, on 6 and 7 September.

The Antonym Game which triggered the first instance of the Hiding Game was in turn suggested to Suzy and Nani by their physical environment, in particular the backseat of the car which had a plastic cover and became hot in the afternoon sun. When one girl said that the seat was 'hot', the other said that it was 'not hot'. On 6 and 7 September, they used 'hot' and 'not hot' as the basis for a word game, which, like other Antonym Games in the data, involved the juxtaposition of words or phrases that differed, as all antonyms do, by only one semantic feature. The sixth and seventh of September were afternoon sessions and it is likely that the car seat was actually hot. Although the hot seat suggested the 'hot/not hot' Antonym Game in the first place, the girls subsequently ignored the referential use of these antonyms. As in the case of some other Antonym Games, the 'hot/not hot' game gained an internal momentum. That is, the polarity of the words was the focus of the routine regardless of the temperature of the seat.[3] It is not surprising therefore that Suzy and Nani talked about whether the seat was 'hot' or 'not hot' on 11 September even though it was a morning session and the seat was probably not hot. (Patterns of Antonym Games which occurred during the first recording of the Hiding Game are shown on the transcription.)

On 11 September, however, the girls were not satisfied with confining the game to contradicting each other about the 'hot/not hot' seat. On this occasion, they incorporated action into the routine by deciding to get down on the floor of the car to escape the 'hot' seat. Nani introduced the new idea, getting down on the floor, by saying, 'Let's get in here . . . Not hot' (see Example 29 below, Utterance 10), and Suzy joined Nani on the floor. Another Antonym Game was incorporated into the discussion of moving down to the floor ('in here') and up from the floor ('outa here'). At no time during this or subsequent Hiding Games was the word 'floor' spoken, even though the floor and the seat were important parts of the Hiding Game. Neither child ever said something like 'Let's get down on the floor from the hot seat.'

Example 29

11 September a.m. (First occurrence of Hiding Game.) (Both girls have been talking to each other and the driver.)

			Antonym Game Patterns[a]	Hiding Game Topic[b]
1.	D:	Ah, it's a lovely day today.		
2.	N:	(giggles)	A_1	1
3.	S:	Not hot.	B_2	
4.	N:	Not hot.	A_2	
5.	S:	Hot.	B_1	Switch
6.	N:	Hot. (giggles)	A_1	
7.	S:	Not hot.	B_2	
8.	N:	Not hot. (giggle) Hot, hot.	$A_{2,1}$	
9.	S:	Oh.		
10.	N:	Let's get in here. Get in here. Get in here. Get in here.	A_3	2
		Not hot. (moves to floor)	A_2	1
11.	S:	Hot. (moves to floor)	B_1	
12.	N:	Let's get out here. Let's get out of here.	A_4	2
13.	S:	Out here.	A_4	2
14.	N:	Let's get outa here.	A_4	2
15.	S:	Let's (?)		
16.	N:	Monster get inna house.	A_3	3,2
17.	S:	Get outa here.	B_4 oppose	2
18.	N:	Let's get *in* here.	A_3	2

(Example 29 continued)

			Antonym Game Patterns	Hiding Game Topic
19.	S:	Out here.	B_3 ⎤ echo	
20.	N:	I wanna get outa here.	A_4 ⎦	
		I wanna get in.	A_3	
21.	S:	Hey		
22.	N:	Let's get in here.	A_3	
		Ow. Let's get outa here.	A_4	
		Let's get outa here.	A_4	
		Let's get outa here.		
		Let's get outa here.		
		Suzy let's get out here.		
		I wanna get in here.	A_3	
		I wanna get in here.		
		Wait. I, I (4) This side, this side, this side, this side. I go this side, this side. Ouch. Ouch.		4
		I wanna get outa here.	A_4	2
		My slipper (slipper is stuck under the front seat)		
		My slipper. My slipper, my slipper		
		(N starts to cry and is calmed by D)		
23.	D:	Don't worry about it. You'll get your slipper when you get out.		
24.	N:	I got it. I got my slipper. There. Let's (?) right here.		
		Outa here. 'Fore the monster	A_4	3
		come in the house. Get in.	A_3	
25.	S:	(?)		
26.	N:	This way, this way.		
		Let's go out here.	A_4	2
27.	S:	Kay.		
28.	N:	(giggle)		
29.	S:	Let's go (?) house.		
30.	N:	(?) house.		
31.	S:	Yeah.		

(Example 29 continued)

			Antonym Game Patterns	Hiding Game Topic
32.	N:	Oh, we go this house.		
33.	S:	Inna	B_3	
34.	N:	Wow (giggle) Look.		
35.	S:	In here. (?)	B_3	
		Monster don't come in here.		3
36.	N:	Come in here. See?		
37.	S:	(?)		
38.	N:	Wind not cloze.		
39.	S:	Window not cloze.		
		(Speech briefly obscured by traffic noises.)		
40.	N:	Hot.	A_1	1
				(start of Game 2)
41.	S:	Hot.	B_1	
42.	N:	Let's get out here	A_4	2
		'fore the monster		3
		come in here. Wow.	A_3	
		Let's get out here	A_4	
		get out here. I want get.		
		Move. Beep-beep. Beep.		
43.	S:	Let's get outa here	B_4	
		'fore the monsters come.		3
44.	N:	Let's get up here,		
		'fore the monsters come.		3
45.	S:	Let's stay here.		
		Let's stay here.		
46.	N:	Huh? Let's go downstairs house.		2
47.	S:	Kay.		
48.	N:	'Fore monsters come.		3
		No, I wanna go *this* house.		2
49.	S:	Oh this house.		2
50.	N:	The monster can't come in here.	A_3	3
		Oh the window is closed.		
51.	S:	And the other window's open.		
52.	N:	Other window, da, *closed*.		
		Other window is closed.		

(Example 29 continued)

	Antonym Game Patterns	Hiding Game Topic

The other window is open.

53.   S: Look, m, Nani, m, Nani.
(Suzy and Nani discuss a dog which they
see outside.)

a. See above, p. 109. 1 = hot, 2 = not hot, 3 = in, 4 = out.
b. See Table 12.

Getting down on (and up from) the floor in response to 'Let's get in here' ('Let's hide' in subsequent games) was the first action triggered by a phrase or sentence that became associated with the set of similar actions and topics which formed the structure of the Hiding Game. This consistent pattern of topics and related actions defined the girls' shared understanding of this activity. Although they did not overtly identify the Hiding Game by giving it a name, they treated it as a unit bounded by understood topics and actions. Like other full routines, the Hiding Game was embedded into the flow of activity which Suzy and Nani considered appropriate to their moods and to the situation they were in in the car. The columns on the right side of the transcription show how Suzy and Nani combined elements of the Antonym Game and the Hiding Game.

The interrelation between the interior dimensions of the car and the girls' conversation and activities suggested that a routine was in progress whenever they were moving around the back seat. By concentrating on the sections of the recorded data that accompanied this movement, I was able to identify the basic structure of the Hiding Game. The topics that were part of the basic structure of the routine were those that Suzy and Nani associated with each other and which coincided with predictable activity (moving around the back seat) by the girls.

I found that the topics that predictably triggered or were associated with certain actions could be put into five main groups. Each of these groups is given a topic number on Table 12. Three of the five are related to the girls' physical environment. Topic 1, 'hot', was related to the seat of the car and had initially come up when the sun had made the seat hot. Topic 2, 'hide, house, up, down, in', was accompanied by movement between the floor (down, in, hide) and the seat (up, out). Topic 4, 'over hear, back, this side', was accompanied by movement from one side of the seat or the floor to the other.[4] While Topic 3, 'monster', did not indicate a physical location, it provided a reason — however imaginary — for their movements. Topic 5, 'slippers',[5] was not directly related to the activity that allowed the girls to use their surroundings in such an enjoyable way but was discussed while they were getting in and out of the 'house'. Several minor topics occurred occasionally and were clearly associated with the main topics and the activity of hiding from the monster. These are shown on the tables.[6] Table 14 also shows the frequency and distribution of topics. Frequency indicates how often a topic was introduced into a game in the course of twenty games. Distribution indicates in which of the games each topic occurred and the relative order of occurrence in each game. Table 15 gives figures and percentages for the occurrence of each of the major topics. The tables reveal that some topics were more likely to occur than others. In a given game, the relative order in which topics occurred remained constant even when one or two topics were skipped in that particular game. I will refer to these tables as I discuss the emergence and development of the Hiding Game.

Table 12: The Hiding Game: Main Topics

Topic 1	'hot, not hot'
Topic 2	'hide, house, down, up, in, out'
Topic 3	'monster'
Topic 4	'over here, back, this side'
Topic 5	'slipper' (clothing)

Table 13: The Hiding Game: Dates of Occurrence

Game Number	Date	Session Number	Example Number	Page Number
1	11 Sept.	7	29	252
2	11 Sept.	7	29	252
3	12 Sept.	8		
4	12 Sept.	8		
5	12 Sept.	8	33	278
6	13 Sept.	9		
7	13 Sept.	9		
8	14 Sept.	10		
9	14 Sept.	10		
10	17 Sept.	11		
11	17 Sept.	11	37	291
12	18 Sept.	12	34, 35	281, 282
13	13 May	39		
14	14 May	40	36	286
15	29 May			
16	30 May	50	39	296
17	12 June	57	38	293
18	13 June	58		
19	18 June	61	40	297
20	20 June	66		

Table 14: The Hiding Game: Frequency and Distribution of Topics

Game Number ↓	Topic → 1 'hot ...'	2 'hide ...'	3 'monster'	4 'over ...'	5 'slipper'
1	A	B	C	D_1	D_2
2	A	C	B		
3		A			
4		A	B, C		A
5		A, D	D	C	B
6	A, D	C		D	
7	A	B	B		B
8	A	B			
9	A				
10		A	B		
11				A	
12		B	A		
13			A_1	A_2	
14		A, D	D	D	C
15			A	A	
16		A		C	
17		A		B	
18		A	B	C	C
19		A	C	B	
20		A		C	B

Key to table: letters represent the order of occurrence in a given game (A = first, B = second, etc.). Where topics were combined and the order of occurrence was clear (i.e. the topics were not embedded in one another), the order is noted in subscript numbers.

Table 15: The Hiding Game: Order and Frequency of Topic Occurrence

Position	Date	Game Total	Topic → 1. 'hot . . .'	2. 'hide . . .'	3. 'monster'	4. 'over . . .'	5. 'slipper'
1st	Sept.	12	6 (50%)	4 (33%)	1 (8%)	1 (8%)	3 (25%)
	M–J	8		6 (75%)	2 (25%)	2 (25%)	2 (25%)
	Total	20	6 (50%)	10 (50%)	3 (15%)	3 (15%)	5 (25%)
2nd	Sept.	12		4 (33%)	4 (33%)		
	M–J	8			1 (13%)	1 (13%)	
	Total	20		4 (20%)	5 (25%)	1 (5%)	
3rd	Sept.	12		2 (17%)	2 (17%)	1 (8%)	2 (25%)
	M–J	8				3 (38%)	
	Total	20		2 (10%)	2 (10%)	4 (20%)	2 (10%)
4th	Sept.	12		1 (8%)	1 (8%)	2 (17%)	1 (8%)
	M–J	8		1 (13%)	1 (13%)	1 (13%)	1 (8%)
	Total	20		2 (10%)	2 (10%)	3 (15%)	1 (5%)
Occurrence	Sept.	12	6 (50%)	10 (83%)	7 (58%)	4 (33%)	4 (33%)
Total	M–J	8		6 (75%)	5 (63%)	7 (88%)	4 (50%)
	Total	20	6 (30%)	16 (80%)	12 (60%)	11 (55%)	8 (40%)

More than one appearance of a topic in a single game is now shown (unless the topic was used in one position, then dropped and then picked up again in a different position). Neither is simple repetition counted. In the figures for total appearances, only one per game is counted.

Since the Hiding Game which took place on 11 September (Example 29) was representative of the games which followed over the following ten months, I will present a full analysis of the 11 September game and refer back to it in subsequent discussions of other games, expansions and innovations. With the exception of Topic 1, 'hot', the structure (the topic and the order in which they occurred) of the first game was virtually the same as the one played on 13 June (see Table 14). On 11 September, the 'hot/not hot' Antonym Game led Nani to suggest moving to the floor (Utterance 10). Nani then introduced the basic topics which were used in subsequent games and which, along with appropriate movements around the car, made up the basic structure of the Hiding Game:

Topic 2:   'in, outa' (N: 10, 12, 14, 18, 20 22)
              'house' (N: 16, 24)
Topic 3:   'monster' (N: 16, 24)
Topic 4:   'this side' (N: 22, 26)
Topic 5:   'slipper' (N: 22, 24)

Suzy repeated and accepted Nani's directions about where to move without adding her own thoughts until Utterance 29 when she picked up two of the topics and used them:

Topic 2:   'house (S: 29)
              'in' (S: 33)
Topic 3:   'monster' (S: 35)

Nani took the initiative again in Utterance 40 by going back to Topic 1, 'hot',[7] and taking up again the main story that pulled all the topics together: 'Let's get out here 'fore the monster come in here' (Utterance 46).

The only topic that was mentioned several times on 11 September but did not occur in subsequent Hiding Games was 'window' (Utterances 38, 19, 50, 51, 52). 'Window' was connected to the story and thereby to the game because of the girls' concern that the monster might come through an open window. In later occurrences of the Hiding Game, other topics were proposed by Suzy or Nani. Because they were both aware of the basic structure of this routine, any new topic had to be explicitly shown to relate to the actions and discussion that revolved around escape from the monster.[8]

The girls' shared concept of what the basic structure of the Hiding

Game was is reflected on Table 14. As this table shows, the frequency
with which the topics were used and the relative order of introduction
changed very little between September 1973 and May and June 1974.
The only major change is the disappearance of Topic 1, 'hot', after
Game 9 (14 September) in spite of the fact that this topic triggered the
emergence of the game and initiated six out of the first nine games (half
of the twelve games that occurred in September).

The 'hot/not hot' exchange was the link between the reality of the
temperature of the seat and the beginning of the game. After the game
became a ritualised routine, either girl could convince the other to get
down on the floor even though the problem of the 'hot' seat was not
mentioned — all that was needed was what had by now become a code
phrase: 'Let's get in here,' 'Let's hide,' or 'Let's get inna house.' In
ordinary ongoing conversation, it would have been necessary to give
some reason for getting down on the floor and to give an explicit direc-
tive such as 'Let's get down on the floor to hide from the monster' in
order to accomplish what the code phrase was able to do.

The eventual disappearance of Topic 1, 'hot', was similar to what
had happened in the 'no-yes' You Say routine (see Chapter 5). In that
case there were two basic steps in the aspect of ritualisation which
resulted in a loss of connection with the real world and which established both routines as Suzy and Nani's private property. First, 'no-yes'
became a unit in itself not dependent on the girls disagreeing about
anything. Second, 'no-yes' was transformed so that its phonetic shape
was different from any real-world use. Once 'no-yes' became [nowɪs],
it was Suzy and Nani's personal property — only they (and the eaves-
dropping researcher) knew where [nowɪs] had come from. In the case
of 'hot/not hot', Suzy and Nani also seemed to use this opposition only
as long as necessary. Once each was sure that the other would respond
to topics other than 'hot', they dropped the topic completely and used
only other topics to start and continue the routine. Just as they shared
the origin of [nowɪs], they also shared the original reason for getting
on the 'not hot' floor from the 'hot' seat.

Over the ten-month period during which Suzy and Nani used this
routine, the most important parts of the story were 'house, hide',
'monster' and 'over here'. The most popular topic was also the one the
girls used most frequently: Topic 2, 'house, hide'. It occurred in 80 per
cent of the Hiding Games (see Table 15) and began the routine in 50
per cent of the twenty games. It was the topic that usually replaced
'hot' when 'hot' was no longer used to introduce the routine. The girls
used Topic 2 to initiate ten out of the fourteen games in which Topic 1,

'hot', did not occur (71 per cent of those games that did not contain 'hot').

In terms of popularity, Topic 2, 'house, hide', was followed by Topic 3, 'monster', which occurred 60 per cent of the time. The third most popular topic was Topic 4, 'over here, back, this side', which occurred 55 per cent of the time. No other topic occurred in more than half of the twenty games. As Table 15 shows, other topics were used infrequently to start the routine. Of those topics which occurred as the second topic of a game, Topic 3, 'monster', was the most popular. The third topic in a game was most likely to be Topic 4, 'this side, back, over here'.

The Hiding Game continued to have the same basic structure in terms of topics mentioned and the order in which the topics occurred from the first occurrence on 11 September until Game 18 on 13 June. The children received no support from any source other than themselves and the fact that their physical environment remained the same. The Hiding Game did not seem to bear any resemblance to other games, e.g. traditional children's games, nor to any specific story they might have heard.[9]

Each girl knew what the other expected of her and usually they responded to each other according to their shared expectations. As a result, the use of topics was consistent and key phrases, such as 'Let's get in here,' had an immediate and predictable effect. On the rare occasions that one of the girls failed in an attempt to initiate the game, the cause of the failure was the other girl's refusal to respond as expected. That is, the second girl refused either to bring up an appropriate topic or to move in an appropriate direction (e.g. to the floor in response to 'Let's hide'). 'Appropriate' here means according to ritual (dyadic) constraints — the behaviour each girl expected of the other within the context of this routine. The following two examples illustrate what happened when one child (Nani in both of these cases) tried unsuccessfully to involve the other in the Hiding Game. Note that Suzy simply ignored what Nani said; she did not get down on the floor and she did not use any of the shared language that she knew Nani expected her to use.

Example 30

8 Oct. a.m.

N: (giggles, squeaky voice) Let's get in here. Let's get inna house.

S: (continues to sing)
(discussion of who will get out of the car first at destination)

Example 31

19 Oct. p.m.

N: Let's get in the house.
S: Same, see, same (reference not known)
(After a pause, Nani tries to initiate another game in which Nani pre-
tends to bump her head. Suzy does not respond immediately. Eventually Nani, by laughing and changing the quality of her voice, involves
Suzy in the 'Bump Head' exchange. As I mentioned above (Example
23), the idea of 'bump my (or your) head' usually made the girls
giggle. I could not find any indication in the data as to why this was
so.)

    On both occasions, Suzy simply refused to respond. Nani did not try
to convince her to play by saying, 'Let's get down on the floor,' instead
of 'Let's get in here' or 'Let's get inna house.' Apparently, Nani assumed that if Suzy would not respond to 'Let's get inna house' by talking
about monsters or by getting down on the floor, then she simply was
not in the mood for playing the Hiding Game. Nani therefore changed
the subject of the conversation. Nani did not, apparently, consider the
possibility that the phrase, 'Let's get in the house' would be meaningless to Suzy. She knew from past experience that Suzy used the Hiding
Game jargon in the same way that Nani herself did and that Suzy would
respond appropriately if she wanted to.
    What Joos (1961) called the intimate style may be the correct way
to characterise the language that Suzy and Nani used to engage in the
Hiding Game. Because they had developed it without external influence, it was an exclusive product of their relationship and their verbal
interaction. The exclusivity of this intimate jargon was clear when a
third child, Eero, joined the girls in the car. Very few of the girls'
usual routines occurred during sessions in which Eero was present. Suzy
attempted to start the Hiding Game during the first session which included Eero.

Example 32

12 Oct. a.m.

1. S: Monster, yeah?
2. E: (laugh)
3. D: Hey, hey, hey, hey, Nani, stay on your side.
4. S: Now my k
5. E: (sings) 'La-a it tastes so good.'
   (Nani asks D to help her take off her sweater)

Eero reacted to the mention of 'monster' by laughing and apparently forgot the subject when he started to sing a part of a television commercial (Utterance 5). It is not clear whether Nani was moving because she wanted to play the Hiding Game or because she was struggling to take off her sweater. Suzy (4) does not seem to be starting to say anything connected with the Hiding Game.

There are two possible reasons for the non-occurrence of further attempts to initiate the Hiding Game in other sessions when Eero was in the car. First, there was simply not enough room for the children to engage in appropriate escape activity. Second, since Eero did not respond appropriately to the jargon, the girls may have realised that he would not be able to participate because he had not been a party to the development of the Hiding Game jargon. The intimate code of the Hiding Game excluded Eero. Suzy and Nani may have felt that the atmosphere was simply different when a third child was present. The girls' ability to take another person's point of view seemed to be operating here. What they expected of each other was different from and more specific than what they expected from a third person. The speech that was recorded when Eero was in the car was not as expressive as when he was not present. This is probably because Suzy and Nani could not understand what was in Eero's head (nor could he understand their point of view) as well as they understood each other.

The structure of the Hiding Game and number of times it appeared in the data were determined by the girls without external intervention. In playing the game, they were able to drop the original reason for getting down on the floor (the 'hot' seat) and to avoid direct reference to the floor apparently because they both accepted the Hiding Game as a unit complete in itself which did not need ordinary explanations. Explanations were made unnecessary by the special code that the girls had invented for their own use and by the ritual constraints they both accepted. They both knew, for example, that 'Let's hide' was an invitation to get down on the car floor and that 'monster' created a make-believe emergency and required imaginary escape attempts.

7.3 Extensions

The overwhelming proportion of successful games out of attempts made (20 out of 23)[10] indicates that playing the Hiding Game was a very popular activity. The popularity of the Hiding Game in its original (11 September) form is also suggested by the fact that Nani and Suzy continued to play the game over a period of ten months. They even continued to play it under threat of adult punishment when the driver (in May and June) told them not to get down on the floor because she thought they were safer on the seat. The remarkable inertia or momentum of the game which derived from the strong attraction it held for them made it difficult for either child to refuse to play. This inertia was typical of other popular routines and an invitation to play was, like a request to share something, tied to the threat to withdraw or promise to extend friendship.[11] Because playing the Hiding Game involved the use of their own special code, it was a product and proof of their intimate relationship. Part of the inertia of the most popular routines was the fact that a refusal to play could be and usually was considered an unfriendly act.[12] The rest of the inertia derived from the fun the girls had in engaging each other in routines.

7.3.1 Expansions

As the consistent use of the same topics and actions shows, the girls made few attempts to change the Hiding Game. This may be related to the possibility that the intimate style is more resistant to change than the more formal casual style. According to Joos's definition of these styles (see Chapter 1, pp. 22-6), the systematic features of intimate style are (1) extraction and (2) jargon (Joos, 1961, pp. 30-1). Extraction means that the speaker extracts a minimum pattern from some conceivable sentence. It is not ellipsis because an elliptical sentence still has wording, grammar and intonation. ('Monster', for example, was too brief to be considered elliptical in the context of the Hiding Game; 'monster' represented a part of the whole story that underlay the game.) If this concept can be applied to a unit larger than a sentence, that is to a routine, and I believe it can, then the Hiding Game was an intimate routine. It was conceivably extracted from a potential casual routine in that the girls could have alluded to non-shared information to help Eero understand that when Suzy said, 'monster', she meant 'Let's get down on the floor and pretend that a monster is chasing us.' Suzy and Nani never tried to explain the game to anyone. For them it came to have only the intimate form. For this reason, they seemed not to consider using a casual form which would have suggested the meanings of parts of the jargon. They seemed even further from using a consultative form which might have included explanations of each part of the jargon. (This is what is done if one person is teaching a game, contract bridge for example, to someone else. The actual playing of a bridge game will not include explanations for why someone says, 'two hearts'.) The only form of the Hiding Game that was available for Suzy and Nani to change was the intimate form that used the special Hiding Game jargon — not the unrealised casual form. If the connections (whatever these may be) between an extracted form and a fuller form of a sentence or a routine are to be maintained, the extracted form can be changed only in superficial ways. In the Hiding Game, for example, the 'monster' element was required because escaping from the beast was the reason for the movement around in the car. Since the intimate form of the routine did not admit mention of moving for the sake of moving, they could not say, 'Let's move around in the car because it's fun.' They also could not change the game to 'Let's sit still,' although Suzy did keep Nani from moving by saying 'No more monster on your side' (see Example 39 below, Game 17). Suzy and Nani may have been reluctant to change the Hiding Game not only because the intimate form of the routine made it more rigid but because the intimacy itself was a way for them to express their feelings of closeness. The invention of the game represented shared experience and their friendship may have stimulated a need to preserve the structure of the routine.

Nevertheless, Suzy and Nani did propose to each other innovations and expansions. Because the Hiding Game was resistant to change, the incorporation of innovations was itself a skill. In order to change the game, Suzy and Nani had to recognise first the difference between old, shared information (that was already part of the ritual) and new ideas that had to be shown to relate to the old; then they had to explain these new relationships.[13] From time to time, Suzy and Nani tried to make changes in the game by introducing new topics or expanding old one and by finding new ways to use the game to control each other's behaviour (e.g. involving each other in the main activities of the game). Expansions of topic and changes in function were often, though not necessarily, connected. Expansions during the first period of data collection (September-November 1973, Games 1-12) usually involved manipulation of linguistic material and the introduction of new topics which were closely related to the basic five topics. The use of the game to control behaviour was more fully exploited during the second period of data collection (May-June 1974, Games 13-20).

One type of expansion involved playing an Antonym Game in which the contrasting words or phrases were part of the Hiding Game jargon. As discussed above, the Hiding Game first occurred as a response to the 'hot/not hot' Antonym Game. Even as the girls started to include the action of getting down on the floor, they used the 'in/out' Antonym Game. (Patterns of both are shown on Example 29 above.) Because the words or phrases that were juxtaposed were part of the basic structure of the Hiding Game, this type of expansion or innovation was easily incorporated into the game.

7.3.2 Innovations

Suzy and Nani found that it was more difficult to introduce topics which were not closely associated with the five basic topics. The child who introduced such a topic was obliged to show how it fitted into the game. If the second child could not connect the new topic with one of the old ones, she would usually say, 'Huh?' 'Huh?' was then accepted by the first child as a request for repetition and/or clarification. Such a request operated as a repair mechanism.[14] A request for repetition during an instance of the Hiding Game had two possible motivations: either the child making the request did not hear what was said, or what was said did not belong to the basic structure of the Hiding Game and the child said, 'Huh?' because she could not figure out how to continue the Hiding Game. The 'Huh?' in this case indicated that some ritual constraint had been violated. The violated constraint was one of those that governed the girls' expectations of topics and procedures that might occur during a Hiding Game.

Example 33 below contains the use of a repair mechanism. In this case, Suzy found that she had to provide some kind of connection to the basic structure of the Hiding Game when she mentioned 'fish' in the middle of the game. The section of data which involved the customary playing of the game is now shown here. Utterance numbers are from the start of the game. This was the third game during the 12 September session. Conversation which was unrelated to the Hiding Game occurred between the three separate games.

Example 33

12 Sept. a.m. (Game 5)

```
 9.  N:  Oh, I go that side. This a way.
10.  S:  Fish. That's a fish in there.
11.  N:  Huh?
12.  S:  There's fish.
13.  N:  Fish.
14.  S:  (sing-song voice) Fishing, fish, fishing time.
         Yeah, I go fish with you.
15.  N:  I go fish with Mommy.
16.  S:  (?) with you.
17.  N:  I go fish with Suzy.
18.  S:  Yeah. Let's go down. No, let's stay inna boat. Let's stay a boat.
         Let's stay a boat house.
19.  N:  House. (squeal)
```

Immediately after Suzy brought up 'fish' (Utterance 10), Nani said, 'Huh?' Suzy merely repeated the essential part of what she had said (12). Nani seemed willing to accept what Suzy had said and went on to accept Suzy's apparent change of subject from 'fish' to 'fishing time' (14) by first saying she would fish with Mommy (15) and then agreeing to fish with Suzy (17). When Suzy was able to bring the fish topic directly back into the Hiding Game by talking about 'going down' (the same phrase used to get down on the floor in the Hiding Game), then about staying in the 'boat' and finally about staying in the 'boat house', Nani squealed to express her delight at arriving at the familiar Topic 2, 'house' (19). Although Suzy responded to Nani's 'Huh?' by repeating and expanding the topic she had introduced in Utterance 10, only the clear return to the Hiding Game drew a strong reaction from Nani in the form of a squeal.

Nani's 'Huh?' signalled that a repair was required because 'fish' not only had no obvious semantic relation to the established Hiding Game topics (and thereby threatened the continuity of the routine) but it also acknowledged a switch from intimate style to consultative style.[15] The child who said 'Huh?' indicated that a statement had been made which represented new information and therefore was not appropriate to the intimate jargon that the girls used to play the Hiding Game.[16] Such new information which requires explanation is, following Joos's definition, appropriate to consultative style but is not tolerated by intimate style. The playing of the Hiding Game involved the use of jargon or a special code in the sense that 'Let's hide!' symbolised but did not express the idea of getting down on the floor. Because 'each intimate group must invent its own code' (Joos, 1961, p. 32) and the introduction of 'fish' did not fit into the set of topics which made up the jargon of this routine, the intimacy involved in playing the game was challenged.

'Huh?' as a repair device was used not only in the way Sacks *et al.* (1974) predicted, i.e. to repair a semantic break, but also to correct the violation of a ritual constraint. New topics had to be shown to be related to the established ones in order for the Hiding Game to continue to be used by the girls to express their feelings about their relationship. 'Huh?' or a similar repair mechanism was not always needed when a new topic was incorporated into the routine. One girl could bring up a new or unrelated topic, discuss it with the second girl, and continue to use the routine in the usual way. On 13 June (Example 34 below), a possible interruption in the form of a cockroach on the floor of the car was integrated into the game. On that occasion, the Hiding Game was initiated by Nani, and Suzy was willing to play until she noticed the bug or 'buggies' on the floor.

Example 34

13 June (Game 18)

1. N: Better *hide*. Hide, yeah?
2. S: Monsters. Monsters, yeah. Buggies.
3. N: Kay, can't go and catch.
4. S: Over there on the middle of the side, a
5. N: Kay. Yeah, yeah. Now we go hide.

The girls were willing to get down on the floor after Suzy noticed the 'buggies'. Suzy delivered 'buggies' with the same voice quality, pitch and intonation as 'monsters', almost as if she were identifying the roach as a kind of monster. Nani said they 'can't go and catch' so the cockroach kept them from going 'over there on the middle of the side' just as the 'monster' kept them on one side or the other. Once the 'buggies' had left, Nani said, 'Now we go hide,' without explaining that although the game had been introduced earlier, the action of getting down on the floor had been delayed. There was also no need to explain which part of Suzy's Utterance 2 was imaginary and which part referred to the real world. The 'buggie' excerpt (Example 34) illustrated how flexible Topic 3, 'monster', was. This topic was also expanded in several ways in Example 35.

Example 35

18 Sept. (Nani speaks as the girls get into the car at the end of pre-school) (Game 12)

 1. N: Monster, Mommy. (growl)
 2. D: Who's a monster?
 3. N: Suzy's a mon ⎰ ster.
 4. S: ⎱ (growl)
 5. N: Mom, Suzy's a monster, Mo ⎰ mmy.
 6. S: ⎱ (growl)
 7. N: Suzy's a monster.
 8. D: Yeah?
 9. N: (softer) Suzy's a monster. (laugh)
10. S: (growl)
11. N: (growl) 'Fraid Mommy.
12. D: Huh?
13. N: I'm 'fraid of a monster.
14. S: (growl, roar)
15. N: (growl, roar)
16. S: Then I'm a lion. (?) tiger.
17. N: No. I'm a, no, I'm a monster. (growl)
18. S: Then I'm a lion, OK?
19. S&N: (growl in unison)
20. S: Let's go in ogre's house.
21. N: Huh?
22. S: Ogre house.
23. N: OK. I wan go (?)'s house. I go (?) house.
     No. I going ogre's house. Yeah.
24. S: Yeah.
25. N: Sit on ogre's house. What's that?

Suzy's monster imitations may have started at the pre-school before the girls got into the car. Nani identified Suzy's growl as a monster noise in Utterance 2 ('Monster, Mommy') and then pretended to be afraid of the monster (' 'Fraid, Mommy', 11). Finally Nani started to growl like a monster too. Suzy suggested that she was a lion (16) while Nani became a monster (17) and they both growled. In Utterance 20

Suzy introduced Topic 2 ('house, hide, get in') but, instead of getting into a house to escape the monster, she wanted to get into the ogre's house. Unlike the quick acceptance which Nani gave the association between growling and monsters, the connection of 'ogre' and 'house' brought a questioning 'Huh?' from Nani. As in Example 33 when Suzy introduced 'fish' into the Hiding Game, Nani's 'Huh?' asked for repetition and/or explanation. In this case Suzy's repetition was sufficient (22). Nani said, 'OK' (23) and agreed to go to the ogre's house. However, Nani ran into difficulty. It is clear from the tape (although I could think of no way to represent it in the transcription)[17] that Nani said 'No' to herself because she was not satisfied with her first two attempts to pronounce 'ogre'. 'What's that?' (25) referred to the microphone. Suzy tried to take it off and to pretend it was a gun. Nani agreed with the idea, but the driver stopped them from taking it off the stand. Although the 'gun' did not occur in connection with the Hiding Game elsewhere, it could have been an extension of the idea of monsters because a gun can be used to shoot them.

In Example 35 above, Topic 3, 'monster,' included the idea of growling like a lion or a tiger, and Topic 1, 'house,' was expanded to include 'ogre's house.' The growling of monsters, lions and tigers and the act of impersonating one of these creatures was easily accepted by both girls; that is, they met each other's expectations and no explanations were needed.[18] 'Ogre's house,' however, kept the game from progressing in two ways. First, it did not fit into the Hiding Game because 'house' was always a place where the girls went to escape the monster and had never been the home of a frightening being. Nani was able to use 'Huh' to tell Suzy that she did not accept or understand the new idea. Although Suzy's repetition of 'ogre house' (22) satisfied Nani, the game was then held up by Nani's struggle to articulate 'ogre'. Nani's ability to monitor and correct her own pronunciation[19] allowed the game to continue.

In addition to 'monster', Topic 5, 'slippers, clothing' was also used in other Hiding Games. This topic occurred in 8 of the 20 Hiding Games and was probably connected with a custom in Hawaii (which was followed in the homes of both girls) which requires that shoes or sandals be taken off before entering a home. Although some people have footwear that is reserved for wearing indoors, many people and most children are usually barefoot indoors. This may be the reason for Nani and Suzy's attention to taking slippers off before they go into their pretend 'house' on the floor of the car. Their attention to taking off sweaters and ponchos may have derived from the fact that the weather in Hawaii is seldom cold enough for anyone to wear one of these indoors. At the pre-school, they were expected to take sweaters off immediately on entering and hang them up.

Although I will discuss only the first eleven utterances of the 14 May Hiding Game with regard to Topic 5, 'slippers', I am including the entire game to show how smoothly the girls negotiated progress from one topic and/or action to the next.

Example 36

14 May a.m.   (Game 14)

1. S: Oh, let's hide, let's hide.
2. N: Oh, let's hide, let's hide.
     (D urges them to sit properly)
3. N: Let's hide, Suzy. Take off your shoes. Let's hide now. Let's hide.
4. S: Hide.
5. N: Take off your shoes like me. I take off my shoes.
6. S: Get my slippers dirty.
7. N: Take off your sweater.
8. S: (?) Nani.
9. N: Yes, do. I take off my sweater. I take off my poncho.[a] Take off yours now. Now let'd let's hide, kay. You don't hide on this (?), OK. I go with you, kay? OK. Down.
10. S: Right down here?
11. N: Hiding right down here. Now let's hide. OK. Kay. We hide these[b] here, OK.
12. S: Live here too. Hide under there.
13. N: No, hide over here. No. See. Because that's small.
14. S: There too.
15. N: This hides, hides here.
16. S: OK.
17. N: No, Eh
18. S: Nani you hide yourself.
19. N: I hide here, OK? I hide this way. You hide this way.
20. S: No, I don't need to. I said. I don't need to. I don' need to. You hide in (?). Hide down here.
21. N: Kay. Are you afraid?
22. S: Unh-unh.
23. N: Well, then kill the monster.

(Example 36 continued)

24. S: Huh?
25. N: Kill the monster then.
26. S: (?)
27. N: I'm the mommy.
28. S: (?)
29. N: You, mommies kill.
30. S: Huh?
31. N: Mommies kill monsters.
32. S: (?)

a. A 'poncho' was considered a kind of sweater by the children. Nani was not wearing both a sweater and a poncho.
b. 'These' refers to the clothing which they just took off.

Towards the beginning of Example 36, Nani insisted that Suzy take off her shoes and her sweater as she herself had done (3). On this occasion, Nani wanted to hide the clothes as well as herself and she wanted Suzy to do the same. Suzy resisted Nani's instructions (6, 8, 10) and forced Nani to repeat herself (7) and explain in some detail, showing Suzy what she was doing (9) and encouraging Suzy to follow her example (11).

By expanding Topic 5, 'slippers', Nani was able to tell Suzy what to do while convincing her to continue to play the game. Suzy was able to resist following Nani's instructions without being completely uncooperative by referring to the Hiding Game topics to give excuses ('Get my slippers dirty.' 6) to request clarification ('Right down here?' 10), and to issue orders ('Nani you hide yourself.' 18). In Utterance 20, Suzy was more reluctant than ever, insisting, 'I don't need to [hide] . . . You hide . . .' Suzy did not, however, refuse to play. She never said, 'I don't want to get down on the floor.' The continuation of the game (21-32) depended on Nani's ability to keep Suzy interested. Since Suzy had offered her resistance within the terms of the game (e.g. 'Hide down there,' 20), Nani was able to keep the game going by expanding one of the main topics, Topic 3, 'monster', in several steps without losing its connection with the basic structure of the Hiding Game and therefore without losing Suzy's interest.

In Utterance 21, Nani accepted Suzy's refusal to 'hide'. However, she tried indirectly to keep Suzy involved by asking her if she were afraid. Even though Suzy answered negatively (22), Nani continued as if Suzy were willing to follow her line of thought.[20] In Utterance 23, Nani went on as if Suzy had responded affirmatively as Nani had expected. Suzy was confused by the suggestion that offensive action, killing the monster, was part of the game. Nani answered Suzy's 'Huh?' by repeating what she had said and, although Suzy still did not seem to understand exactly what she meant, Nani went on to her next step which appeared at first to be completely unrelated to the Hiding Game. She said, 'I'm the mommy' (27). At this point Suzy seemed to be thoroughly confused. Nani, however, had a definite logic which she revealed over the course of several utterances. She showed that being a mommy could be considered part of the Hiding Game because that role gave one the power to kill the monsters.

Unfortunately the data do not show whether Nani's manoeuvres would have resulted in the continuation of the game because the car arrived at the pre-school and the girls had to scramble to put on their shoes and sweaters. Nani, however, had succeeded in maintaining Suzy's interest and involvement by discussing being afraid, killing the monster, being a mommy, and finally assuming the role that gave her the power to kill the frightening monster. Recognition of the Hiding Game's basic structure was strong enough for Suzy to follow Nani's steps. Nani knew that each point she was making was connected to the convention, the Hiding Game, which she shared with Suzy. Suzy did not discourage her and additional explanation would have been redundant within the context of the situation: the established routine and their intimate relationship.

The use of the Hiding Game as a means of telling the other child what to do was not always as elaborate as on 14 May; it could be accomplished more directly. This use of the routine was more easily realised as the game became a familiar activity, but it did occur in the earlier games. One example of this occurred during Game 11 on 17 September. This was the first time that either girl had used the Hiding Game jargon to convince the other to allow her to do something. Example 37 occurred at the end of the game.

Example 37

17 Sept. (Game 11)

S: (?) going this, side.
N: Oh, oh, I going this side.
S: You go that side?

Example 37 continued

N: I go with you, kay?
S: No. No. No.
N: Yes.
(crying)

Both girls ended up crying because Nani tried to use the game to invade the side of the car that Suzy wanted to stay on alone. Although Nani tried to make Suzy agree with her by talking about 'this side' and 'that side', Suzy simply refused. On this occasion, the Hiding Game did not achieve the agreement that Nani wanted.

On other occasions, after the Hiding Game had become a familiar part of the girls' conversations, it was used quickly and calmly if not always effectively to state desires indirectly. On 29 May, for example, Nani wanted to sit on Suzy's side so she said, 'Monster on my side. I come your side.' Suzy did not want Nani to come to her side so she said, 'No more monster on your place.' This use of the Hiding Game jargon is similar to the code used in playing a game like contract bridge. The special meaning of 'Monster on my side' is like the special meaning of 'two hearts' in a bridge game. It conveys a message that would have a different meaning outside the context of the game. Furthermore, successful use of the code depends on knowing that the other 'players' will understand that the special meaning rather than the general meaning is intended.

In Example 38, Nani, using the Hiding Game jargon, directed Suzy to stay on one side of the car because Nani was pretending to paint.

Example 38

12 June (Game 17)

1. N: You hide in there while I'm painting. OK? You hide in there while I'm painting.
2. S: Hide in there?
3. N: No, hide in your own place, in there, because I'm painting on this side. Go in that side and hide. Inside in there. No, you gottu[a] go in here. Yes, you gottu. You hide in there because I goin' when I get through painting and then I hide.
4. S: How 'bout I stay like this?
5. N: Hm?

Example 38 continued

6. S: How 'bout I stay like this?

a. *tt* is actually an alveolar flap, [gaDu].

Nani tried very hard to convince Suzy to 'hide' while she 'painted'. Even when she was most insistent about what Suzy 'gottu' do, she never used any word but 'hide'. Apparently she felt that 'hide' was more convincing than a term which did not belong to the Hiding Game jargon. On this occasion, however, Suzy was unmoved and, after asking for clarification ('Hide in there?'), she insisted on staying 'like this'. Suzy's reluctance to pursue the Hiding Game did not lead Nani to be more direct. Instead of either telling Suzy what she wanted her to do directly or continuing the Hiding Game, Nani initiated role play and continued in that context to tell Suzy what to do. The expressive function of the shared language was thus a useful tool for Suzy and Nani. For instance, they could use the Hiding Game jargon to compose indirect directives. When Nani failed to gain Suzy's co-operation in playing the Hiding Game, she tried another kind of shared language — the language they used in pretending to be other people. (Space does not permit a discussion of their role-play routine.)

One type of expansion of the Hiding Game was the incorporation of the threat of adult intervention. To the extent that Nani and Suzy did not let this threat interfere with their game, this type of expansion is similar to the incorporation of 'buggies' (Example 34 above). The threat was considered and rejected at the point in the game where one child convinced the other to 'hide', but it was not closely associated with one of the main topics. The girls knew that adult intervention could end a game as it had on 14 May (Example 34) when the driver would not let the girls remove the microphone to use it as a 'gun'. Not only were the girls not supposed to touch the microphone but the driver had told them (before the second series of recordings began on 8 May) that it was not safe for them to move around the back of the car. This directly restricted the activity involved in playing the Hiding Game. In spite of this restriction (or perhaps stimulated by it), the girls continued to play the game. The threat of adult punishment did not appear to influence their behaviour. Although they played the game eight times during May and June, they discussed the possibility of punishment only twice (Examples 39 and 40 below). On both occasions, Nani convinced Suzy to play in spite of this threat.

In Example 39 below, Nani joined Suzy on the floor. They discussed how crowded it was down there. Suzy said she did not want to 'squash' her legs. They repeated 'squish-squash' for a while. Nani then made the following suggestion:

Example 39

30 May (Game 16)

N: Aw right. I go that side. You go this side.
S: No, she might spank me.
N: I go this side and my mommy won't spank me.

Nani's reassurance was sufficient to calm Suzy's fears about the driver being angry because they were 'hiding'. They continued to sit on the floor and discuss legs and 'squish-squash' until they arrived at the pre-school. In Example 40, the enjoyment of the Hiding Game was again more important than fear of adult reprisal. On this occasion, Nani's imitation of her mother's speech either amused Suzy to the extent that she forgot her fear or Nani succeeded in making the adult's presence less important to Suzy than she had considered it in Utterance 4.

Example 40

18 June (Game 19) (quotation marks (5) indicate that Nani lowers her voice and speaks gruffly — a 'Papa Bear' voice)

1. N: Kay, we better hide in here, kay. Kay? Hide it[a] here. Come and hide it here. I put our slippers here. That we just did (?) yesterday.
2. S: (?)
3. N: Kay now. No you better sit here so we could hide.
4. S: No, your mommy said not, (?) get angry at me again.
5. N: No, *la*ter she will say, 'I'm angry at you.'
        (belly laugh)
6. S: (giggle)
7. N: OK, let's hide these.[a] You, hide. There's monster.
8. S: Here. Want this[a] there?
9. N: OK, now hide, hide.
10. S: Hide.

Example 40 continued

11. N: Hide now. Hide.
 (D tells them to sit on the seat. The game appears to be over but they continue to discuss 'hide', and 'put on slippers'.)

a. 'It' and 'these' refer to objects, probably slippers, which were often involved in the process of 'hiding'. See discussion above of clothing as a topic.

Although the driver enforced the regulation against sitting on the floor, Nani's imitation of her mother allowed the Hiding Game to continue — at least the girls continued to discuss Topic 1, 'hide', and Topic 5, 'slippers', even if they were prevented from 'hiding' on the floor.

Several answers are possible for the question of why the children's behaviour was not restricted by fear of adult disapproval in the above two conversations (Examples 39 and 40) while on 12 September the very thought of being scolded or spanked brought tears (data not shown).

(1) The children may have discovered that the driver was too busy driving to be much of a threat. This was clearly indicated in Example 38 when Suzy appealed to the driver to mediate a dispute and the driver said she could not help because she was driving. Nani reinforced the driver: 'No, no, she driving. Cannot talk to her now.'

(2) They were not as easily intimidated in May as they were in September. There is no independent evidence to support this except that they were older and bigger.

(3) They are enjoying the Hiding Game too much to stop. The data indicate that the game had an inertia for the girls and they tried to keep it going as much as their ingenuity and circumstances allowed.

Whatever combination of the three possible answers is closest to what motivated the children's behaviour on these occasions, the existence of the Hiding Game was well established in their relationship with each other and with their physical environment.

The Hiding Game was a routine developed by Suzy and Nani which had a characteristic structure identified by a set of topics and related actions which were based on an underlying narrative. Because its structure and style were easily recognised and accepted by both children, the girls were able to incorporate certain expansions and innovations into the basic structure of the Hiding Game. The structure of the game depended on the behaviour they expected of each other. By knowing what was in the other's mind, each girl was able to use the language of the game expressively for amusement, to exercise control over the other and the direction of the conversation, and to indicate the closeness of their relationship.

Through a process of ritualisation, the Hiding Game developed the base which made expansion and innovation possible. During this process, the girls learned what they could expect of each other when they were engaged in the routine. They no longer had to explain to each other the topics that were included in the game. Furthermore, they could initiate and use the routine quickly. Like the other ritualised routine I examined, the You Say routine, the Hiding Game became a quick and easy way for Suzy and Nani to direct the course of their conversation. The routine was the product and sign of their close relationship. As such, hesitancy in engaging in it could be construed as rejection of their friendship. This also seemed to add to the attraction the Hiding Game had for both Suzy and Nani.

So much of the conversation involved in playing the Hiding Game was structured by established custom that a high degree of co-operation was possible without the need for repair devices such as requests for repetition and explanation. This provided a base on which the girls could build innovations and practise certain skills. The incorporation of innovations was itself a skill because it involved recognising the difference between old, shared information and new ideas that had to be shown to relate to the old. For example, the girls used 'Huh?' to indicate that a new idea had occurred which violated ritual constraints that governed the intimate style of the special code they had developed in order to play the game. The effective use of 'Huh?' in their conversation required skill in recognising and indicating violations of ritual constraints and in repairing such violations by showing the relevance of apparently new information (e.g. 'Mommies kill') to one of the established topics ('Mommies kill monsters.') (See Example 36 above).

While Suzy and Nani played the Hiding Game, they experimented with linguistic forms as well as underlying linguistic relationships such as the relationship between old and new information. Associations between lexical items occurred frequently. The girls connected semantically related items such as 'monster', 'lion' and 'tiger', all of which were associated with growling noises (Example 35). Antonym Games were another form of experimentation with lexical items. These occurred frequently in Hiding Games in forms such as 'in/out' (11, 12 and 17

September), 'hot/not hot' (11, 13 and 14 September); and 'this/that'
11, 12 and 13 September). The occurrence of semantically related
items and Antonym Games was not restricted to the Hiding Game.
Indeed, the Hiding Game seemed to incorporate many of the types of
short routine and correction activity that were discussed in previous
chapters. Of all the routines, the Hiding Game best exemplified the
girls' ability to understand each other's expectations and their skill
in using language expressively to respond to those expectations.

Notes

1. 'Topic' continues to mean 'conversational topic', i.e. what is being talked
about, and does not refer to other meanings such as grammatical topic, topic-
comment, etc. For uses of the term 'topic', see S. Scollon (1975).
2. (Boggs, 1975, p. 8). Also see above, Chapter 1, footnote 6.
3. The tendency for routines to develop momentum or inertia as a result of
the girls' attraction to them and to subsequently lose whatever connection they
originally may have had to the 'real world' was discussed above, pp. 106-7.
4. A 'side' of the floor is the area behind one of the front bucket seats which
is bounded by the wall of the car and the drive shaft tunnel. The tunnel made a
bump down the centre of the car and was quite high relative to the girls' size. It
also separated the bench seat in the back into 'sides' because it could be felt under
the centre of the seat.
5. 'Slippers' refers to sandals which have no buckles or straps. Suzy and Nani
usually wore this type of footwear.
6. Some of these minor topics are discussed in section 7.3.2.
7. This is shown on Table 4 as a separate game, Game Number 2. There were
five sessions which included more than one Hiding Game. The games were clearly
separated by intervening conversational topics and always started in the same way
whether an individual game was the first or the second in a session. That is, either
Suzy or Nani began a game by introducing a topic that led to both girls getting
down on the floor. To introduce the game Suzy and Nani were most likely to use
Topic 1, 'hot', or Topic 2, 'Let's hide/Let's get in here,' although they used Topic
3, 'monster', on two occasions (Games 12 and 15).
8. Introduction and testing of innovations is discussed in section 7.3.2.
9. For an example of how a story in a book affected the girls' conversation,
see Example 19, 'Jason', in section 4.4.
10. The three attempts that failed are Examples 30, 31 and 32.
11. See Appendix A (Table VI) and Appendix B, Analysis of 3 June session,
for further discussion on how Suzy and Nani felt about being someone's friend.
12. See discussion of Pittenger *et al.* in Chapter 1, pp. 27-8.
13. Weiman pointed out that at the level of the two-word utterance in Stage II
children, new or contrasting information receives the most stress (1974; referred
to in Dale, 1976, pp. 27-8). The work of Chafe (1970) and others made Weiman
aware of the grammatical importance of new information. Dale pointed out the
significance of the new-old distinction in verbal interaction: 'even early in language development, children are sensitive to the distinction between new and old
information, a distinction at the heart of conversational communication' (1976,
p. 28). Indicating new information by means of stress shows that the child has
begun, as early as Stage II, to take into consideration another person's point of

view, that is, to know what is new and what is old within another's experience. At their more advanced stage, Suzy and Nani were conscious of new-old distinctions in the narrow context of a ritualised routine.

14. 'Repair mechanism' has been used in the literature (Sacks *et al.*, 1974) to refer to any word or phrase that seeks to return a conversation to its expected form (p. 101). A person who speaks for a long time might be interrupted to keep a dialogue from turning into a monologue. Requests for repetition are repair devices in the sense that they allow someone who does not understand the conversation to have another chance to figure out what is being discussed and to resume his position as a participant.

Goffman (1976) called the use of requests for 're-runs' corrective action. He pointed out that such corrective action is accomplished by conversational and ritual constraints, but not by grammatical constraints. See also pp. 50-3, 60, 74, 80, 101, 103.

15. Joos (1961, p. 29) explained that casual and consultative styles include 'public information'. While casual style takes such information for granted, consultative style states it as fast as needed. In the Hiding Game, 'Huh?' signalled that some information was neither irrelevant (intimate style) nor understood (casual style) but needed to be provided immediately so that the routine could continue in its customary intimate style. Furthermore, the girls seemed to understand that they were working within a format such as the one they had for the Antonym Game (see pp. 106-13). The Hiding Game format existed only within their society of two and would cease to exist if either of them failed to acknowledge the ritual constraints that defined the format. In Goffman's framework (see p. 103), the violation of a ritual constraint demands corrective action. In the case of the Hiding Game, failure to correct a violation would result in the demise of the routine.

16. This use of 'Huh?' by the listener provided the speaker with an outside view of her speech. George Grace (1976, Ch. VII, p. 7) has called this phenomenon 'metalinguistic feedback'. The ability of the girls to provide each other with metalinguistic feedback and to adjust their speech according to the feedback each received from the other was an important part of their interaction. See above, section 1.2.

17. Although the transcription fails in this regard, the use of (?) is helpful here in showing what Nani's 'No' is in response to.

18. Suzy and Nani grouped these three creatures (and perhaps 'ogre' too) as if the girls thought they belonged together. This set might share semantic features such as [+frightening, +animal, +growlers].

19. See section 4.2 on correction of pronunciation, for more on this type of correction activity.

20. This is similar to what Pawley and Syder (1975) call 'accepting the lure'. That is, once one participant has responded appropriately, the speaker is then free to continue either to the benefit or the detriment (as in the case of a joke) of the respondent. In this case, Suzy continued to accept the 'lure' by continuing to use the Hiding Game jargon and thus staying involved in the routine. Just as being suspicious of the 'lure' in adult conversation might be construed as unfriendliness, Suzy might also have challenged the friendliness of the conversation by not acknowledging the jargon of the routine.

8 CONCLUSIONS

As we have seen, Suzy and Nani were capable communicators. Whether their dialogue seemed adult-like or child-designed, they created and sustained a social *ambiance* that was unique. This creation of theirs was the object of this study. In our examination of some of the units which the girls developed, we observed their understanding of rules of grammatical construction and rules of conversational construction. Such units, which I called routines and correction activities, provided a focal point from which we could view language from several angles. From one angle, we could see the individual child struggling to identify and codify the structure of the language she needed. Nani's problems with *wanna* (Chapter 4) were an example of this. From another angle, we could see individuals using language as a means of relating to each other. The Hiding Game, as well as less elaborate routines, were examples of this. From still another angle, we could look at the nature of shared language itself:

> Most of the uniquely human forms of social behavior are dependent on shared language, so that the structure of language use in society may be related to societal functioning in unique ways. If this is the case, sociolinguistics will contribute a new dimension to social sciences rather than further exemplification of the otherwise known (Ervin-Tripp, 1964a, p. 258).

In investigating the structure of language use within the dyad made up of Suzy and Nani, I was able to identify units which the girls treated as separate from their ongoing conversation. The identification of these units focused my description on types of language which depended heavily on co-operative behaviour. Such behaviour is a prerequisite not only to social interaction in a general sense, but also to the establishment of more intimate types of social interaction.

Within the description of each unit I discussed, it was possible to examine the relationship between the girls' knowledge of rules of grammatical construction and their understanding of rules of conversational usage. With reference to this relationship, Ervin-Tripp and Cook-Gumperz have said:

169

We can argue that the social development of the child and linguistic development have a mutual dependence; his communicative needs motivate his development of formal means. On the other hand, his strategies are constrained by his capacities to handle formal devices available in his grammar, phonology, and sociolinguistic norms around him (1974, p. 3).

In examining Suzy and Nani's routines and correction activities, it was possible to take some tentative steps towards describing the interdependence between social and linguistic (as well as cognitive) development. At certain points, the girls' ability to carry on a conversation contributed to the refinement or adjustment of linguistic forms. The resolution of how to pronounce 'package' (section 4.2.2) was an example of this. In that case the ability to construct cohesive discourse allowed the girls to continue their conversation until each could figure out what the other was talking about.

Their ideas about how a conversation should progress also contributed to their ability to construct routines. The Antonym Game, for example, could be a shared activity only if each child understood conversational turn-taking. Knowledge of opposites was a necessary but not sufficient condition for this routine; the sharing of this knowledge could be enjoyed only when the girls incorporated it into a routine by means of turn-taking.

Co-operative construction of a routine such as the Antonym Game involved more than knowledge of grammatical structure and of conversational structure. It also involved the ability to use language in non-referential ways. In the case of the Antonym Game, the girls used their awareness of language as an *object* of communication when they focused on the polar opposition between the antonyms. They were able to communicate with each other that playing with antonyms was fun to do and that words could be used in games as well as in the normal, non-game, referential way.

Fitting words into games or making up games out of words involves a use of language which Slobin (1975) called 'expressive' and identified as an advanced step in the development of language. The use of language in non-referential ways was evident not only in the use of language as the focus of a game, but also in the development of routines over time. When some routines, such as the Hiding Game and the You Say routine, occurred repeatedly, the structure of these routines changed in predictable ways. As the girls repeated these routines, they seemed to enjoy them more. They giggled more and used them as symbols of their friendly (and sometimes unfriendly) feelings towards each other. If either girl tried to change such a routine, which I call a ritualised routine, the other might have become offended by the introduction of an unfamiliar element. In this way, familiar parts of a routine could be better expressions of friendliness than innovations could be. In this process of change, which I call ritualisation, a routine became not only a better vehicle for the expression of feeling, but also often became streamlined. It came to be initiated more quickly and with little or no explanation. This conforms to another of Slobin's predictions: that a language will become 'quick and easy' as it develops. This certainly was true of Suzy and Nani's shared language.

As Suzy and Nani's routines developed more abbreviated forms and depended more on the girls' private historical perspective, the meaning of the language that they shared became less transparent. Words like 'house' and 'monster', for example, came to represent parts of the narrative that underlay the Hiding Game. In the history of the 'no-yes' You Say routine, 'no-yes' not only lost all sense of disagreement between speakers, but also lost some of its normal phonological characteristics when the girls changed 'no-yes' to [nowɪs].

The loss of referential meaning and of transparency and the gain of expressiveness and abbreviated forms indicated, according to Slobin's (1975) model, that Suzy and Nani's shared language as it occurred in ritualised routines was advanced in its development. In Slobin's model, expressiveness and abbreviation do not develop until *after* clarity and processibility have been established. The skills that the girls exhibited in inventing and expanding ritualised routines were similar to the skills they used in constructing correction activities. These skills included monitoring each other's speech, suggesting corrections and correcting themselves. At no point is it possible to say that grammatical rules alone or rules of usage alone were influencing the shape of the data. The examination of these data suggests that there is no clear division between these two types of rules in the conversation of young children. This conclusion can be extended to a view of the language acquisition process as a whole. A child does not learn to speak 'any and all sentences of her language' in random order. Such a child would be a social monster (Hymes, 1974, p. 75). The development of non-monsters is clearly a patterned, highly organised process. Although we are forced to isolate patterns in order to examine them and describe them, we must not forget that they never occur in isolation. At the present time, there are no doubt many patterns that we cannot observe simply because they are too deeply embedded in other, more easily observed patterns. In dealing with the language of children, we focus on the way in which a child goes about learning to interact verbally with her environment. We watch her learning the rules of grammar in the context of social situations. We can then see how she extends her knowledge of grammar by constructing conversation. Much of the value of descriptions of this process derive from the ability of the researcher to keep track of the circumstances that support and influence the shape of the data.[1]

In the study described here, I maintained the role of a semi-involved observer. In collecting data for this study, I felt that it was important to ensure that only the children's skills and interests would be considered and that contamination of direct adult influence be eliminated as much as possible. I found a suitable setting in a natural, everyday activity that would have occurred in exactly the same form whether or not this study was undertaken (except, of course, for the presence of the recording equipment). Fortunately, the setting, daily car rides between home and the children's pre-school, was well suited physically for recording speech data. The children were 'captive'. They could not go outside the range of the tape-recorder. I, too, was captive. The activity (riding in the car) could not have taken place without me. The fact that I was Nani's mother ensured that my participation would add nothing unnatural to the situation. At the same time, my preoccupation with driving prevented me from becoming an intrusive investigator and from interfering with the naturalness of the situation.

The children's conversation which provided the data for this study took place with a minimum of adult interference or influence. The fact that I could find complex patterns in such data raises, I believe, a number of questions about the ways in which children's speech has traditionally been evaluated. Complexity, for example, has always been assumed to be indicative of maturity. I do not doubt that this is a valid definition of maturity. The assumption I find questionable is that maturity can be measured by surface complexity. Adults simply do not speak in full sentences at all times. Nor do they always exhibit on the surface all their knowledge of their language every time they open their mouths to speak. One reason why this is the case is that maximally clear and processible language is cumbersome, slow and over-redundant. Whenever possible, adults choose concise and expressive language. According to Slobin, the qualities of conciseness and expressivity are characteristics of language in late stages of development. Conciseness and expressivity may therefore be important measures of how maturely a child uses her language.

Children are usually not given credit on a maturity scale for using ellipsis appropriately, for understanding the humour of language play such as punning, understatement or over-statement or for inventing their own language games. They are usually assumed to have no meta-linguistic awareness. As I have shown, it is possible to collect naturalistic data to show how children employ language in unexpectedly mature ways. It seems to me that further research is needed to discover how early in a child's development she becomes aware of choices between full and elliptical forms and how soon she knows that such choices are related to the intimacy or formality of the situation. We need to know how children learn what information is 'old' and what is 'new' to the person to whom they are speaking — and also what words and other means of expression are known to larger and smaller groups or only to oneself. We need to know which sentences normal children learn and how and why they learn those particular sentences instead of 'any and all the sentences of their language' in random order. I believe that such research will lead to a better understanding of the process of language acquisition.

Note

1. For a discussion of the need for students of human behaviour to remain aware of the 'ecology' that maintains a 'niche' for every behavioural pattern, see Hood, Cole and McDermott, 1978.

To mom I Love you
Do you Love me?
I LIKe you
Do you LIKe me?
yes I Love you
yes I LIKe you
Love 12 auko
LIKe12 auk 12 I
HI mom HI NANI
From NANI

2 August 1976

APPENDICES

Appendices are usually used to present relevant information which does not fit into the main body of the discussion. My use of appendices follows this tradition. The first of the two appendices, Tables of Contrasting Words and Phrases, is a listing of some of the smallest units Suzy and Nani used in building routines. The second appendix, Analyses of Complete Sessions, is included to show how Suzy and Nani were able to weave routines into the flow of their conversation in the course of individual sessions.

It was not possible to include all of the relevant data in the discussion of each type of routine because including a large quantity of data would have made the discussion difficult to follow. For this reason, discussion of various points was illustrated by means of appropriate excerpts rather than complete data from entire sessions or long lists of words and phrases. The data included in these appendices illustrate some of the variety of terms that Suzy and Nani enjoyed manipulating and the number of times each type of manipulation occurred. Analyses of complete sessions are included to give the reader some sense of Suzy and Nani's verbal interactions during the ride to and from pre-school and home. I also hope that the data presented here will prove useful to other researchers.

APPENDIX A: TABLES OF CONTRASTING WORDS AND PHRASES

In order to compile the information displayed on these tables, I first went through the data looking for contrasting words and phrases. I was primarily interested in contrast which was a product of the interaction between Suzy and Nani. I therefore included in these tables only those examples of contrast within the speech of one speaker that was in some way relevant to the interaction. Some examples occurred in the interaction as part of dialogues and also outside the interaction as part of monologues. In such cases I listed all occurrences and indicated which had appeared as part of a monologue. One example of this was 'up/down' which occurred as part of a monologue on 28 August (Nani only) and 29 August (Suzy only) and as an Antonym Game on 2 November (see section 5.2, Example 22). I have included this information in Table I, Opposites, because I believe that the appearance of 'up/down' in monologues is related to the appearance of 'up/down' in Antonym Games.

After I found all of the examples that I thought should be listed, I tried various ways to divide the lists into tables. I considered approaches such as Casagrande's and Hale's thirteen types of semantic relationships which they identified in Papago folk definitions (1967). Casagrande and Hale intended these thirteen categories to 'reflect the semantic principles implicit in their construction' (p. 165). I tried to accomplish the same goal in setting up a basis for dividing the words and phrases I had found. Suzy and Nani's reactions to each other's speech were the primary factors in determining the 'semantic principles' for establishing categories for the six tables I decided to use.

The six tables in this appendix are based on usage in discourse. Since the data were not elicited but were spontaneous conversation, they can provide only such information as happened to occur in the flow of Suzy and Nani's conversation. I limited my initial compilation to contrasting words and phrases because I felt that these were more likely to provide an insight into the semantic principles that were psychologically real in the girls' linguistic systems. I believe that semantic principles can be inferred from words and phrases which are contrasted in dialogue in much the same way that Fromkin has found that the 'psychological reality of discrete units' can be substantiated by the examination of speech production (including errors) (1971, pp. 29-30). Fromkin showed that the relation between a 'correct' form and an 'error' in adult speech revealed that some small units such as semantic features are psychologically real. Casagrande and Hale established thirteen categories of folk-definitions to reflect those properties of the defined terms which the Papago culture considered salient. They further believe that investigation into semantic relationships can 'illuminate similarities and differences in the ways men cognitively organize the world' as they understand it (p. 192). The goals of Fromkin and Casagrande and Hale are clearly similar. Both linguists and anthropologists are attempting to describe how the human mind works.

My tables of contrasting words and phrases are an attempt to describe − in a very restricted sense − the way the human mind works during an early stage of development. My data were limited to whatever Suzy and Nani wanted to talk about. My choice of what to include in these tables was therefore limited by the girls' interests. Furthermore, I could not be sure about what the girls meant by what they said unless they used words and phrases in opposition or association. The semantic principles that I was able to infer were therefore limited not only to *what* topics the girls talked about but also *how* they talked about them. This is one reason why I have six categories while Casagrande and Hale have thirteen. I have also used syntactic information to establish semantic opposition. Table V, Assertion/Counter-assertion, for example, lists whole sentences in some cases to illustrate semantic opposition. All tables include reference to how a given term was related to the discourse in which it occurred. Casagrande and Hale suggested that certain grammatical patterns may be associated with particular semantic relations. This association is reflected in some of the six categories I have set up. Table IV, Assertion/Denial, contains many examples of negation that follow the expected pattern, DO + *not*. I tried to lay these tables out in a manner which reveals as many of the relations between semantics, syntax and discourse as possible.

The six tables are as follows:

I. Opposites. Words and phrases listed in this table are the kind that made up Antonym Games. They are terms which are differentiated by polarised features.

II. Comparatives. This is a short list. It is included to indicate some of what the girls knew about relative quantity and quality.

III. Possession. The purpose of this table is to show what objects the girls referred to in terms of possession. This list also shows how often they contrasted the idea of *yours* and *mine*.

IV. Assertion/Denial. When one child asserted something, the other often (32 times) flatly denied it. This is closely related to Antonym Games. I have listed 'no/yes' here, although it also belongs in Table I, Opposites.

V. Assertion/Counter-assertion. The data included here are similar to that in Table IV, Assertion/Denial, except that the cases of denial here were always accompanied by counter-assertions that were sometimes rather elaborate.

VI. Associated Words and Phrases. This table includes data which are types of association other than the kinds of opposition shown in the other five tables.

Key to Tables

Data are roughly organised to give the reader some idea of the range of associations that occurred in Suzy and Nani's conversation. Data within each table are grouped to suggest various subcategories. In many cases, several cross-category classifications are possible. The order in which the data are presented suggests some of these.

Example number: if the word or phrase has been discussed elsewhere, the number it was given there is presented in the left column (e.g. no. 21).

Routine: if the word or phrase occurred as part of a routine, the abbreviation for that routine is given after the example number (if any) on the left side of the table. Abbreviations for routines are as follows:

HG Hiding Game
AG Antonym Game
CA Correction Activity
YS You Say
SR Short Routine

Date: the date that the word or phrase was recorded. If the contrasting words or phrases appeared more than once on one day (separated by other verbal interchange), the number of times is indicated; for example, 30 Oct. (2x) means twice on 30 October.

Words and Phrases: all occurrences of the same set of words or phrases are listed together in chronological order. The numbers 1, 2 and 3 across the top indicate which word or phrase was spoken first, which second, and which third on the date given. If more than three utterances were involved (excluding repetition), the additional utterances are numbered and placed in the right-hand column under reference (e.g. (4)

'doo-doo'). These tables do not indicate how many utterances were involved in each opposition or association. The phrases were in fact spoken once or twice on some occasions and repeated many times on other occasions. Italics indicate stress.

Reference: if the word or phrase occurred with reference to other elements in the discourse, this reference is shown. When the reference is the exact quotation from the data, quotation marks are used. Quotation marks are omitted when a paraphrase is given. Additional information, such as cross-references to other tables, is provided in parentheses.

Abbreviations

N   Nani
S   Suzy
E   Eero (His participation is noted in the reference column.)
D   Driver

Table I: Opposites

Example and/or Routine	Date	Word or Phrase 1	2	3	Reference
No. 21, HG	30 Aug.		not hot	hot	(N only)
HG	6 Sept.		not hot	hot	(S only)
HG	7 Sept.		not hot	hot	
No. 29, HG	11 Sept.		not hot	hot	
HG	13 Sept.		not hot	hot	
HG	14 Sept. (2x)		not hot	hot	
HG	8 Oct.		not hot	hot	
No. 22, AG	28 Aug.	going up	gown down		
No. 29, HG	29 Aug.	and up	and down		
HG	2 Nov.	up	down		'here'
HG	11 Sept. (2x)	in	outa		'house'
No. 29, HG	12 Sept.	get outa	go in	over to	'downstairs the house'
HG	11 Sept.	get out here	stay here		'the house'
HG	12 Sept.	come in here	get outa		
HG	12 Sept.	there	there	here	
HG	19 June	down here	over there		
HG	28 June	right *here*	over there	over *here*	(slippers; sit)
HG	17 Sept.	back	over and over		'slippers'
HG	28 June	on	off		

Table I. (Continued) Opposites

Example and/or Routine	Date	Word or Phrase			Reference
		1	2	3	
No. 29, HG	14 June	this	the other		'store'
HG	11 Sept.	this	that		'side'
HG	12 Sept. (3x)	this	that		'house'
	13 Sept.	this	that way		'way'
	17 Sept.	this	that		'side'
	28 Aug.	this	that		'one'
	2 Nov.	like this	not like that		(how to do something)
	30 May	this	that		
	7 Sept.	sleep	wake up		(S and N; E not present)
	18 Sept.	sleep	wake up		'baby'; 'not dark' (N only)
	12 Oct.	waking up	sleeping		(N, S and E)
	25 Oct.	waking up	sleeping		(N, S and E)
	11 Sept. (2x)	closed	not closed		'window' 'The other window is open'
	17 Sept. (2x)	closed	not closed		'window'
	8 Oct.	closed	not closed		'window'
	29 Oct.	closed	not closed		'window'

Table I. (Continued) Opposites

Example and/or Routine	Date	1	2	3	Reference
	6 June	dead	not dead		'doctor'
	31 May p.m.	heavy for you	not for me		
	29 May	funny	not funny		
	10 June	lot	one		'candy' (19 June 'plenty')
	21 May	little bit	a lot		'hair'
	14 June	all	one		
	13 May	*big*	*big*	*small*	'shawl' 'small' for 'baby'
	31 May p.m.	big	little		'jingle bell'
	31 May p.m.	noisy	not noisy		
No. 20, CA	8/30	grandma/mommy	grandpa/father		

Table II: Comparatives

Example and/or Routine Date	Word or Phrase 1	2	3	Reference
31 May	little bit rain	raining harder		'poncho' (cf. Table I, 'small/big')
19 June	kiss	enough kisses		(paper elephant)
22 May	bigger now	bigger now		'call Mommy'
19 June	fat	big, big fat	fatter	
19 June	louder			(loudly)

Table III: Possession

Date	Example and/or Routine			Reference
	1	Word or Phrase 2	3	
14 Sept.	my friend	not your/my friend		(N only)
17 Sept.	my friend	not my friend		
11 Oct.	my friend	talking now		
16 Oct.	my friend	not my friend		
19 Oct.	my friend	not my friend		
24 Oct.	my friend	not my friend		
25 Oct.	my friend	not my friend		
29 Oct.	my friend	not my friend		
30 Oct. (2x)	my friend	not my friend		
2 Nov.	my friend	not my friend		
15 May	my friend	not my friend		'not talk to you' (come to house)
30 May	my friend	not my friend		
31 May a.m.	my friend	not your friend		'if you hit' (house)
31 May p.m.	my friend	not your friend		
3 June	my friend	not your friend		'if you give me'; 'house'
13 June	my friend	not your friend		(4) 'Toddy's'
14 June	are you my friend	no	mommy's?	'your place'
17 June	not you friend	tomorrow who?	Toddy can't go	(S to D:) 'N is my
19 June	somebody's your	Gwynnie's	Toddy's	friend. You wait for her.'
7 June	friend hold hands	friend, come my house		

Table III. (Continued) Possession

Eample and/or Routine	Date	Word or Phrase			Reference
		1	2	3	
	7 June	friend now?	tomorrow	angry?	
	21 June	friend now, today	yeah, kay?		
HG	13 May	*my* side	your side		
	20 May	my own song			
	4 Oct.	It's not yours.	It's mine	no	(4) *'Yes, it's mine.'*
No. 28, YS	21 June	your	my	my *own own*	'name'
No. 27, YS	17 June	I make hula lesson with you	you gonna go your *own*	hula lessons	
	3 June	my *own* zoo	your zoo		
	3 June	my own zoo	my own zoo too		
	10 June	my house	my own house		
	10 June	my house	*my* house		
	4 Oct.	no, that's my book	no	yes, that's my book	'I eat it all up.'
	4 Oct.	it's not yours	no	it's mine	
	28 Aug.	my *dolly*	*your* dolly		

Table III. (Continued) Possession

Example and/or Routine	Date	Word or Phrase			
		1	2	3	Reference
	12 Sept.	*your* dolly	no my *dolly*	Nani's dolly	
	14 May	your car	no, it's Mommy's car and *my* car		

Table IV: Assertion/Denial

Example and/or Routine	Date	Word or Phrase			Reference
		1	2	3	
No. 23, YS	30 Aug.	no	yes		
No. 24, YS	15 May	no	yes		
No. 26, YS	20 May	no	yes		
	10 June	no	yes		
	4 Oct.	talk	don't talk		'friend'
	2 Nov.	talk	don't talk		
	24 June	don't talk to me	don't talk to my mommy	don't talk sassy to me	
	31 May a.m.	hear	don't hear		'noisy'
	14 Sept.	you don' *have*, I *have*	I get[a] some 'candy'		
	29 Aug.	got	don't have		'crackers at home'
	18 May	you can't see	yes, I can		'a rainbow'
	19 May	I don't like	I like		'air' (window open)

a. *Get* as it was used here meant 'have' which is a common HCE meaning. *Got* which occurred on 29 Aug. meant 'have' in the conventional GAE sense.

Table IV. (Continued) Assertion/Denial

Example and/or Routine	Date	Word of Phrase			Reference
		1	2	3	
No. 17, CA	21 May	1 saw	but I didn'	I *did*	'Miz Sizon' (a teacher)
	20 June	you *did*			'spit'; 'bubbles'
	19 June	hurts	sore	no hurt	
	7 Sept.	borrow	take	no, I didn't	'picture' (cf. Table V)
	20 May	I saw	I didn't		'play outside'
	31 May p.m.	I too	I didn't sawed you		(relative: aunties, etc.)
	17 June	saw	didn't see		
	6 June	open	didn't open		
No. 9, CA	21 May	then don't	I no going		
	14 June	you gotta give me that kind	cannot have it all		'hit people'
	10 May	you can't see	yes, I could		
	3 June	I didn't paint	I did		

Table IV. (Continued) Assertion/Denial

Example and/or Routine	Date	1	Word or Phrase 2	3	Reference
	4 Oct.	don't throw	I don't wanna don't throw		
	13 June	give me that	no		
	30 Aug.	don't touch	no		
	7 Sept.	you took my picture	no, I didn't		
	17 Sept.	I go the beach too	no		
	13 May	say *cheese*	I won't		(cf. Table VI, 'cheese/ pizza', 'happy/funny face')
	7 Sept.	you be quiet	I don' wan' I said already not		
	21 June	wet	wet	not	'grass'; 'You have to see if it's wet.'

Table V: Assertion/Counter-assertion

Example and/or Routine	Date	Word or Phrase 1	2	3	Reference
	15 May	who is your friend?			(cf. Table III for more on 'friend')
	17 June	don't talk to me	not gonna tell who's your friend then?	I'm not gonna let you talk to me	
	10 June	not goin' to be your friend	OK then I'm goin' be Wendy's friend		
	7 Sept.	okolele	I'm not		(derogatory children's chant; from *okole*, 'rear end' in Hawaiian; see Table VI, footnote)
No. 5, SR	13 May	donkey-donkey	I'm not	mushi-mushi	
	20 June	squeezing	squashing		
	12 Sept.	scold	spank		
	28 June	run	I'm gonna *walk*		
	8 May	sing	not talk		

Table V. (Continued) Assertion/Counter-assertion

Example and/or Routine	Date	Word or Phrase			Reference
		1	2	3	
	4 Oct.	you shush	that's a bad word	shut up	(4) doo-doo
	20 June	marigold	berry gold	*small* berry doo-doo	(4) strawberry doo-doo
	12 Sept.	pink	red		(colour of slippers)
	25 Sept.	red	blue		
	15 May	(colours of barettes)			('white', 'yellow', 'red', 'blue': S,N,D)
No. 6, SR	10 May 13 May 19 June	(red, green; stop, go)			(traffic light)
	6 June	grape purple			(colours of lollipops)
	28 June	I have sweater at school	I have slippers on		
	14 June	triangle	square		(role play: shopkeeper)

Table V. (Continued) Assertion/Counter-assertion

Example and/or Routine	Date	1	Word or Phrase 2	3	Reference (cf. Table IV)
	31 May p.m.	It's mine	just want to borrow it		
	20 June	spit	bubbles		
	31 May p.m.	popcorn	wasn't popcorn, just water		
No. 16, CA	18 June	gas	water		(liquid in container)

Table VI: Associated Words and Phrases

Example and/or Routine	Date	Word or Phrase			Reference
		1	2	3	
No. 35, HG	18 Sept.	monster	ogre		(growls, roars)
No. 35, HG	18 Sept.	monster	lion	tiger	
No. 34, HG	13 June	monster	buggie		(cockroach on car floor)
	4 Sept.	horse	pony	horse-pony	
	13 May	say *cheese*	I won't (?) pizza too		(photograph)
	13 May	don't make funny face	make *happy*	say cheese too	(N tried to make S smile)
	30 Oct.	skida bite	where you fall down		(wound on S's knee)
No. 15	30 Oct.	heads	hands		
	25 Oct.	I got grandma	And I have *shoes*	yeah, you and me have shoes yeah?	
	14 May	*poncho*	*coat*	*sweater*	

Table VI. (Continued) Associated Words and Phrases

Example and/or Routine	Date	1	Word or Phrase 2	3	Reference
No. 11, CA	22 May	poncho	shawl		'I want it to be a shawl'
	4 Sept.	you sit back	I sit inna back too		
	29 Oct.	inna back	(D: behind us)	by my *house*	'the sun
	23 May	right here	far away	next to you	(4) 'far away from over here' (5) 'next to you' (6) 'far away from Waikiki' 'my house'
	3 June	too far away	little bit far away	not far away	(distance between S's home and school)
No. 17	21 May	last night	last time, this morning	long time ago	
	3 June	tomorrow	now	already	'paint(ed)'
	3 June	tomorrow	next week	lotta times	

Table VI. (Continued) Associated Words and Phrases

Example and/or Routine	Date	Word or Phrase 1	2	3	Reference
	3 June	tomorrow	this time		
	7 Sept.	Sh-h-h	not sleeping		
	18 Sept.	'time to wake up'	not dark	not nighttime	(N only)
	28 Sept.	*night*time	time to get up	time to sleep	(4) 'time to wake up' (5) 'waking time' (6) 'pillow'
	18 Sept.	baby	candy		
	1 Nov.	baby	bottle	drink, milk	
	5 Oct.	baby	sister		(role play)
	27 Sept.	baby	sister		(song)
	29 Aug.	*crackers*	*grapes*		
	15 Oct.	lemons	bananas	melon	

Table VI. (Continued) Associated Words and Phrases

Example and/or Routine	Date	Word or Phrase 1	2	3	Reference
	15 Oct.	cookie	cracker		
	16 Oct.	cookie	cracker		
	1 Nov.	chair	bed	home	'tired' (need a place to) 'lay down'
	25 Sept.	open window	cold out	open the door	
	17 Sept.	swim	kick	pass	
	10 May	rainbow	cloud		
No. 33, HG	14 Sept.	fish	water	boat	(4) 'houseboat'
	18 June	water	makes filled up		'the car'
	24 May	I'm *sweaty*	(D:) how come?	because I got wet neck	
No. 6, SR	13 May	cross(red)	green says go	red says stop	(traffic light)
No. 14, CA	4 Oct.	hear, read, see	read		'my book'

Table VI. (Continued) Associated Words and Phrases

Example and/or Routine	Date	Word or Phrase			Reference (N and E)
		1	2	3	
	26 Oct.	that's pau[a] all pau	that's all	that's all	(made out of paper napkin)
	21 June	puka[a]	ring	washcloth	
	18 Sept.	tummy	okolele,[a] no okole		

a. These three words are from Hawaiian. Even though the native Hawaiian-speaking population is very small now and none of the children had any direct contact with it, they all seem to be aware of the existence of words having the same meaning in Hawaiian and English.

'That's pau' is equivalent to 'That's all' (i.e. finished, used up, over). One child seemed to be acting as translator.

A *puka* is a hole. A paper napkin (which is what they were playing with) folded in the shape of a doughnut could be described in terms of the hole in the middle or the ring around the hole. It could also be opened up and called a 'washcloth'.

Okolele (cf. Table V) is a word from a popular (derogatory) children's chant. It is based on *okole*, which means 'rear end'. *Tummy* was apparently associated with *okole*, but the child said *okolele* by mistake and corrected herself.

APPENDIX B: ANALYSES OF COMPLETE SESSIONS

Up to this point, I have used excerpts from various sessions to illustrate aspects of the data. One aspect of the data which could not be illustrated by the use of excerpts is the way in which Suzy and Nani embedded routines in the flow of ongoing conversation. Appendix B will examine this aspect of the girls' verbal interaction. In the two complete sessions which I have chosen to analyse here, Suzy and Nani co-operated closely. Not all sessions involved as much co-operation as the two I will discuss, but most sessions included similar elements. I chose these two sessions (12 June and 3 June) because they seemed to be among the richest in the units I described above (Chapter 3-7). I will discuss the 12 June session first, because it contained more of the units the reader is already familiar with.

In my study of the data, the analysis of a complete session necessarily followed the identification and analysis of smaller units: short routines, correction activities and full routines. I will refer back to earlier discussions in which these were examined. The discussion of each session is divided into five sections.

1. Outline. Each full session analysis will begin with a brief outline of the session. This outline is based on divisions I have made in the data. These divisions are based primarily, but not exclusively, on changes in conversational topic. Where topics change completely and relatively abruptly I have indicated a sequence boundary (a horizontal line across the transcription) and assigned a roman numeral to each sequence. Where topics flow into one another and there is a minimum of overlap, I have indicated a sub-sequence boundary (not shown in the transcription) and assigned an upper-case letter (shown on the outline) under the appropriate roman numeral. The boundaries between sequences and between sub-sequences were sometimes not sharp because a topic could be referred to even after it was no longer the main focus of the conversation. Sequence and routine boundaries may or may not have coincided. Topics sometimes occurred which suggested to the girls a related routine. The reverse also happened; a routine could suggest a related topic. In such cases, I showed the routine as a sub-sequence and the related material which preceded or followed it as a separate sub-sequence.

2. General analysis of the session. This will summarise the tone of the session — whether the girls felt friendly, competitive, argumentative, etc. — and some of the main verbal events that took place.

3. Complete transcription. The only analysis that will accompany this transcription will be lines indicating sequence boundaries.

4. Utterance analysis. Different sections will be treated differently depending on whether the data have been discussed elsewhere. Detailed analyses will not be repeated.

5. Summary.

(a) Analysis of Session of 12 June a.m.

1. Outline

Utterance Numbers	Sequence	Sub-sequence	Conversation Topic
1—6	I		'painting', 'my side'[a]
7—64	II		S and N agree to disagree
7—11		A	'long-dress'[b]
12—38		B	'down to the floor'
39—42		C	'go down'
43—64		D	'will/won't'
65—73	III		opening windows

a. See Example 38.
b. See Example 13.

2. General Analysis

The tone of the 12 June session was very friendly and co-operative. This did not, however, inhibit the ongoing competition between Suzy and Nani. They were still very interested in maintaining influence over each other without either violating the closeness of their relationship or giving up too much personal independence. The second of the three sequences of this session was by far the longest (53 of the 73 utterances that make up the session) and was made up of the children's successful efforts to maintain conflicting points of view.

I divided the sessions into three sequences. The first (1-6) was an attempt to start the Hiding Game and has been discussed elsewhere (Example 38). The second sequence (7-64) concerned the long dresses or muumuus the girls were wearing and will be discussed in detail below. The last (65-73) was short and concerned opening the car windows and arriving at school.

The second sequence is of special interest because it was a dispute throughout which the girls maintained different positions. This also happened in shorter sequences ('last time', Example 17; 'red light/green light', Example 6). In these shorter conversations, the girls came to an agreement in the content of what they were saying, but the *tone* remained that of a dispute. In the 12 June session, they did not wish to agree with each other. They managed to continue to disagree by changing the meaning of what they were saying without changing the key phrase: 'down to the floor'.

The focus of the discussion was the fact that a long dress covers one's legs and the hem of the dress ends up near the floor. The meaning of the key phrase, 'down to the floor', changed as the conversation progressed; each child maintained her own point of view even though the meaning of the phrase changed, with the girls consistently disagreeing on whatever meaning(s) was/were in operation at any given moment. Whenever agreement seemed imminent, one of the girls changed the meaning of the phrase (see discussion of Utterances 39-44 below). Sequence II includes the entire 'down to the floor' discussion. It falls into four sub-sequences:

A	(7-11)	Topic, 'long dress', is introduced.
B	(12-38)	'Long dress down to the floor/way, way down'.
C	(39-43)	'Won't go down; mommy zipped it'
D	(44-64)	'will/won't'

The following examination will illustrate (1) the children's grasp and manipulation of meaning according to the context that affected the interpretation of the key phrase and (2) how they maintained different points of view.

3. Complete Transcription

Suzy's mother, Pam, is outside the car helping Suzy get in. Pam and D briefly discuss topics which do not occur again. N gives S something which S gives to her mother. The car door slams and the car starts. Both S and N are wearing long muumuus.

1. N: You hide in there while I'm *pain*ting. OK? You hide in there while I'm *pain*ting.
2. S: Hide in there?

3. N: No, hide in your own place, in there because I'm painting this side. Go in *that* side and *hide*. Inside in, in there. No, you gottu go in here. Yes, you gottu. You hide in there because I goin' when I get through painting, you, then I hide.

(short pause)

4. S: How 'bout I stay like this?

5. N: Hm?

6. S: How 'bout I stay like this?

(short pause)

7. N: Yeah, here, OK, now. You be the *dad*dy and I be the *mom*my.

8. S: But I have a muumuu on *too*.

9. N: Kay. OK then [bli bli], both be the *mom*my.
        OK. Here Suzy. OK come here, and *paint* here.

(short pause)

10. N: My turn now. *My* turn. Kay. It's *my* turn. Enough *paint*. Wa. Now you *hide* in there. This is my, *hap*py dress. I gotta happy dress like *you*. I gotta happy dress like you.

11. S: I don' have a happy dress. I don' have a happy dress. (?) in my dress.

12. N: Oh, eh (laugh) you're wearing a long dress down to the *floor*.

13. S: No. Look. (stands up and falls down as car turns)

14. D: Sit on the seat, kids.

15. N: Wow (as Suzy falls on the floor) See.

16. D: That's why.

17. N: See what *hap*pens to *you*.

18. S: See. Look. It can't go 'way 'way *down*.
        Cannot go 'way 'way *down*.

19. N: (?)

20. S: If I stand up, if I stand up it won't go 'way 'way *down*.

21. N: If *I* don', if *I* stand up, if *I* stand up I will blow *away*.

22. S: Huh?

23. N: If *I* stand up I will blow a*way*.

24. S: What?

25. N: If I stand up I will blow away.

26. S: Blow away?

27. N: Yes.

28. S: Blow, away outside?

29. N: Yeah.

30. S: Outside?

31. N: Yeah-eah.

32. S: Outside?

33. N: Yeah.
34. S: Outside?
35. N: Yeah, yeah.
36. S: And I will stand up my dress won't go down.
37. N: Hm? Hm?
38. S: If I stand up my dress won't go down.
39. N: If I stand up my dress won't go down. No. No. No. Unh-Unh.
        No. No, see it doesn't.
40. S: I see it goes *down*.
41. N: *See*, it's *not*.
42. S: I *see* it going *down*.
43. N: No, because see, because no, my mommy *zip*ped it.
44. S: Look. Try look. Try put your legs like this. See look. It goes
        down.
45. N: So? So look. My dress doesn't go down.
46. S: Nani's mommy.
47. D: Unh-huh?
48. S: Is Nani's muumuu go down?
49. D: I don't know. I can't see.
50. S: Try see.
51. D: I *can't*. I'm *dri*ving.
52. N: No, no, she's *dri*ving. Cannot *talk* to her *now*.
53. S: My muumuu goes, if *I* stand up, my muumuu will go down.
54. N: If *I* stand up, my muumuu won't go down.
55. S: Huh?
56. N: If *I* stand up *my* muumuu won't go down.
57. S: Your muumuu won't go down?
58. N: No, your will go down.
59. S: It *will* go down?
60. N: No, yours go down.
61. S: My *will*.
62. N: *My won*'t.
63. S: Mine *will*.
64. N: Mine *won*'t. (pause, then faster and faster)
        Mine will, mine won't, will, will mine will my won't, my won't.
    (short pause)
65. S: You can open your window and I'll open my window.
66. N: No-o-o, my mom,
67. S: Like this. Like this.
68. N: No-o-o
69. S: Pretend to.

70. N: I don' wannu. No, you roll up your window and they in the car, because my window is open here. And you open your window.
71. S: Look. (?)
(pause)
72. S: Here and here and here. We're at school.
73. N: I going first.

4. Utterance Analysis

Sequence I.

1. N: You hide in there while I'm *pain*ting. OK?
You hide in there while I'm *pain*ting.
2. S: Hide in there?
3. N: No, hide in your own place, in there because I'm painting this side. Go in *that* side and *hide*. Inside in, in there. No, you gottu go in here. Yes, you gottu. You hide in there because I goin' when I get through painting, you then I hide.
(short pause)
4. S: How 'bout I stay like this?
5. N: Hm?
6. S: How 'bout I stay like this?
(short pause)

This sequence has been discussed in detail elsewhere as an extension of the Hiding Game (pp. 162-3). The session starts off in a friendly mood. Nani has given Suzy a present and, in 1 and 3, uses the familiar Hiding Game code-word, 'hide'. Suzy accepts the jargon (She doesn't say, 'I won't get down on the floor.'), but maintains her independence by making a counter-suggestion (4, 6). Nani's self-correction of *you* to *I* (3) is similar to correction of pronouns elsewhere (Example 12). Nani's 'Hm?' functions as a request for a re-run. Perhaps she was surprised by Suzy's counter-suggestion.

Sequence II, Sub-sequence A.

7. N: Yeah, here, OK now. You be the *dad*dy and I be the *mom*my.
8. S: But I have a muumuu on *too*.

Nani introduces role play. This is her second attempt to get Suzy to do what she wants.
Again, Suzy refuses Nani's suggestion without saying that she will not co-operate. To do this, she raises a technical point: daddies do not wear muumuus. This is the first mention of what both girls

9. N: Kay. OK then [bli bli],
        both be the *momm*y. OK.
        Here Suzy. OK come here,
        and *paint* here.

are wearing: long dresses.
Nani concedes the technical
objection and alters her proposal
but does not give up the idea of
their pretending to be parents.
Nani is prepared to compromise
on two points: they will both be
the mommy and will both paint.
[bli bli] could be a conflation of
'we'll both be.'

10. N: My turn now. *My* turn. Kay.
        It's *my* turn. Enough *paint*.
        Wa. Now you gotta *hide* in
        there. This is my, *hap*py
        dress. I gotta happy dress
        like *you*. I gotta happy dress
        like you.

Nani ends the discussion of painting and mentions 'hide' for the
last time in this session.
'Happy dress' was discussed as an
example of the idiosyncratic use
of words (Example 18). Suzy is
not wearing her 'happy dress',
but she has worn it previously.
Suzy apparently does not understand Nani's use of 'happy dress'.

11. S: I don' have a happy dress.
        I don' have a happy dress.
        (?) in my dress.

Sub-sequence B.

12. N: Oh, eh (laugh) you're wearing
        a long dress down to the
        floor.

13. S: No. Look. (stand up and falls
        down as car turns)

Nani says that a long dress goes
down to the floor.
Suzy objects. Then she stands up
to show how her dress will behave
She does this to support her
claim that her dress does not go
'down to the floor'.

14. D: Sit down on the seat, kids.
15. N: Wow (as Suzy falls to the
        floor) See.
16. D: That's why.
17. N: See what *hap*pens to *you*.

14-17 are concerned with Suzy's
fall. This is related to the main
topic ('long dress down to the
floor') because (1) Suzy wanted
to stand up to show that her
dress does not reach the floor,
and (2) Suzy's spill may have
suggested 'blow(ing) away' to
Nani (21-35).

18. S: See. Look. It can't go 'way
        'way *down*. Cannot go 'way

Suzy finishes making the point
she started at 13 (before she fell).

'way *down*.

To her, 'down to the floor' means ' 'way 'way down', that is, touching the floor.

19. N: (?)   ^a

Nani is confused. She initiates a repair sequence (comprised of 19 and 20). (For more on the use of 'Huh?' and (?) as requests for repetition, see sections 4.4.2 and 7.3.2.)

20. S: If I stand up, if I stand up it won' go 'way 'way *down*.

Suzy repeats her claim, thus completing the repair sequence and amplifying her point.

21. N: If *I* don', if *I* stand up, if *I* stand up, I will blow a*way*.

Nani introduces a new idea, possibly suggested by Suzy's fall (13-17). The girls discuss the idea of blowing away through 35.

22. S: Huh?

Suzy initiates a repair sequence by asking for clarification of 21.

23. N: If *I* stand up I will blow a*way*.

Nani repeats, completing repair sequence.

24. S: What?

Suzy asks for further clarification; Nani's repetition did not satisfy her.

25. N: If I stand up I will blow away.

Nani repeats again but does not stress 'I' and 'away' this time.

26. S: Blow away?

Suzy seeks clarification again.

27. N: Yes.

Nani's answer is minimal. 22-35 are

28. S: Blow, away outside?

repair sequences. Suzy either does

29. N: Yeah.

not understand what Nani is

30. S: Outside?

saying or is questioning whether

31. N: Yea-eah.

'blow away outside' is reasonable.

32. S: Outside?
33. N: Yeah.

34. S: Outside?
35. N: Yeah, yeah.

Nani may be getting impatient with having to repeat.

36. S: And I will stand up my dress won't go down

Suzy stops asking Nani to repeat and/or clarify. She returns to the same point she made in 20 before Nani talked about blowing away.

a. Brackets indicate repair sequences

37. N: Hm? Hm?

Nani initiates a repair sequence. The abrupt return to an earlier idea surprises her.

38. S: If I stand up my dress won't go down.

Suzy completes the repair sequence.

Sub-sequence C.

39. N: If I stand up my dress won't go down. No. No. No. Unh-unh. No. No, see it doesn't.

Nani reverses the position she took at 12. (This reversal indicates the start of Sub-sequence C.) Nani now says what Suzy said in 20, 36 and 38.

40. S: I see it goes *down*.

Suzy now supports what Nani said in 12. At this point they have exchanged points of view and still disagree. The polarity of the dialogue is maintained. It is not clear at this point whether 'go down' still means 'toward the floor' for Nani and 'touching the floor' for Suzy, but these meanings do not seem to apply here.

41. N: *See* it's *not*.

Nani repeats her new (39) position.

42. S: I *see* it's going *down*.

Suzy repeats her new (40) position.

43. N: No because see, because no, my mommy *zip*ped it.

Nani reveals the new meaning she has given the 'down to the floor' phrase. It now means 'fall down' (or 'fall off'). The dress will not fall off because it is zipped up.

44. S: Look. Try look. Try put your legs like this. See look. It goes *down*.

Suzy has adopted Nani's original meaning (12): 'down to the floor' means 'towards the floor'. The use of *try* here is a commonly used HE expression which is a polite form, an 'auxiliary of the imperative' (Reinecke and Tokimasa 1934, p. 123). Thus, the *to* is not missing here, and this is a perfectly acceptable adult sentence. Suzy uses 'try' the same way in (50).

Sub-sequence D.

45. N:	So? So look. My dress doesn't go down.	Nani repeats the position she took in 39. Sub-sequence D involved a new approach: Suzy's appeal to the adult (46). 45 could also be considered the last utterance of Sub-sequence C.
46. S:	(calls to D) Nani's mommy.	Suzy begins appeal for adult help.
47. D:	Unh-huh?	
48. S:	Is Nani's muumuu go down?	Suzy wants the adult to intercede.
49. D:	I don't know. I can't see.	Adult refuses to get involved.
50. S:	Try see.	Suzy appeals again.
51. D:	I *can't*. I'm *dri*ving.	Adult refuses again.
52. N:	No, no, she's *dri*ving. Cannot *talk* to her *now*.	Nani reinforces adult's refusal which suits Nani because Nani seems to be enjoying Suzy's confusion.
53. S:	My muumuu goes, if *I* stand up, my muumuu will go *down*.	Suzy repeats her position: her muumuu goes down toward the floor, covering her legs.
54. N:	If *I* stand up, my muumuu won't go down.	Nani repeats her position: her muumuu won't fall off.
55. S:	Huh?	Suzy initiates a repair sequence.
56. N:	If *I* stand up, *my* muumuu won't go down.	Nani repeats 54 and completes repair sequence.
57. S:	Your muumuu won't go down?	Suzy initiates another repair sequence.
58. N;	No, your will go down.	Nani says their dresses will behave differently. She agrees that she and Suzy disagree.
59. S:	It *will* go down?	Suzy initiates yet another repair sequence.
60. N:	No, your will go down.	Nani completes repair sequence by answering Suzy's question.
61. S:	My *will*.	61-64 is an Antonym Game. Up to 61, both girls had used normal intonation and pitch. In 61, Suzy stresses 'will' by making the vowel long. In 62 and 63, the vowels are even longer. Finally (64), Nani chants the contrasting phrases,
62. N:	*My won't*.	
63. S:	Mine *will*.	
64. N:	Mine *won't* (pause, then faster and faster and faster) Mine will, mine won't, will, will mine will my won't,	

my won't.

speaking faster and faster. The 'will/won't' Antonym Game marks the end of Sub-sequence D and of Sequence II in the session.

(short pause)

Sequence III.

65. S:	You can open your window and I'll open my window.	Suzy initiates new activity, opening windows.
66. N:	No-o-o, my mom,	Nani starts to resist the idea.
67. S:	Like this, like this.	Suzy does not acknowledge Nani's resistance.
68. N:	No-o-o.	Nani continues to resist.
69. S:	Pretend to.	The 'pretend' ploy has been noted by Garvey (1975; referred to by Ervin-Tripp, 1974, pp. 191-2). Suzy hopes Nani will co-operate if the proposed activity involves imaginary windows instead of real ones.
70. N:	I don' wannu. No, you roll up your window and they in the car, because my window is open here. And you open your window.	Nani does not accept the idea of pretending to open windows. She says her window is already open and Suzy should open the one on her own side.
71. S:	Look (?)	
(pause)		
72. S:	Here and here and here. We're at school.	72-3 concern the arrival at the school. Being the first one out was always important to the girls. Nani seems to have the last word.
73. N:	I going first.	

5. Summary

Suzy and Nani were friendly but competitive during the 12 June session. Nani tried to start the Hiding Game, but Suzy was not interested. The longest sequence in the session involved a discussion of the meaning of 'down to the floor'. Two days after 12 June Suzy and Nani both used this phrase to mean a dress which went down towards the floor (but did not touch the floor). On 12 June, however, the discussion of long dresses included a series of alternate meanings of 'down to the floor'. 'Down to the floor' had at least three meanings on 12 June: (1) covering the legs, going towards the floor (Utterance 12, 40); (2) touching the floor (13, 18); and (3) falling down or off (39, 40).

When Suzy and Nani included three alternate meanings of 'down to the floor' in their discussion, they seemed to treat the meanings as they did alternative lexical, syntactic or phonetic forms in their correction activities. The girls' use of the three meanings followed the format of correction activities. This format included a presentation of alternatives (words, phonetic shapes; syntactic configurations). In correction activities (as in Antonym Games and other routines), Suzy and Nani exchanged positions or traded responses (e.g. antonyms). They did not seem to care who was right about the phonetic shape of a word (e.g. 'please', Example 7), whether 'hot' was more correct or better than 'not hot' (Example 21), or which of the three possible meanings was the best one for 'down to the floor'. Therefore, it did not matter to them who used which phonetic shape, antonym or meaning. What did matter to them was that they continued to disagree. That is, each seemed to feel compelled *not* to say what the other said. One of the revealing features of their agreement to disagree was that their conversation did not dissolve into nonsense. They always knew what the focus of their disagreement was. Sometimes they eventually chose one of the alternatives; sometimes they did not. In the case of the 'down to the floor' dress that was discussed on 12 June, they both agreed that a 'down to the floor' dress was a 'long dress'. They reached this agreement two days later on 14 June.

Example 13

14 June (both girls are wearing muumuus)

1. N: Is it a long dress?
2. S: Yes.
3. N: I'm wearing a long dress.
4. S: I too.
5. N: Is that one is a down-to-the-floor dress?
6. S: Uh-huh.
7. N: Is it a down-floor dress?
8. S: Uh-huh, mines down.

On 14 June, the semantic content of *long* or *down to the floor* was overtly agreed upon. It is possible that the girls had discussed the topic between the 12 June morning sessions and the 14 June morning session (although they did not in the 13 June morning session). Even if the topic came up between the two sessions during which it was recorded, the content of the 12 June discussion almost certainly affected the use of the phrase on 14 June. The connection between the 12 June and 14 June sessions is likely because the girls agreed so quickly on 14 June and also because there was a tendency for topics which came up more than once to occur on consecutive or nearly consecutive days. (The first three You Say routines occurred within six days of each other, for example.) The dates that appear on the tables of contrasting words and phrases (Appendix A) also illustrate this tendency. On 14 June, Suzy and Nani seemed to have lost interest in disagreeing, although they were still interested in long dresses. It is also possible that they no longer wanted to disagree about the meaning of 'down to the floor' because that phrase had developed a special value for them since they had shared the fun of disagreeing about what it meant. Now that they could agree that 'down to the floor' was synonymous with 'long', they could use the terms interchangeably in a way that no one else could. Since there are no other examples of 'down to the floor' in the data, this special phrase cannot be compared with the special jargon which the girls had invented for playing the Hiding Game. It seems likely, however, that 'down to the floor' was an expression of the girls' on-going relationship in a way that was similar to the Hiding Game jargon. The 'will/won't' Antonym Game at the end of the discussion of 'down to the floor' dresses may have been an indication of loss of interest in the topic. In any case, the Antonym Game seemed to serve as a de-escalating device or a device to change the conversational topic. The girls continued to try to tell each other what to do in the last sequence when Suzy wanted Nani to open her window and Nani refused, telling Suzy to open her own window.

(b) Analysis of Session of 3 June p.m.

1. Outline

Utterance Numbers	Sequence	Sub-sequence	Conversation Topic
1–14	I		'car smells/stink'
15–37	II		painting at pre-school
38–114	III		being friends
38–40		A	'horsie'

Outline continued

Utterance Numbers	Sub-sequence	Conversational Topic
41–4	B	'friend'/'house'
45–55	C	N not going to S's house
56–61	D	'hula lesson'
62–7	E	plans that exclude S
68–78	F	N rejects S's invitation to go to the zoo
79–83	G	N tries to be included in S's plans
84–93	H	N reverses position; won't include S
94–9	I	ladder, stairs
100–1	J	S tries to change topic
102–6	K	talk
107–14	L	more zoo plans; S includes N: N excludes S

2. General Analysis

The third of June was an afternoon session. Throughout most of the 3 June session Suzy and Nani competed. When Suzy attempted to re-confirm the closeness of her relationship with Nani, Nani failed continuously to acknowledge this closeness. Nani rejected Suzy's contention that the car smelled 'stink' (Sequence I). Nani also resented the fact that Suzy had painted at school, but she had not (Sequence II, 15-37). Her resentment may have contributed to her rejection of Suzy throughout the remainder of the session. The discussion of painting at school and the preceding comments on the strange odour in the car (1-14) are the only topics which are not directly connected to Suzy's unsuccessful attempts to gain Nani's acceptance. In spite of Nani's relentlessness (which is softened somewhat when Nani says she will join Suzy (Sub-sequence G, 79–83), neither child was upset or angry. This was a calm, relaxed conversation with a great deal of underlying opposition and contradiction.

3. Complete Transcription

1. S: Stink.
2. D: What?
3. S: This smells stink.
4. D: No? What smells stink?
5. N: This car smells stink?
6. D: No. Why should the car smell stink?
7. N: See, my mommy said it's not *stink*.

Complete Transcription continued

8. D: Well, what do you mean? Well, it smells like a car. Don't all cars smell, kind of, a little,

⎧ (?)

9. S: ⎨ Over here stink. Over here stink.

10. D: Oh, yeah? What kind of stink?

(pause)

11. S: Smells like, smell like it's, smell like it's, doo-doo.

12. D: Smells like doo-doo?

13. S: Uh-huh.

14. D: Oh, really, that's interesting. Hum.

15. N: Know *what*?

16. D: I dunno, what?

17. N: Know what. I just paint, but. But I *di*dn't *paint*.

18. D: You just paint but you *di*dn't paint, well did you paint or not?

19. N: No. Because. Miz Sizon, Sizon say (sing-song) 'You paint to*mor*row, kay?' OK. So. Miz Sizon said I paint to*mor*row.

20. D: OK.

21. N: Next week. Or tomorrow. But la' time, you gottu take me to school ag*ai*n. Mommy you

⎧ got

22. S: ⎨ Know what? Know what?

23. N: No, I'm talking to my *mom* ⎧ my.

24. S: ⎨ Know what Nani's mommy?

25. D: I dunno. What?

26. S: I painted *now*.

27. D: You painted. Today?

28. S: Yeah.

29. N: She painted holes and, and, the dark-dender holes.

30. S: I painted *holes*. I painted *holes*, Nani's mommy.

31. D: You painted holes.

32. S: Yeah.

33. D: I see.

34. N: But *I* didn't paint. I goin' paint *one*. Not everybody. But *every*body *pain*ted al*rea*dy.

35. S: And *I*. I paint *too*.

36. N: But *I* didn't. Every has, everybody has to.

37. S: Everybody has to (?)

38. N: Hor*sie*, horsie.

39. S: Where? No, horsie is over there. Like see?
40. N: No.
41. S: *Please*, I be your *friend*.
42. N: No, I don' wanna be your friend because
43. S: { I'm
       { I let you go my *house*.
44. N: I don' *wan*na go your house.
45. S: Why?
46. N: Be*cause*.
47. S: Because *why*?
48. N: Because I don' wannu.
49. S: Cause you have a (?)?
50. N: Because I got, I got, *tir*ed. (?)
51. S: Why?
52. N: Because, cause your home too far a*way*.
53. S: Huh?
54. N: Because your home too far away from the school.
55. S: My home is not far away. My house is, is, a *little* bit far away.
(short pause)
56. N: You're not going to my house, and you're not going come to my
       hula lesson cause { (?)
57. S: { (?) Tomorrow
       I'm gonna come Lani's house, yeah? Tomorrow, I
       { go Lani's house.
58. D: { I don't know. We'll see.
59. N: No, next week, and lotta times I, lotta times I going to go to hula
       lessons, yeah, Mom? Yeah, Mommy?
60. D: Yes, Nani.
61. S: Eh, Leilani don' go to hula lessons then, then I go her house.
62. N: No, you're *not*. Because. We. Tomorrow I gon have a pic*nic*.
       Tomorrow I gon have a *play*ground. And then, tomorrow, I gon
       go to the zoo and have a, *pro*gram. Yeah? Yeah, Mommy I gotta
       go to the (?) to the zoo to have program, yeah?
63. D: I don't think they started yet, honey, but I'll find out. I think
       they start in a
       { few weeks.
64. N: { My mommy goin' tell *me*, see my mommy telled me. *Wait*.
       Wait a minute, my mommy ha' to say something. It's not yet,
       on yet. What she said. See? (sing-song) 'She said that.' Is on. See
       she said the movie is on here. Is on the zoo. I going go to the *zoo*.
       Yeah? Mommy, I gonna go to the zoo. Yeah, Mom?

65. D: Sure, we'll go to the zoo.
66. N: *Yeah*. See my mommy said I could go to the *zoo*. I'm gonna go to the zoo. I am going. I *am*. I am going onna zoo. You're not going to the zoo. Not going go to the zoo, yeah? Mommy, Suzy's not going to the zoo, yeah?
67. D: *I* don't know.
68. S: I going s, to see a big, big tiger.
(pause)
69. N: No.
70. S: Yes, I am to*mor*row when I go with my *aun*tie and *un*cle.
71. N: *Not*.
72. S: And my mommy.
73. N: *No*.
74. S: And, and, and, my grandma and *e*verybody gonna come and, and you too, you could come too.
75. N: No, I gottu go my own zoo.
76. S: No, I gottu go my own zoo, *too*.
77. N: I not going far away with you.
78. S: I going far away with my *gran*dma and *gran*dpa, and, and *aun*tie and uncle.
79. N: Tomorrow I go your zoo.
80. S: And Maile and
81. N: Tomorrow I go your zoo, OK?
82. S: Huh?
83. N: Tomorrow, OK? Kay. I go your zoo to*mor*row.
(pause)
84. N: I cannot go your zoo too, this time, I got *lot* of *work* to do at home. When I get through doing my ⎰ *hu*la.
85. S: ⎱ (?) At home.
86. N: Yeah. No, I just going do, hula (sigh) on the stage, but not today. Yeah? Mommy, I'm not going on the stage, yeah?
87. D: Not today. Maybe next Sunday.
88. S: That's right. That's right. Next Sunday.
89. N: I goin' on the stage on Sunday. (?) on the stage?
90. S: Next weekend Lani have something?
91. N: Something new for the stage?
92. S: I don' have anything new for the stage.
93. N: You gottu *buy* some. My mommy buyed some for me to go on the stage.
94. S: Lani, maybe my m, mommy may m, my mommy will buy, a, us a ladder, a ladder and (?) Kay, maybe, kay?

95. N: I got a ladder
96. S: Let's (?), kay?
97. N: No, the *stairs* to climb up. Stairs.
98. S: (?)
99. N: Jus' little tiny stairs. Jus' (?), jus' stairs, this *much* stairs.
100. S: (?) play, I think. You have to *play* first.
101. N: But.
102. S: Let's stop *talk*ing. I'm *tire*d talking.
103. N: But, let's stop talking for a *little* while and then we stop talking.
104. S: Kay.
105. N: Know what you could be talk?
106. S: Uh-huh.
107. N: Know what I goin' go to the zoo, um, next week.
108. S: Yeah?
109. N: Yeah, is I goin' on the zoo next week, too? Next week.
110. S: My mommy and daddy, my mommy and daddy going to the zoo next week with *you* and I *too*. I goin' too with you.
111. N: But I'm going go my *own* zoo, that's my zoo, is why, is why.
112. S: I'm going to your zoo.
113. N: But your, your zoo is too far away.
⎡ You go your own zoo.
114. S: ⎣ Is *Sun*day, is Sunday today.
(arrive at Suzy's home)

4. Utterance Analysis

Sequence I.

1. S: Stink.

'Stink' is a popular HE expression used by adults and children. It can be an adjective: a person with a 'stink ear' is one who does not seem to hear well. As an adverb, 'stink' is never heard as 'stinky' except when non-creole speech is preferred. Nani used 'stinky' as an adverb in talking to her grandmother (a non-HE speaker) who visited (from the US mainland) two months after this conversation was recorded (field notes).

2. D: What? ⎤ D initiates a repair sequence.
3. S: This smells stink. ⎦ S completed repair sequence.

4. D: No? What smells stink?   D asks for further clarification.

5. N: This car smells stink?   N completes repair sequence for S
                                          at the same time questioning S's
                                          judgement.

6. D: No. Why should the car   D also rejects S's opinion. Asks for
    smell stink?   elaboration.

7. N: See, my mommy said it's   N continues to support D against S
    not *stink*.   (N and D have, of course, a vested
                                          interest — it is their car).

8. D: Well, what do you mean?   D softens her objection somewhat.
    Well, it smells like a car.   Asks for further elaboration.
    Don't all cars smell, kind
    of, a little, ⌈ (?)

9. S: ⌊ Over here   S provides further details (the exact
    stink.   location).
    Over here stink.

10. D: Oh. Yeah? What kind of   D asks for more details.
     stink?

(pause)

11. S: Smells like, smells like it's,   S specifies type of smell.
     smell like it's, doo-doo.

12. D: Smells like doo-doo?   D still questions S's opinion. Asks
                                           her to confirm.

13. S: Uh-huh.   S confirms.

14. D: Oh. Really, that's interes-   D accepts S's judgement.
     ting. Hum.

Sequence II.

15. N: Know *what*? ⌉   N requests the floor.
16. D: I dunno, what? ⌋   D acknowledges N's summons.

17. N: Know what. I just *paint*, ⌉   Nani uses stress to explain what she
     but. But I *did*n't *paint*. ⌋   cannot explain by means of syntax.
                                           She seems to mean, 'I almost pain-
                                           ted, but I didn't.'

18. D: You just paint but you ⌉   D requests clarification.
     *did*n't paint, well, did
     you paint or not?

19. N: No. Because. Miz Sizon, ⌋   N answers D's question. Uses direct
     Sizon say (sing-song) 'You   speech, mimicking the teacher, in-
     paint to*mor*row, kay?' OK. stead of indirect speech which is
     So. Miz Sizon said I paint   more complex syntactically.
     to*mor*row.

20.	D:	OK.	D concurs.
21.	N:	Next week. Or tomorrow. But la' time, you gottu take me to school a*gain*. Mommy you ⌠got	N is concerned about getting her turn; asks for reassurance that D will take her back to school so she can collect her turn at painting.
22.	S:	⌡Know what? Know what?	S requests the floor.
23.	N:	No, I'm talking to my *mom* ⌠my.	N resists S's efforts to gain the floor; uses possession of D to do this.
24.	S:	⌡Know what Nani's mommy?	Accepts N's possession of D but repeats request for the floor anyway.
25.	D:	I dunno. What?	Awards S the floor and her attention.
26.	S:	I painted *now*.	S uses present-time term, now, to express recent past.
27.	D:	You painted. Today?	D repeats what S said and asks for confirmation.
28.	S:	Yeah.	S confirms D's interpretation of S's 26.
29.	N:	She painted holes and, and, the dark-dender holes.	N expands S's statement of what she did (26).
30.	S:	I painted *holes*. I painted holes, Nani's mommy.	S confirms what N said in 29.
31.	D:	You painted holes.	D repeats what S says she did (requests confirmation).
32.	S:	Yeah.	S confirms.
33.	D:	I see.	Acknowledges S's 32.
34.	N:	But *I* didn't paint. I goin' paint *one*. But *e*verybody *pain*ted al*ready*.	N seems to be upset that she did not paint yet. She uses 'already' to indicate past time. Her use of 'everybody' seems contradictory. She uses stress instead of saying 'almost everybody', 'everybody else', or 'everybody but me'.
35.	S:	And *I*. I painted *too*.	S repeats her advantage.
36.	N:	But *I* didn't. Every has, everybody has to.	N is not satisfied with 'every', corrects herself. This is a short lexical correction activity (cf. section 4.4). Even though N does not use the phrases mentioned above (comment on 34), she knows the difference between *every* and *everybody*.

37. S:	Everybody has to (?)	S agrees that everyone (including N) will paint.

Sequence III, Sub-sequence A (horsie)

38. N:	Hor*sie*, horsie.	N introduces new topic.
39. S:	Where? No, horsie is over there. Like see?	S is interested in new topic. Adds information.
40. N:	No.	N will not share topic.

Sub-sequence B ('friend'/'house')

41. S:	*Please*, I be your *friend*.	S pleads, offers powerful bribe. friendship.
42. N:	No, I don' wanna be your friend because ⎰ I'm	N rejects bribe.
43. S:	⎱ I let you go my *house*.	S expands bribe
44. N:	I don' *wan*na *go* your house.	N rejects expansion of bribe.

Sub-sequence C (N will not go to S's house)

45. S:	Why?	S asks for explanation.
46. N:	Be*cause*.	N does not give reason.
47. S:	Because *why*?	S asks for elaboration.
48. N:	Because I don' wannu.	N gives reason.
49. S:	'Cause you have a (?)?	S suggests reason, asks for clarification.
50. N:	Because I got, I got, *tir*ed. (?)	N gives another reason.
51. S:	Why?	S repeats request for reason.
52. N:	Because, 'cause your home is too far away.	N gives another reason.
53. S:	Huh?	S asks for clarification.
54. N:	Because your home is too far away from the school.	N expands reason given in 52.
55. S:	My house is, is, a little bit My house is, is, a little bit far away.	S rejects explanation as not true.

(short pause)

Sub-sequence D ('hula lesson')

56. N: You're not going to my house, and you're not going come to my hula lesson 'cause ⎰ (?)

N rejects S as a friend by not letting her come to her house; she then brings up a topic that S is sensitive about — S is jealous of N's hula lessons. (See example 27).

57. S: ⎱ (?) Tomorrow I'm gonna come Lani's house, yeah? Tomorrow, I go ⎰ Lani's house.

S tries to be included; seeks reassurance of friendship by asking if she will go to N's house.

58. D: ⎱ I don't know. We'll see.

D fails to provide reassurance.

59. N: No, next week, lotta times I, lotta times I, lotta times I going to go to hula lessons, yeah, Mom? Yeah, Mommy? ⎤

N continues to exclude S; asks D for confirmation.

60. D: Yes, Nani. ⎦

D confirms that N will go to hula lessons.

61. S: Eh, Leilani don' go to hula lessons then, then I go her house.

S tries to find a way to get to N's house.

Sub-sequence E (N makes plans that exclude S)

62. N: No, you're *not*. Because. We. Tomorrow I gon' have a pic*nic*. Tomorrow I gon' have a *play*ground. And then, tomorrow, I gon' go to the zoo, and have a, program. Yeah? Yeah, Mommy, I gotta go to the zoo to have a program, yeah? ⎤

N will not include S in anything.

63. D: I don't think they started yet, honey, but I'll find out. I think they start in a ⎰ few weeks.

D confirms some of N's plans. 'They' refers to weekly concerts at the zoo during the summer. Nani calls the concerts 'programs'. N insists on making plans, asking D for confirmation.

64. S: ⎱ My mommy goin' tell *me*, see my mommy told me. *Wait*. Wait a

minute my mommy ha'
to say something. It's
not yet, on yet. What
she said. See? (sing-song)
'She said that.' Is on. See
she said the movie is on here.
Is on the zoo. I going to the
zoo. Yeah? Mommy, I gonna
go to the zoo. Yeah, Mom?

65. D:	Sure, we'll go to the zoo.	D confirms some of N's plans.
66. N:	*Yeah.* See my mommy said I could go to the *zoo.* I'm gonna go to the zoo. I am going. I *am*. I am going ona zoo. You're not going to the zoo. Not going to the zoo, yeah? Mommy Suzy's not going to the zoo, yeah?	N acknowledges D's confirmation of her plan to go to the zoo. Then she asks D to also confirm the fact that Suzy is not going to the zoo.
67. D:	*I* don't know.	D will not participate in excluding S.

Sub-sequence F (N will not join S)

68. S:	I going s, to see a big, big tiger.	S starts to defend herself by telling *her* plans.
(pause)		
69. N:	No.	N contradicts S.
70. S:	Yes, I am to*mor*row when I go with my *aun*tie and *un*cle.	S reasserts.
71. N:	*Not.*	N contradicts S.
72. S:	And my mommy.	S continues to list people included in her plans.
73. N:	*No.*	N contradicts S again.
74. S:	And, and, and, my grandma and *ev*erybody gonna come and, and you too, you could come too.	S includes N in her list of participants in her plans. Either S is more charitable than N or still is trying to find something that N will do with her.
75. N:	No, I gottu go my own zoo.	N still refuses to join S (there is really only one zoo in Honolulu).
76. S:	No, I gottu go my own zoo, *too.*	S claims to have whatever N claims to have.

77. N: I not going far away with you.   N will not join S. Uses same reason as she used in 52 and 54 for not going to S's house. 'Far away' may be related to S's pending move to New Jersey where her grandparents live. Her other set of grandparents live in Honolulu.

78. S: I going far away with my ˙ grandma and grandpa, and, and auntie and uncle.   'Far away' may or may not refer to N.J. here. S lists participants in her plans. Stress emphasises the listing aspect.

Sub-sequence G (N tries to be included in S's plans)

79. N: Tomorrow I go your zoo.   This the first time N has offered to do anything with S. Perhaps S's list finally made her feel excluded.

80. S: And Maile and   S continues her list.

81. N: Tomorrow I go your zoo, OK?   N repeats offer, seeks acceptance of offer.

82. S: Huh?   S is surprised by N's sudden change of heart (perhaps S didn't hear 79). S asks for repeat.

83. N: Tomorrow, OK? Kay. I go your zoo tomorrow.   N repeats offer, answers her own request for acceptance of offer.

(pause)

Sub-sequence H (N reverses again; won't join S)

84. N: I cannot go to your zoo too, this time, because I got a lot of work to do at home. When I get through doing my   N returns to attitude she had before 79; she won't join S. She also brings up hula again. (See Sub-sequence D, 56-61).

85. S: ⎰ hula.
       ⎱ (?) at home.   S's intentions not clear. N treats this as a request for repetition.

86. N: Yeah. No, I just going do, hula (exaggerated sigh) on the stage, but not today. Yeah? Mommy I'm not going on the stage, yeah?   N continues return to hula topic. Asks D to confirm what she is saying.

87. D: Not today. Maybe next Sunday.   D confirms what N said. (On some Sundays, N did perform with her

			hula class. There were stairs leading to the stage. See Utterance 97.)
88.	S:	That's right. That's right. Next Sunday.	S emphasises that N's plans are for *next* Sunday.
89.	N:	I goin' on stage on Sunday. (?) on the stage?	N repeats what D said, asks for confirmation.
90.	S:	Next weekend Lani have something?	S echos N's request for confirmation.
91.	N:	Something new for the stage?	N seems to be working on S's jealousy again.
92.	S:	I don' have anything new for the stage.	N seems to have succeeded in making S feel excluded.
93.	N:	You gottu buy some. My mommy buyed some for me to go on the stage.	N gives advice.
94.	S:	Lani, maybe my m, mommy maybe m, my mommy will buy, a, us a ladder, a ladder and (?) Kay, maybe, kay?	S seems to feel so left out that she even expresses her hopes hesitantly. She asks N to confirm only a 'maybe'. (End of Sub-sequence H; 94 could be considered part of Sub-sequence I.)

Sub-sequence I (ladder, stairs)

95.	N:	I got a ladder.	N continues to boast.
96.	S:	Let's (?), kay?	S wants to be included.
97.	N:	No, the *stairs* to climb up. Stairs.	N associates ladder with stairs.
98.	S:	(?)	S may not have known about the stairs N meant.
99.	N:	Jus' little tiny stairs. Jus' (?), jus' stairs, this *much* stairs.	N treats 98 as request for clarification and describes the stairs.

Sub-sequence J (S tries to change the topic).

100.	S:	(?) play, I think. You have to *play* first.	S presents a new topic, a new plan: *play*.
101.	N:	But	N objects.

Sub-sequence K (talk about not talking)

102. S: Let's stop *talk*ing. I'm *tir*ed talking.	S wants to stop talking, perhaps because she knows that she cannot talk N into agreeing with her.
103. N: But. Let's stop talking for a little while and then we stop talking.	N seems to have the same problem expressing two opposite but related events as she had in explaining that she did not paint, but everyone else did. (See Sequence II, 15-37.)
104. S: Kay.	S agrees.
105. N: Know what you could be talk?	N keeps S talking, sets up the introduction of the next topic.
106. S: Uh-huh.	S agrees, keeps the conversation going (is ready for the next topic).

Sub-sequence L (more zoo plans)

107. N: Know what I goin' go to the zoo, um, next week.	N introduces change of topic by returning to her zoo plans.
108. S: Yeah?	S accepts change of topic by responding with a question which tells N to go ahead.
109. N: Yeah, is I goin' on the zoo next week too? Next week.	N specifies time for trip to zoo: next week.
110. S: My mommy and daddy, my mommy and daddy going to the zoo with *you* and I *too*. I goin' with you.	S makes yet another list of participants in the zoo trip, including N.
111. N: But I'm going go to my *own* zoo, that's my zoo, is why, is why.	N still will not join S in S's plans.
112. S: I'm going to your zoo.	S is still willing to join N.
113. N: But your your zoo is too far away. ⎰ You go your own zoo.	N ignores S's offer to come to *her* (N's) zoo and argues against S's zoo.
114. S: ⎱ Is Sunday, is Sunday today.	S tries new argument to be included in N's plans, but does not have time to explain it.

(arrive at S's home)

5. Summary

The entire 3 June session was a kind of tug-of-war between Suzy and Nani. As each topic came up, the girls took opposing positions. Some sections seem to be similar to data collected by Watson-Gegeo and Boggs (1976) which contain what they call a 'contradicting routine' among part-Hawaiian children (see Chapter 2, footnote 20). In this routine, as in Suzy and Nani's conversation of 3 June, the children seemed intent on disagreeing and on challenging each other's claims and assertions. In this particular session (and elsewhere as well) Suzy and Nani seemed especially concerned with the status each had with the other. Although Suzy did not leave for New Jersey for several weeks after this session (the last recorded session was not until the end of June), it was not clear on 3 June exactly when she would stop going to the pre-school. The question 'Are you my friend?' seemed to be implied by the various ways in which each girls attempted to make plans that would either exclude or include the other.

The 3 June session was similar to the 12 June session in that maintaining conflicting points of view was a major characteristic of both sessions. In neither session did the children become angry or upset by the conflict. They actually put some effort into perpetuating it. A significant difference between the two examples is that on 3 June the issue, being included or excluded, was something they both were genuinely concerned about while on 12 June they seemed more interested in confusing each other by changing the meanings of the words 'down to the floor'. However, even though being someone's friend was very important, Suzy did not get upset when Nani excluded Suzy from her plans and refused to accept Suzy's invitation to go to *her* zoo. In spite of Nani's tactics, Suzy merely tried to withdraw from the interaction (102). She did not feel strongly about not talking, apparently, because Nani easily persuaded her to keep talking. It is, of course, possible that Suzy was not easily riled by such treatment, but on the other occasions, she was adamant about how she was to be treated.

Suzy and Nani discussed being someone's friend sixteen times during the recorded sessions. Usually at least one of the girls became angry enough to say, 'I'm not your friend', or to refuse to do something as a price for the other's friendship at some time during these discussions. On five of these occasions, Suzy was the one who took this position. Bearing in mind that it is possible that Suzy was just in a good mood on 3 June, another possibility should be considered: that the girls encouraged such conflict between themselves. It enabled them to pass the time without getting bored and it required verbal exchange that involved much of their linguistic skills. They did not get into trouble with the driver and they could engage in verbal manoeuvres without running into the frustration of being confined to the car.

BIBLIOGRAPHY

Bar-Adon, Aaron and Leopold, Werner F. (eds.). *Child language: a book of readings* (Prentice-Hall, Englewood Cliffs, New Jersey, 1971)

Bates, Elizabeth. 'Peer relations and the acquisition of language' (MS., 1975) in M. Lewis and L. Rosenblum (eds.), *Friendship and peer relations: the origins of behavior*, vol. 3 (Wiley and Sons, New York, forthcoming)

Bauman, Richard and Sherzer, Joel (eds.). *Explorations into the ethnography of speaking* (Cambridge University Press, Cambridge, 1974)

Bellugi, Ursula. 'The acquisition of negation', (Doctoral dissertation, Graduate School of Education, Harvard University, 1967)

Berko Gleason, Jean. (see Gleason, Jean Berko)

Bernstein, Basil. 'Social class, linguistic codes, and grammatical elements', *Language and speech*, vol. V (1962), pp. 224-37

——, 'Elaborated and restricted codes: their social origins and some consequences', *American Anthropologist*, vol. 66 (1964) (Pt. 2), pp. 55-69

——, 'A sociolinguistic approach to socialization: with some reference to educability, in F. Williams (ed.). *Language and Poverty* (Markham, Chicago, 1970)

Bever, Thomas. *A survey of some recent work in psycholinguistics. Specification and utilization of transformational grammar*, ed. by W. Plath (Scientific report no. 3, Air Force Cambridge Research Laboratories, Cambridge, Mass., 1968)

——, 'The cognitive bases for linguistic structures' in J.R. Hayes (ed.), *Cognition and the development of language* (Wiley and Sons, New York, 1970), pp. 279-362

——, 'Psychologically real grammar emerges because of its role in language acquisition' in Daniel P. Dato (ed.), *Developmental psychology: theory and application* (Georgetown University Roundtable on Language and Linguistics) (Georgetown University Press, Washington, D.C., 1975) pp. 63-76

Blackburn, Thomas R. 'Sensuous and intellectual complementarity in science' in Robert E. Ornstein (ed.), *The nature of human consciousness* (W.H. Freeman and Co., San Francisco, 1973), pp. 27-40

Bloom, Lois. *Language development: form and function in emerging grammars* (MIT Press, Cambridge, Mass., 1970)

——, Hood, L., and Lightbrough, P. 'Imitation in language development: if, when, and why', *Cognitive psychology*, vol. 6 (1974), pp. 380-420

Boggs, Stephen. 'Development of verbal disputing in part-Hawaiian children' (MS., 1975)

Bowerman, Melissa. *Early syntactic development* (Cambridge University Press, Cambridge, 1973)

Brennis, Donald, and Lein, Laura. ' "You fruithead" a sociolinguistic approach to children's dispute settlement' (MS., 1977) in Susan Ervin-Tripp and Claudia Mitchell-Kernan (eds.), *Child discourse* (Academic Press, New York, 1976), pp. 49-66

Brown, Roger. *A first language* (Harvard University Press, Cambridge, Mass., 1973)

——, and Berko, Jean. 'Word association and the acquisition of syntax', *Child development*, vol. 31 (1960), pp. 1-14

——, and Fraser, Colin. 'The acquisition of syntax' in Charles N. Cofer, and Barbara Musgrave (eds.), *Verbal behavior and learning: problems and processes* (McGraw-Hill, New York, 1963), pp. 158-201

——, Fraser, Colin, and Bellugi, Ursula. 'Explorations in grammar evaluation' in Ursula Bellugi and Roger Brown (eds.), *The acquisition of language* (Monographs of the society for research in child development, vol. 29, no. 92 (1964)), pp. 79-92

——, and Hanlon, Camille. 'Derivational complexity and order of acquisition in child speech' in J.R. Hayes (ed.), *Cognition and the development of language* (Wiley and Sons, New York, 1970), pp. 11-53

——, and Bellugi-Klima, Ursula. 'Three processes in the child's acquisition of syntax' in A. Bar-Adon and W.F. Leopold (eds.), *Child language: a book of readings* (Prentice-Hall, Englewood Cliffs, New Jersey, 1971), pp. 307-18

——, Cazden Courtney, and Bellugi-Klima, Ursula. 'The child's grammar from I to III' in A. Bar-Adon and W.F. Leopold (eds.), *Child language: a book of readings* (Prentice-Hall, Englewood Cliffs, New Jersey, 1971), pp. 382-412

Bruner, Jerome S. 'From communication to language — a psychological perspective', *Cognition*, vol. 3, no. 3 (1974/5), pp. 255-87

Carr, Elizabeth. *Da kine talk* (University of Hawaii Press, Honolulu, 1972)

Casagrande, Joseph B. and Hale, Kenneth. 'Semantic relations in Papago folk-definitions' in D. Hymes and W. Bittle (eds.), *Studies in southwestern ethnolinguistics* (Mouton, The Hague, 1967), pp. 165-93

Chafe, Wallace. *Meaning and the structure of language* (University of Chicago Press, Chicago, 1970)

Chomsky, Carol. *Acquisition of syntax in children from 5 to 10* (MIT Press, Cambridge, Mass., 1969)

Chomsky, Noam. *Syntactic structures* (Mouton, The Hague, 1957)
——, *Aspects of the theory of syntax* (MIT Press, Cambridge, Mass., 1965)

Chou-Allender, Susan. 'On the augmentation with English of the communicative competence of a Filipino child in Hawaii' (MA thesis, University of Hawaii, 1976)

Cole, Michael, Hood, Lois, and McDermott, Ray. 'Ecological Niche Picking: Ecological Invalidity as an Axiom of Experimental Cognitive Psychology' (unpublished MS., Rockefeller University, New York, n.d.)

Cross, Toni G. 'Some relationships between mothers and linguistic level in accelerated children', Stanford papers and reports, no. 10 (September 1975), pp. 117-33

Crystal, David. 'Review of a first language by Roger Brown', *Journal of child language*, vol. 1, no. 2, (1974) pp. 289-306

Dale, Philip S. *Language development: structure and function* (Holt, Rinehart and Winston, New York, 1976)

Derwing, Bruce L. *Transformational grammar as a theory of language acquisition* (Cambridge University Press, Cambridge, 1973)

Dore, John. 'Holophrases, speech acts and language universals', *Journal of child language*, vol. 2, no. 1, (1975), pp. 21-40

Ervin-Tripp, Susan M. 'An analysis of the interaction of language, topic, and listener' (1964a) in J. Gumperz and D. Hymes (eds.), 'The ethnography of communication', *American anthropologist*, vol. 66, no. 6 (1973), Part 2, pp. 86-102; in A.S. Dil (ed.), *Language acquisition and communicative choice* (Stanford University Press, Stanford, 1973), pp. 239-61

——, 'Imitation and structural change in children's language' in C. Ferguson and D. Slobin (eds.), *Studies of child language development* (Holt, Rinehart and Winston, New York, 1964b), pp. 391-406

—— in A.S. Dil (ed.), *Language acquisition and communicative choice: Essays by Susan M. Ervin-Tripp* (Stanford University Press, Stanford, 1973)

——, 'The comprehension and production of requests by children', *Papers and reports on child language development*, no. 8 (1974) pp. 188-96 (Stanford University)

——, 'Wait for me, Roller Skate!' in Susan Ervin-Tripp and C. Mitchell-

Kernan, *Child discourse* (Academic Press, New York, 1977), pp. 165-88

——, and Cook-Gumperz, Jenny. *The development of communicative strategies in children* (NIMH Grant Application MH26163, University of California, Berkeley, 1974)

——, and Mitchell-Kernan, Claudia (eds.). *Child discourse* (Academic Press, New York, 1977)

Ferguson, Charles A. 'Diglossia', *Word*, no. 15 (1959), pp. 325-40

——, and Slobin, Dan I. (eds.). *Studies of child language development* (Holt, Rinehart and Winston, New York, 1973)

——, and Farwell, Carol B. 'Words and sounds in early language acquisition', *Language*, vol. 51, no. 2 (1975), pp. 419-39

Fillmore, Charles. 'The case for case' in Emmon Bach and Robert Harms (eds.), *Universals in linguistic theory* (Holt, Rinehart and Winston, New York, 1968), pp. 1-87

Fischer, Susan D. 'Child language as a predictor of language change: a case study' in *Working papers in linguistics*, vol. 8, no. 1 (1976), pp. 71-104 (University of Hawaii)

Flavell, John H. *Cognitive development* (Prentice-Hall, Englewood Cliffs, N.J., 1977)

Forman, Michael L. 'Questions on CAUSE and transposition in the development of pre-school children's speech' in *Working papers in linguistics*, vol. 3, no. 5 (1971), pp. 119-28 (University of Hawaii)

——, Peters, Ann M., and Scollon, Ronald T. 'Early language acquisition in the Hawaii continuum' (MS., University of Hawaii, 1975)

Fox, James J. 'Our ancestors spoke in pairs: Rotinese views of language, dialect, and code' in Richard Bauman and J. Sherzer (eds.), *Explorations into the ethnography of speaking* (Cambridge University Press, Cambridge, 1974) pp. 65-88

Fromkin, Victoria. 'The non-anomalous nature of anomalous utterances', *Language*, vol. 47, no. 1 (1971), pp. 27-52

Gardner, Beatrice, and Gardner, Allen. 'Teaching sign language to a chimpanzee', *Science*, no. 165 (1969), pp. 664-72

Garvey, Catherine. 'Requests and responses in children's speech', *Journal of child language*, vol. 2, no. 1 (April 1975), pp. 41-63

——, and Hogan, R. 'Social speech and social interaction: egocentrism revisited', *Child development*, no. 44 (1973), pp. 562-8

Givón, Talmy. 'Topic, pronoun, and grammatical agreement' in Charles N. Li (ed.), *Subject and topic* (Academic Press, New York, 1976), pp. 149-88

Gleason, Jean Berko. 'Fathers and other strangers: men's speech to young children' in Daniel P. Dato (ed.), *Developmental psychology: theory and application* (Georgetown University Roundtable on Language and Linguistics) (Georgetown University Press, Washington, D.C., 1975), pp. 289-97

——, and Weintraub, Sandra. 'The acquisition of routines in child language: "trick or treat" ', *Language in society*, vol. 5, no. 2 (1976), pp. 129-36

Gleitman, L.R. and Gleitman, H. *Phrase and paraphrase: some innovative uses of language* (W.W. Norton, New York, 1970)

Goffman, Erving. 'Replies and responses', *Language in society*, vol. 5, (1976), pp. 257-313

Grace, George. 'Ethnolinguistic notes', I-XV (1976), I-XII (1977), XIII-XV (1977) (MS.)

Gruber, Jeffrey. 'Topicalization in child language', *Foundations of language*, vol. 3 (1967), pp. 37-65

Halliday, M.A.K. *Explorations into the functions of language* (Arnold, London, 1973)

——, 'Review of sociolinguistics: a cross-disciplinary perspective' (Center for Applied Linguistics, Washington, D.C.), *Language in society*, vol. 3, no. 1 (1974), pp. 94-103

——, 'Anti-languages', *American Anthropologist*, vol. 78, no. 3 (1976), pp. 570-84

——, *Learning how to mean: explorations into the development of language* (Elsevier, New York, 1977)

——, and Hasan, Ruqaiya. *Cohesion in English* (Longman, London, 1976)

Harris, Zellig. *Structural linguistics* (University of Chicago Phoenix Books, Chicago, 1951)

Hayes, John R. (ed.). *Cognition and the development of language* (Wiley and Sons, New York, 1970)

Hollos, Marida. 'Comprehension and use of social rules in pronoun selection by Hungarian children' in Susan Ervin-Tripp and C. Mitchell-Kernan (eds.), *Child discourse* (Academic Press, New York, 1977)

Huxley, Renira, and Ingram, Elisabeth (eds.). *Language acquisition: models and methods* (Academic Press, New York, 1971)

Hymes, Dell. 'The ethnography of speaking' in T. Gladwin and W.C. Sturtevant (eds.), *Anthropology and human behavior.* (Anthropological Society of Washington, Washington, D.C., 1962), pp. 13-53

—— (ed.). *Pidginization and creolization of languages* (Cambridge University Press, Cambridge, 1971)

——, 'On communicative competence' in J.B. Pride and J. Holmes (eds.), *Sociolinguistics: selected readings* (Penguin, Baltimore, 1972), pp. 269-93

——, *Foundations in sociolinguistics: an ethnographic approach* (University of Pennsylvania Press, Philadelphia, 1974)

Iwamura, Susan. 'The acquisition of phonology' (MS., 1972)

Jefferson, Gail. 'Side sequences' in D.N. Sudnow (ed.), *Studies in social interaction* (Free Press, New York, 1972), pp. 294-328

Joos, Martin. *The five clocks* (Harcourt, Brace and World, New York, 1961)

Keenan, Elinor Ochs. 'Conversational competence in children', *Journal of child language*, vol. I (1974a), pp. 163-83

——, 'Again and again: the pragmatics of imitation in child language', paper presented at the annual meetings of the American Anthropological Association (1974b)

——, 'Evolving discourse: the next step' (MS., 1975a)

——, 'Making it last: repetition in children's discourse' (MS., 1975b) in Susan Ervin-Tripp and C. Mitchell-Kernan (eds.), *Child discourse* (Academic Press, New York, 1977), pp. 125-38

——, and Klein, Ewan. 'Coherence in children's discourse', paper presented at LSA summer meetings (1974)

——, and Schieffelin, B. 'Topic as a discourse notion: a study of topic in the conversation of children and adults' in Charles Li (ed.), *Subject and topic* (Academic Press, New York, 1976), pp. 335-84

Kimball, Solon T., and Watson, James B. *Crossing cultural boundaries: the anthropological experience* (Chandler, San Francisco, 1972)

Klima, Edward and Bellugi-Klima, Ursula. 'Syntactic regularities in the speech of children' in A. Bar-Adon and W. Leopold (eds.), *Child language: a book of readings* (Prentice-Hall, Englewood Cliffs, New Jersey, 1971), pp. 412-23

Krashen, Stephen. 'Formal and informal linguistic environments in language acquisition and language learning' (MS., n.d.)

Labov, William. 'Finding out about children's language' in *Working papers in communication*, vol. I, pp. 1-30 (Pacific speech association and department of speech-communication, Honolulu, 1970)

——, 'On the inadequacy of natural languages: I, the development of tense' (MS., 1971)

Lakoff, George. 'On syntactic irregularity' (Report NSF-16, The computation laboratory, Harvard University, Cambridge, Mass., 1965)

Macnamara, John. 'Cognitive basis of language learning in infants',

Psychological review, no. 79 (1972), pp. 1-14

McCawley, James. 'The role of semantics in grammar' in Emmon Bach and Robert Harms (eds.). *Universals in linguistic theory* (Holt, Rinehart and Winston, New York, 1968), pp. 124-69

——, *Acquisition models as models of acquisition* (Proceedings of 1975 NWAVE conference) (forthcoming)

——, 'Some ideas not to live by' (MS., 1976)

McNeill, David. *The acquisition of language* (Harper and Row, New York, 1970)

Merritt, Marilyn. 'On questions following questions in service encounters', *Language in society* , vol. 5 (1976), pp. 315-57

Metcalfe, J. 'An investigation of speech sound discrimination in children' (PhD dissertation, Stanford University, 1962)

Moore, T.E. (ed.), *Cognitive development and the acquisition of language* (Academic Press, New York, 1973)

Moskowitz, A.I. 'The 2-year-old stage in the acquisition of English phonology', *Language*, no. 46 (1970), pp. 426-47

——, 'The acquisition of phonology' (unpublished PhD dissertation, University of California, Berkeley, 1972)

Nelson, Katherine. *Structure and strategy in learning to talk* (Monographs of the society for research in child development, vol. 38, nos. 1-2 (1973)) (serial no. 149)

——, 'The nominal shift in semantic-syntactic development', *Cognitive psychology*, no. 7 (1975), pp. 461-569

Newport, Elissa. 'Motherese: the speech of mothers to young children' in N. Castellan, D. Pisoni and G. Potts (eds.). *Cognitive theory: volume II*. (Lawrence Earlbaum Associates, Hillsdale, N.J. 1976)

Nooteboom, S.G. 'The tongue slips into patterns' in A.L. Sciarone *et al.* (eds.), *Layden studies in linguistics and phonetics* (Mouton, The Hague, 1969), pp. 114-32

Odo, Carol. 'English patterns in Hawaii', *American speech*, no. 45 (1972), pp. 234-9

Ornstein, Robert E. (ed.). *The nature of human consciousness* (W.H. Freeman, San Francisco, 1973)

Pawley, Andrew, and Syder, Frances. 'Accepting the lure' (MS., 1975)

Perlman, Alan. 'Grammatical structure and style-shift in Hawaiian pidgin and creole' (PhD dissertation, University of Chicago, 1973)

Piaget, Jean. *The language and thought of the child* (1926) (Harcourt, Brace and World, New York, 1971)

Pittenger, Robert E., Hockett, Charles, and Danehy, John. *The first five minutes* (P. Martineau, Ithaca, New York, 1960)

Reinecke, John E., and Tokimasa, Aiko. 'The English dialect of Hawaii', *American speech*, no. 9 (1934), pp. 48-58, 122-31

Reisman, Karl. 'Contrapuntal conversations in an Antiguan village' in R. Bauman and J. Sherzer (eds.), *Explorations into the ethnography of speaking* (Cambridge University Press, Cambridge, 1974), pp. 110-24

Sacks, Harvey, Schegloff, Emmanuel, and Jefferson, Gail. 'A simplest systematics for the organization of turn-taking for conversation', *Language*, vol. 4, no. 1 (1974), pp. 696-735

Sanches, Mary. 'How to talk with a child: from interactional rules', paper presented at the American Anthropological Association meetings (1975)

Schegloff, Emmanuel. 'Sequencing in conversational openings', *American anthropologist*, no. 70 (1968), pp. 1075-95

——, and Sacks, Harvey. 'Opening up closings', *Semiotica*, no. 8 (1973), pp. 289-327

Schlesinger, I.M. 'Production of utterances and language acquisition' in Dan I. Slobin (ed.), *The ontogenesis of grammar* (Academic Press, New York, 1971), pp. 63-101

Scollon, Ronald. 'One child's language from one to two: the origins of construction' (PhD dissertation, University of Hawaii, 1974)

——, 'Language to the crib' (MS., 1975)

——, *Conversations with a one year old: a case study of the developmental foundation of syntax* (University of Hawaii Press, Honolulu, 1976)

Scollon, Suzanne. 'On the notion of topic in conversational analysis' (MS., 1975)

Shatz, Marilyn and Gelman, Rochelle. *The development of communicative skills: modifications in the speech of young children as a function of listener* (Monographs of the society for research in child development, vol. 38, no. 5 (1973)) (serial no. 152)

Shuy, Roger (ed.). *Sociololinguistics: current trends and prospects* (Georgetown University Roundtable on Language and Linguistics) (Georgetown University Press, Washington, D.C., 1972)

Slobin, Dan I. 'Cognitive prerequisites for the development of grammar' in C. Ferguson and D. Slobin, *Studies in child development* (Holt, Rinehart and Winston, New York, 1973)

——, 'Language change in childhood and history', Language behavior research laboratory working paper, no. 41 (University of California, Berkeley, 1975), pp. 1-37

Sudnow, D.N. (ed.). *Studies in social interaction* (Free Press, New

York, 1972)

Tsuzaki, S. 'Coexistent systems in language variation' in D. Hymes (ed.), *Pidginization and creolization of languages* (Cambridge University Press, Cambridge, 1971), pp. 327-39

Vanderslice, Ralph, and Pierson, Laura Shun. 'Prosodic features of Hawaiian English', *The quarterly journal of speech*, vol. LIII, no. 2 (1967), pp. 156-66

Watson, James B. 'Talking to strangers' in S.T. Kimball and J.B. Watson (eds.), *Crossing cultural boundaries: the anthropological experience* (Chandler, San Francisco, 1972), pp. 172-81

Watson, Karen Ann. Transcripts for doctoral dissertaion (1972)

——, 'The rhetoric of narrative structure: a sociolinguistic analysis of stories told by part-Hawaiian children' (PhD dissertation, University of Hawaii, 1973)

Watson-Gegeo, Karen Ann, and Boggs, Stephen T. 'From verbal play to talk story: the role of routines in speech events among Hawaiian children' (MS., 1976) in S. Ervin-Tripp and C. Mitchell-Kernan, *Child discourse* (Academic Press, New York, 1977), pp. 68-90

Weiman, L.A. 'The stress pattern of early child language' (unpublished PhD dissertation, University of Washington, 1974)

Weir, Ruth. *Language in the crib* (Mouton, The Hague, 1961)

INDEX